Reimagining the Higher Education Student

Drawing on the perspectives of scholars and researchers from around the world, this book challenges dominant constructions of higher education students. Given the increasing number and diversity of such students, the book offers a timely discussion of the implicit and sometimes subtle ways that they are characterised or defined. Topics vary from the ways that curriculum designers 'imagine' learners, the complex and evolving nature of student identity work, through to newspaper and TV representations of university attendees.

Reimagining the Higher Education Student seeks to question the accepted or unquestioned nature of 'being a student' and instead foreground the contradictions and 'messiness' of such ideation. Offering timely insights into the nature of the student experience and providing an understanding of what students may desire from their Higher Education participation, this book covers a range of issues, including:

- Impressions versus the reality of being a Higher Education student
- Portrayals of students in various media including newspapers, TV shows and online
- Generational perspectives on students, and students as family members

It is a valuable resource for academics and students both researching and working in higher education, especially those with a focus on identities, their importance and their constructions.

Rachel Brooks is Professor of Sociology at the University of Surrey, UK, and an executive editor of the *British Journal of Sociology of Education*.

Sarah O'Shea is a Professor and Director of the National Centre for Student Equity in Higher Education (NCSEHE) which is hosted by Curtin University, Australia.

The Society for Research into Higher Education (SRHE) is an independent and financially self-supporting international learned Society. It is concerned to advance understanding of higher education, especially through the insights, perspectives and knowledge offered by systematic research and scholarship.

The Society's primary role is to improve the quality of higher education through facilitating knowledge exchange, discourse and publication of research. SRHE members are worldwide and drawn from across all disciplines.

The Society has a wide set of aims and objectives. Amongst its many activities the Society:

• is a specialist publisher of higher education research, journals and books, amongst them Studies in Higher Education, Higher Education Quarterly, Research into Higher Education Abstracts and a long running monograph book series.

The Society also publishes a number of in-house guides and produces a specialist series "Issues in Postgraduate Education".

• funds and supports a large number of special interest networks for researchers and practitioners working in higher education from every discipline. These networks are open to all and offer a range of topical seminars, workshops and other events throughout the year ensuring the Society is in touch with all current research knowledge.

• runs the largest annual UK-based higher education research conference and parallel conference for postgraduate and newer researchers. This is attended by researchers from over 35 countries and showcases current research across every aspect of higher education.

SRHE

Society for Research into Higher Education
Advancing knowledge Informing policy Enhancing practice

73 Collier Street
London N1 9BE
United Kingdom

T +44 (0)20 7427 2350
F srhe@srhe.ac.uk
🐦 @srhe73

www.srhe.ac.uk

Director: Helen Perkins
Registered Charity No.313850
Company No.00868820
Limited by Guarantee

Registered office as above

Society for Research into Higher Education Series

This exciting new series aims to publish cutting edge research and discourse that reflects the rapidly changing world of higher education, examined in a global context. Encompassing topics of wide international relevance, the series includes every aspect of the international higher education research agenda, from strategic policy formulation and impact to pragmatic advice on best practice in the field.

Series Editors:
Jennifer M. Case, Virginia Tech, USA
Jeroen Huisman, Ghent University, Belgium

Changing European Academics
A Comparative Study of Social Stratification, Work Patterns and Research Productivity
Marek Kwiek

The Education Ecology of Universities
Integrating Learning, Strategy and the Academy
Robert A. Ellis and Peter Goodyear

Designing Effective Feedback Processes in Higher Education
A Learning-Focused Approach
Naomi Winstone and David Carless

Exploring Diary Methods in Higher Education Research
Opportunities, Choices and Challenges
Edited by Xuemeng Cao and Emily F. Henderson

For more information about this series, please visit: https://www.routledge.com/Research-into-Higher-Education/book-series/SRHE

Reimagining the Higher Education Student

Constructing and Contesting Identities

Edited by Rachel Brooks and
Sarah O'Shea

Routledge
Taylor & Francis Group

LONDON AND NEW YORK

First edition published 2021
by Routledge
2 Park Square, Milton Park, Abingdon, Oxon, OX14 4RN

and by Routledge
52 Vanderbilt Avenue, New York, NY 10017

Routledge is an imprint of the Taylor & Francis Group, an informa business

British Library Cataloguing-in-Publication Data
A catalogue record for this book is available from the British Library

Library of Congress Cataloging-in-Publication Data
Names: Brooks, Rachel, 1971- editor. | O'Shea, Sarah, editor.
Title: Reimagining the higher education student : constructing and contesting identities / edited by Rachel Brooks and Sarah O'Shea.
Description: First Edition. | New York : Routledge, 2021. | Includes bibliographical references and index.
Identifiers: LCCN 2020043960 (print) | LCCN 2020043961 (ebook) | ISBN 9780367426514 (Hardback) | ISBN 9780367426538 (Paperback) | ISBN 9780367854171 (eBook)
Subjects: LCSH: College students--Psychology. | College students--Attitudes. | Education, Higher--Aims and objectives. | Identity (Psychology)
Classification: LCC LB3609 .R45 2021 (print) | LCC LB3609 (ebook) | DDC 378.1/98--dc23
LC record available at https://lccn.loc.gov/2020043960
LC ebook record available at https://lccn.loc.gov/2020043961

ISBN: 978-0-367-42651-4 (hbk)
ISBN: 978-0-367-42653-8 (pbk)
ISBN: 978-0-367-85417-1 (ebk)

Typeset in Galliard
by SPi Global, India

We dedicate this book to current and future (possible) university students including our own children:
Hannah, Martha and Daniel
Hannah and Tom

Contents

Illustrations

Figures

Tables

Acknowledgements

We would like to thank all those who contributed chapters to this collection, and the series editors, Jeroen Huisman and Jenni Case, for their support. In addition, Rachel is grateful to the European Research Council for the award of a Consolidator Grant (reference 681018_EUROSTUDENTS) that funded the time she spent on the book (and the chapter she co-authored with Anu Lainio). Equally, Sarah wishes to acknowledge the support of the Australian Research Council (ARC) and the National Centre for Student Equity in Higher Education (NCSEHE), both of which funded research aligned with the focus of this book.

Editors

Rachel Brooks is Professor of Sociology at the University of Surrey, UK, and an executive editor of the *British Journal of Sociology of Education*. She has published widely on numerous topics in the sociology of higher education, including international student mobility, student politics, and the experiences of students with caring responsibilities. She is currently leading a large European Research Council-funded project ('Eurostudents') that is exploring the ways in which higher education students are understood across Europe. Her recent books include: *Education and Society: Places, Policies Processes; Materialities and Mobilities in Education* (with Johanna Waters); and *Sharing Care: Equal and Primary Caregiver Fathers and Early Years Parenting* (with Paul Hodkinson).

Sarah O'Shea is a Professor and Director of the National Centre for Student Equity in Higher Education (NCSEHE) which is hosted by Curtin University, Australia. Sarah has spent over twenty-five years working to effect change within the higher education (HE) sector through research that focuses on the access and participation of students from identified equity groups. She has published widely within the broad field of educational equity including how under-represented student cohorts enact success within university, navigate transition into this environment, manage competing identities and negotiate aspirations for self and others. She is currently completing a large national grant funded by the Australian Research Council (ARC) exploring the capitals and capabilities that underpin university persistence for students who are the first in their family to attend university.

Contributors

Kim Allen is a University Academic Fellow in Sociology at the University of Leeds. An interdisciplinary feminist researcher, her research is located at the intersections of youth studies, sociology, and the cultural studies of education. She has published widely on issues including: youth aspirations and transitions; educational inequalities; and representations of class and gender in popular culture. She is co-author of *Celebrity, Aspiration and Contemporary Youth: Education and Inequality in an Era of Austerity* (Bloomsbury Press 2018).

Elisa Alves is trained as a social scientist with a diverse background in Political Science, Economics, Sociology and Education. Currently she is a doctoral fellow of the Portuguese Foundation for Science and Technology (FCT), completing her PhD on international student mobility at IGOT (the Institute for Geography and Spatial Planning) at the University of Lisbon, where she is also a teacher and associate researcher.

Matthew Bunn is a Research Fellow at the Centre of Excellence for Equity in Higher Education (CEEHE) at the University of Newcastle, Australia. His work is centred on understanding entrenched inequalities within Australian Higher Education. His areas of interest include problems of individualisation, the theorisation of social and individual agency and the durability of social class. Dr Bunn also works on building stronger communication between research and practice, including through CEEHE's National Writing Program for Equity Practitioners, mentoring equity practitioners to support their writing to communicate back into institutional and academic spaces.

James Burford researches across the areas of International Higher Education, Researcher Development and Gender and Sexuality Studies. His recent projects have focused on academic mobility to Thailand, the spatialities of doctoral education and academic conferences as sites of pedagogy and knowledge production. James' NZARE-award winning doctoral research explored the affective-politics of doctoral education in Aotearoa New Zealand. James is a Lecturer in Research Education and Development at La Trobe University, Australia.

Kay Calver is a Senior Lecturer in Education, Children and Young People at the University of Northampton and a Senior Fellow of the HEA. She is the Programme Leader for the BA (Hons) Childhood and Youth programme and teaches on a number of undergraduate modules. Her research interests include youth transitions, inequality and the concept of fateful moments and critical turning points. Her doctoral thesis examined the educational experiences of pregnant and mothering young women. Kay has a professional background in special educational needs, sexual health and widening participation.

Emily Danvers is a Lecturer in Education at the University of Sussex. Her research interests are the 'everyday' exclusions faced in higher education, specifically on how disadvantaged groups experience exclusion beyond the level of access and via the micro and seemingly ordinary moments e.g. via pedagogies, practices, policies, relationships and assessment. Between 2017-19, along with Tamsin Hinton-Smith she was seconded to lead an evaluation of a regional widening participation initiative (NCOP) focusing on low-attainment postcodes.

Paola R.S. Eiras is a third year PhD researcher at the Department of Sociology, University of Surrey – UK. Paola has approximately 15 years of experience in teaching in higher education (HE), mostly in intercultural contexts (China, Australia, Brazil and the UK). Her PhD research was on Chinese students' cultural identity constructions in a transnational university in China. With a background in Biomedicine and Linguistics, her research interests include: internationalisation of higher education, transnational higher education, cultural studies and impact of globalisation on local contexts and societies, interdisciplinary methodological (and epistemological) approaches to research.

Kirsty Finn is Reader in Teaching and Learning at Manchester Metropolitan University. A sociologist of Higher Education, Kirsty undertakes research around student and graduate experiences of transition, (im)mobility and personal life and belonging. She is author of two books, *Personal life, young women and higher education: A relational approach to student and graduate experiences* (Palgrave 2015) and *Everyday mobile belonging: Theorising higher education student mobilities* (Bloomsbury 2019).

Leanne Fray is a Senior Research Fellow at the University of Newcastle in the Teachers and Teaching Research Centre. A former primary school teacher, Dr Fray has extensive experience in qualitative and mixed methods research. Recently she has been involved in several major research projects including the implementation of a randomised controlled trial evaluating the impact of Quality Teaching Rounds on student outcomes, and a longitudinal study of student education and career aspirations. Her research interests include improving student access and participation in higher education.

Jennifer Gore is a Laureate Professor, and Director of the Teachers and Teaching Research Centre at the University of Newcastle and Visiting Professor at the University of Oxford. Her research focuses on quality and equity, teacher development, pedagogical reform, and enhancing student outcomes. Her current agenda focuses on the impact of Quality Teaching Rounds on teachers and students and the formation of educational aspirations during schooling.

Tamsin Hinton-Smith is a Senior Lecturer in Higher Education in the School of Education and Social Work at the University of Sussex where she is also Co-Director of the Sussex Centre for Gender Studies. Tamsin is a sociologist by background, whose broad expertise lies within the sociology of gender and education inequalities. She has a longstanding focus on higher education participation inequalities, including internationally, and in terms of geographical inequalities; young people from Gypsy; Roma and Traveller backgrounds; care leavers; and lone and teenage parents. Tamsin has interests in both developing pedagogic contexts, and wider cultures of belonging and inequality within institutions.

Henk Huijser (SFHEA) is a Senior Lecturer, Curriculum and Learning Design in the Learning and Teaching Unit at Queensland University of Technology. Henk has a PhD in Screen and Media Studies and has held many academic development roles in Australia, the Middle East and China. His research interests include learning and teaching in higher education, problem-based learning, and cultural diversity. He is the co-author (with Megan Kek) of Problem-based learning into the future.

Nicola Ingram is Professor of Sociology of Education at Manchester Metropolitan University. She has published widely on issues of social class inequality in education and her recent books include: *Working-Class Boys and Educational Success: Teenage Identities, Masculinities and Urban Schooling* (Palgrave MacMillan 2018); *Educational Choices, Aspirations and Transitions in Europe* (Routledge 2018); *Higher Education, Social Class and Social Mobility: the Degree Generation* (Palgrave MacMillan 2016).

Russell King is Professor of Geography at the University of Sussex. He has a wide background in research on migration, including student migration and mobility. His research on internationally mobile students has been published in several international journals including *European Urban and Regional Studies; Globalisation, Societies and Education; Journal of Ethnic and Migration Studies; Population, Space and Place; and Transactions of the Institute of British Geographers.*

Anu Lainio is a PhD candidate at the Department of Sociology at the University of Surrey, UK. Her doctoral research examines media representations of higher education students across six European countries. Her research is part of the European Research Council funded Eurostudents project. Anu is also a research assistant for the Eurostudents project. Her research interests are in international and comparative higher education, student identities and media studies.

Matt Lumb is Associate Director of the Centre of Excellence for Equity in Higher Education (CEEHE) at the University of Newcastle, Australia. His work focuses on developing and supporting pedagogical spaces in higher education at the nexus of equity research and practice. A sociologist of higher education, his research interests include program evaluation, policy analysis, and social justice methodologies. His PhD with CEEHE investigated the unintended consequences of university outreach into marginalised school communities.

Sarah McDonald is a PhD candidate in the Education Futures unit at the University of South Australia. Her doctoral research focuses on how the intersection between gender and class interacts with higher education, and how this interaction impacts upon the construction of feminine identities for young women transitioning into university. Her research interests are in gendered subjectivities, social mobility, social barriers, and inequalities in education.

Bethan Michael-Fox works as an Associate Lecturer for the Open University, teaching English literature, interdisciplinary and reflective learning modules. She also holds the visiting academic status of Honorary Associate in the School of English and Creative Writing at the Open University and is undertaking a three year Visiting Research Fellow role at the University of Bath's centre for Death and Society (CDAS). She is the editorial officer for *Mortality*, published by Taylor and Francis, a Senior Fellow of the HEA and a Fellow of the RSA.

Kate O'Connor is a Lecturer in Education at La Trobe University, Australia. Her research is concerned with digital transformations in higher education, with a particular focus on issues relating to curriculum, policy and governance. It engages with questions relating to the impact of new management practices on education and curriculum construction, the understandings and assumptions about knowledge and students evident in new policies and practices, and the implications and opportunities of new research data management practices for qualitative research.

Sally Patfield is a Postdoctoral Researcher in the Teachers and Teaching Research Centre at the University of Newcastle. Sally has over 15 years' experience working in various educational contexts, including as a primary teacher in NSW public schools, in arts education at the local government level, and across professional and academic roles in higher education. Sally's doctoral research investigated school students who would be the first in their families to enter higher education, which was awarded the

Ray Debus Award for Doctoral Research in Education by the Australian Association for Research in Education.

Grace Sykes is Programme Director and Lecturer in Sociology at the University of Leicester. Her research and teaching interests focus broadly on the lives of young people and university students, with particular emphasis on education and health related transitions and risks/risky behaviour. She has a genuine passion for participatory qualitative research and developing visual/creative methods with young people.

Eloise Symonds holds a PhD in Educational Research from Lancaster University. Her research explores the transformation of power relationships between undergraduates and academics through the introduction of conflicting subjectivities and their associated behaviours in the current university climate. Guided by her background in the humanities, Eloise's research utilises critical discourse analysis to explore these conflicting relationships and subjectivities through discursive formations. Prior to her PhD studies, Eloise studied for her Master of Arts in Modern and Contemporary Literature at Birkbeck College, London and her Bachelor of Arts in English at the University of Leicester.

Thornchanok Uerpairojkit is a researcher in Policy Studies and the Sociology of Education. Her main area of interest is Thailand's education system and its policy processes, with a specialisation in policy-practice engagement. Thornchanok's recent research projects include work on learning outcomes in Thai basic education, and the experiences of academic migrants in Thai higher education. She has recently had work published on democracy and Thai education, and the policy environment for academic migration to Thailand. Between 2016-2018, Thornchanok lectured at the Faculty of Learning Sciences and Education, Thammasat University, Thailand. She is currently pursuing her doctoral studies at King's College London, UK.

Series Editors' Introduction

This series, co-published by the Society for Research into Higher Education and Routledge Books, aims to provide, in an accessible manner, cutting-edge scholarly thinking and inquiry that reflects the rapidly changing world of higher education, examined in a global context.

Encompassing topics of wide international relevance, the series includes every aspect of the international higher education research agenda, from strategic policy formulation and impact to pragmatic advice on best practice in the field. Each book in the series aims to meet at least one of the principle aims of the Society: to advance knowledge; to enhance practice; to inform policy.

In this edited volume, Rachel Brooks and Sarah O'Shea offer a compelling set of contributions from authors across Europe, Australia and Asia, all writing on how students are or can be conceived of. The contributions convincingly illustrate the complexities revolving around the identities and roles of students, how pervasive some imaginaries of "the student" are and how this affects students, but also how it is contested by them. The broad range of theoretical perspectives and (often innovative) methods used, significantly increases our understanding of the contemporary student and will undoubtedly influence the future academic debate on this important topic.

Jennifer M. Case
Jeroen Huisman

Chapter 1

Reimagining the higher education student

An introduction

Rachel Brooks and Sarah O'Shea

The value of exploring constructions of students

Over the last 30 years, higher education systems across the world have massified and, as a result, the student body has become increasingly diverse. While there has been some important work that has highlighted how the heterogeneity of this population has affected the learner identities taken up by students (e.g. Reay et al., 2010) – often related closely to their social characteristics and institutional settings – we still know relatively little about how students themselves understand their identity as students, and how they are constructed by other social actors. *Reimagining the Higher Education Student* brings together research from an international group of scholars to assess critically and, in some cases, challenge pervasive understandings of students, including how they are imagined through dominant discourses and policies. With contributions from East Asia, Australia and Europe that span disciplines and fields, the book offers timely insights into the nature of the higher education student experience and provides a better understanding of what students may desire from their higher education participation.

In this introductory chapter, we discuss some of the dominant constructions of students that have been addressed by recent scholarship. This overview is, however, necessarily selective, and there are various other understandings of students that we have had to omit. We then briefly outline how the chapters in this book contribute to and extend this body of work.

Dominant constructions of the higher education student

Students as learners

In much of the literature, within education and other cognate disciplines, it is often assumed that students are first and foremost learners. There is clearly a substantial amount of research devoted to enhancing the teaching and learning that takes place within higher education institutions, typically underpinned by the belief that this is the primary function of the sector. However, over recent years, some scholars have suggested that the place of learning has been usurped by other priorities and considerations, often linked to broader debates about the marketisation of higher education in many parts of the world. Writing with respect to Europe, for example, Moutsios (2013) has contended that, as a result of reforms across the continent over the late 20th century and start of the 21st century, students have come to be understood as consumers rather than learners. Some researchers have suggested that a shift to more highly marketised systems, particularly those in which students pay fees, has had a direct impact on how the process of learning is understood by both students and staff. Molesworth et al. (2009), examining developments in the UK, have argued that students have come to conceptualise learning in highly transactional terms – as a product to be bought, rather than a process that requires a considerable amount of effort on their part and that might, in places, be difficult and challenging. In such analyses, the previously dominant construction of student as learner is seen to have come under significant pressure through the reconfiguration of the higher education sector along market lines.

Nevertheless, as we will discuss further below, other studies have shown how such arguments are not played out in all contexts. Some students may actively reject their construction as consumers or customers on the basis that it undermines their commitment to learning as a two-way process, requiring considerable responsibility on both sides (Tomlinson, 2017). Indeed, research conducted by Brooks and Abrahams (2020) across six European nations has indicated that 'learner' was central to the identities of many students in a wide variety of different national and institutional contexts. Their participants spoke, for example, of the ways in which they believed the academic subjects they were studying had come to define them, and how they valued highly the more open-ended approach to learning that they had encountered within higher education, contrasting this with the less flexible and more prescribed approach they felt had been required at school. They also emphasised strongly the hard work that they had had to put in to their studies, seeing this often as closely allied to their learner identity.

Students as consumers

As we have already mentioned, over recent years, various scholars – as well as a range of social commentators – have asserted that students should be understood less as learners and more as consumers. Typically such arguments are advanced as part of a critique of the neo-liberalisation of the higher education sector. In countries such as Australia, the US and the UK, high fees are often seen to have inculcated more consumerist behaviour on the part of students and led to their clear positioning as consumers by both higher education institutions and policymakers. This has been brought into sharp relief in the UK by the government's encouragement of students unhappy with their degree programme to seek redress through the Competition and Markets Authority – a governmental body that ensures that 'consumers get a good deal when buying goods and services HE, and businesses operate within the law' (CMA, 2020, n.p.). In countries in which fees are either not payable by higher education students or have been kept at a low level (such as across much of mainland Europe), similar arguments about the emergence of new forms of student identity are nevertheless advanced, suggesting that the widespread introduction of principles of new public management (even if payment has not shifted to the individual) has had a similar effect of encouraging a broad range of higher education stakeholders to view students as consumers of an educational product (Kwiek, 2018; Moutsios, 2013).

There is now, however, an emerging body of work that questions some of these assumptions and provides a more nuanced account of the impact of market mechanisms within higher education. Research conducted in the UK by Tomlinson (2017), for example, has shown that while some students have embraced a consumer identity that informs their approach to their studies, a considerable number of their peers actively reject this construction on the grounds that it fails to recognise the effort they themselves put into their learning and has the potential to undermine their relationships with lecturers. A third group of students in Tomlinson's research held more ambivalent positions: they had internalised the discourse of student rights but still distanced themselves from the position of the consumer. While they believed that they were increasingly important stakeholders, with considerable bargaining power, they also acknowledged that they had personal responsibility for their learning. Similarly, cross-national research has indicated that relatively few students readily identify as consumers. Brooks and Abrahams (2020), for example, contend that of the six nations in their research – Denmark, England, Germany, Ireland, Poland and Spain – it was only in Spain that students constructed themselves as consumers. Here, however, this was not an understanding that they embraced; rather, they believed that it had been foisted upon them by government policy and institutional practices. Nevertheless, it is interesting to note that in numerous ways the Spanish higher education system is less marketised than that of many other countries in Europe (Lazetic, 2019). In seeking to explain the distinctiveness of the Spanish responses, Brooks and Abrahams (2020) maintain that the stage of marketisation is significant. There may, for example, be heightened sensitivity and resistance to such ideas because they are relatively new and not yet firmly established in all parts of the higher education system. Moreover, the combination of relatively high fees payable by many Spanish students and widespread dissatisfaction with the quality of education received (evident in Spain but not elsewhere) may have caused more students to question the basis for fees (i.e. a consumerist system, in which higher education is understood, at least partially, as an individual good) than in nations where students are generally happy with the education they are receiving. Research has suggested that constructions may differ at the institutional level, too, with higher status and more financially secure universities better able to insulate themselves from the pressures of marketisation and thus protect their students from being positioned as consumers (Naidoo et al., 2011).

Students as citizens

The construction of 'student as consumer' is often held in tension with that of 'student as citizen'. While the former is typically associated with higher education systems that treat a degree as a private good and personal investment, the latter is more commonly linked to systems that emphasise the public value of a degree. When higher education is conceived of as a public good, then students are recognised for the contribution they make to societal development and progress, and the reinvigoration of a public sphere. Nixon (2011) argues that there are three 'human goods' of higher education linked to this public orientation: capability (acquiring the resources necessary to achieve various goals), reason (learning to take other people's interests into account to resolve collective problems) and purposefulness (taking action, cognisant of the interests of oneself and others). Despite the increasing convergence of higher education systems around more marketised models (as discussed above) and the observed decline of the public good as both an idea and an ideal (ibid.), evidence suggests that some students continue to place importance on their role as citizens (O'Shea & Delahunty, 2018) and see a key purpose of higher education as preparing them to contribute to society, although this appears to be more marked in countries where higher education is publicly funded (Brooks et al., 2020b).

Related to the construction of students as citizens is the understanding of them as significant political actors. In many societies, there is now an assumption that students *should* be politically active, driving social change and challenging enduring inequalities, and students are often criticised – by journalists, higher education staff and other interested parties – when they are perceived not to be acting in this way (Brooks et al., 2020a). Nevertheless, as Williams (2013) has argued, this conceptualisation of students as political actors became common only in the 1960s and is frequently based on a misreading of that particular period – a misreading that incorrectly assumed that a majority of students were involved in the US and European campus protests of the 1960s and early 1970s (Sukarieh & Tannock, 2015). Such contemporary constructions also tend to operate with a relatively narrow understanding of political engagement. While involvement in on-campus activities associated with *formal* politics tends to be limited, and students' unions in a number of countries of the world have become less 'activist' in their orientation (e.g. Nissen & Hayward, 2017; Rochford, 2014), students nevertheless have a relatively high level of political interest (Abrahams & Brooks, 2019; Brooks et al., 2020a) and graduates are more likely than others to be politically engaged in later life (Olcese et al., 2014). Moreover, comparative work in Australia, US and UK has shown that small student societies can play an important role in encouraging students to develop their political identity and emerge as 'student citizens' (Loader et al., 2015).

Students as (current and future) workers

Studies across the Anglophone Global North have indicated that, within national policy, students are frequently constructed as 'future workers', typically as part of a broader discourse in which the primary purpose of higher education is increasingly presented as labour market preparation, and are assumed to be motivated primarily by employment-related concerns (e.g. Allen et al., 2013; Moore & Morton, 2017; Waters, 2009). Nevertheless, evidence suggests that such assumptions are not played out in uniform ways across all countries and that the extent to which students are constructed as 'future workers' is often related to national models of higher education funding. Indeed, Antonucci (2016) distinguishes between three main models and discourses. In what she calls the 'social investment' model, which typifies Anglo-Saxon countries such as England (and also Australia, New Zealand and US, although they were not covered by her research), students are constructed by policymakers explicitly as investors in their future careers and, as such, are expected to make significant private contributions to their higher education fees and living costs. In contrast, in the 'public responsibility' model of higher education funding, which characterises the Nordic countries, and the 'minimal public intervention' model prevalent in continental and southern Europe, the language of investment and the portrayal of students as workers-in-the-making are largely absent from public discourse and thus, perhaps, less likely to be taken up by students themselves and other social actors in these countries.

Such national differences also play out with respect to the extent to which students are constructed as workers *during* their studies. There is now a large body of scholarship that has shown how, across the world, many full-time students engage in part-time work – to finance their studies and/or to help differentiate them from other graduates of mass higher education systems (Callender, 2008; Hall, 2010; Neill, 2015) – and that such work often has a negative impact on both academic performance and well-being (e.g. Beffy et al., 2009; Body et al., 2014; Callender, 2008). This research has also indicated however that such impacts are unequally distributed: students in countries where there is less state support for higher education and/or who come from less privileged families are more likely than their peers to work during their studies (Antonucci, 2016; Darmody & Smyth; 2008; Moreau & Leathwood, 2006). There are also interesting differences between students in the extent to which they see themselves as a worker as opposed to a student. For example, within Europe, research that has asked students who have engaged in paid work during their studies whether they identify primarily as a student or worker has indicated that the percentage choosing the latter is much higher in some countries than others (Eurostudent, n.d.). For example, in Poland, 48.4 per cent of students claimed that they identified primarily as a worker, compared with 25 per cent in Ireland and only 9 per cent in Denmark (ibid.). It is likely that such differences can be explained with reference to the societal value that is attached to having a higher education qualification. In Poland, for example, the apparent belief among the population at large that a degree has low labour market value (Kwiek, 2018) may encourage students to foreground their worker identity rather than that associated with their studies (see also Beerkens et al. (2011) who have made similar arguments with respect to Estonia).

Students as socialites

Finally, students have often been viewed – by others, if not often by themselves – as socialites, 'party animals' or even hedonists, interested primarily in the social opportunities afforded by higher education. This particular construction tends to be stronger in nations with a dominant 'residential' model of higher education, in which it is common for students to leave their parental home in order to pursue their students and live in dedicated student accommodation or shared private houses. Williams (2013) has argued that this particular construction has a long history, dating back at least to the first half of the 20th century. However, some scholars have suggested it has taken on new significance in contemporary society, as some higher education institutions have chosen to stress their 'party credentials' as a means of differentiating themselves from their competitors and thus attracting students who prioritise social life over study. This is articulated well in Armstrong and Hamilton's (2013) ethnography of a large state university in the US, entitled *Paying for the Party*. They identify various 'pathways' that students can take through the university but argue that it is the 'party pathway' which is dominant. It is, they suggest 'the main artery through the university', and the primary means of attracting 'those whose dollars fuel the university' (p. 21). By stressing the highly developed social life of the campus and the correspondingly modest academic demands, the university targets extremely affluent students with middling academic records. Armstrong and Hamilton explain:

> Building the social side of the party pathway involves creating big-time sports teams and facilities, as well as other 'recreational' aspects of student life (e.g. fitness and student centres). It means establishing ways of policing student revelry that protect life, property and reputation without putting too much of a damper on student socialising. Most centrally, it requires solving the puzzle of how to systematically, and in large-scale fashion, generate 'fun'.
>
> (p. 15)

They go on to argue that this institutional prioritisation of partying had a particularly negative impact on the students from less affluent backgrounds in their research. These young people typically did not have the resources to fund the kind of social life that was normalised in the university and yet often failed to fulfil their promise academically because of the relative lack of support that was given to both learning and preparation for employment across the institution.

Clearly, constructing (some) students in this way – as primarily interested in partying – will not be played out in all national or institutional contexts, particularly in countries where it is much more common for students to remain in their own home for higher education and/or study on a part-time basis. Nevertheless, research has suggested that students often believe that they are seen as hedonists by others (Brooks & Abrahams, 2020), and that policymakers in some nations – while not necessarily using the same language – have been explicit in their belief that students need to improve their commitment to their degree programmes by working both harder and faster (e.g. Brooks, 2019; Sarauw & Madsen, 2020; Ulriksen, 2020).

The contribution of this book

The following 14 chapters of this book articulate in important ways with the scholarship discussed in this introduction. For example, contributions engage with the construction of students as: learners (Chapters 2, 3, 7 and 9); consumers and customers (Chapters 2 and 4); citizens (Chapter 4); workers (Chapters 2, 4 and 8); and socially oriented (Chapters 2, 6 and 10) – bringing new perspectives to bear on the debates we have outlined above. The chapters also, however, consider other constructions – for example, the positioning of students as: 'preservers of culture' (Chapter 4); 'deserving' (Chapter 5); 'traditional' or from 'widening participation' backgrounds (Chapters 5 and 6); a risk or 'at risk' (Chapter 10); family members (Chapter 11); fragile (Chapter 12); and 'international' (Chapters 13 and 14). They also consider how constructions have altered over time (Chapter 4) and how specific generational lenses can inform how students are understood (Chapters 4 and 12). Moreover, by drawing on a wide range of different national contexts, they enable us to explore further the extent to which conceptualisations of students vary spatially – a theme we return to in the concluding chapter.

References

Abrahams, J., & Brooks, R. (2019). Higher education students as political actors: evidence from England and Ireland. *Journal of Youth Studies* 22:1, 108–123. doi:10.1080/13676261.2018.1484431.

Allen K., Quinn, J., Hollingworth, S., & Rose, A. (2013). Becoming employable students and 'ideal' creative workers: exclusion and inequality in higher education work placements, *British Journal of Sociology of Education* 34:3, 431–452. doi:10.1080/01425692.2012.714249.

Antonucci, L. (2016). *Student Lives in Crisis. Deepening Inequality in Times of Austerity*. Bristol: Polity Press.

Armstrong, E., & Hamilton, L. (2013). *Paying for the Party. How College Maintains Inequality*. Cambridge, MA: Harvard University Press.

Beerkens, M., Magi, E., & Lill, L. (2011). University studies as a side job: causes and consequences of massive student employment in Estonia. *Higher Education* 61: 679–692. doi:10.1007/s10734-010-9356-0.

Beffy, M., Fougère, D., & Maurel, A. (2009). The impact of students' paid employment on pursuit and completion of university studies. *Économie et Statistique* 422: 31–50.

Body, K., Bonnal, L., & Giret, J.-F. (2014). Does student employment really impact academic achievement? The case of France *Applied Economics* 46:25, 3061–3073. doi:10.1080/00036846.2014.920483

Brooks, R. (2019). The construction of higher education students within national policy: a cross-European comparison. *Compare: A Journal of Comparative and International Education* (Advance online access). doi:10.1080/03057925.2019.1604118

Brooks, R., & Abrahams, J. (2020). European higher education students: contested constructions. *Sociological Research Online* (Advance online access). doi: 10.1177/1360780420973042.

Brooks, R., Gupta, A., Jayadeva, S., Abrahams, J., & Lazetic, P. (2020a). Students as political actors? Similarities and differences across six European nations. *British Educational Research Journal* 46:6, 1193–1209. doi:10.1002/berj.3628

Brooks, R., Gupta, A., Jayadeva, S., & Abrahams, J. (2020b). Students' views about the purpose of higher education: a comparative analysis of six European countries. *Higher Education Research and Development* (Advance online access) doi:10.1080/07294360.2020.1830039.

Callender, C. (2008). The impact of term-time employment on higher education students' academic attainment and achievement. *Journal of Education Policy* 23:4, 359–377. doi:10.1080/02680930801924490

CMA [Competition and Markets Authority] (2020). *About Us.* Available online at: https://www.gov.uk/government/organisations/competition-and-markets-authority/about (Accessed June 18 2020)

Darmody, M., & Smyth, E. (2008). Full-time students? Term-time employment among higher education students in Ireland *Journal of Education and Work* 21:4, 349–362. doi:10.1080/13639080802361091.

Eurostudent (n.d.). *Eurostudent VI Database.* Available online at: http://database.eurostudent.eu (Accessed November 26 2019)

Hall, R. (2010). The work-study relationship: experiences of full-time university students undertaking part-time employment. *Journal of Education and Work* 23:5, 439–449. doi:10.1080/13639080.2010.515969.

Kwiek, M. (2018) Building a new society and economy: high participation higher education in Poland, in: Cantwell, B., Marginson, S. & Smolentseva, A. (eds). *High Participation Systems of Higher Education.* Oxford Scholarship Online. doi:10.1093/oso/9780198828877.003.0012.

Lazetic, P. (2019). Students and university websites – consumers of corporate brands or novices in the academic community?. *Higher Education* 77:6, 995–1013. doi:10.1007/s10734-018-0315-5

Loader, B., Vromen, A., Xenos, M., Steel, H., & Burgum, S. (2015). Campus politics, student societies and social media, *The Sociological Review* 63:4, 820–839. doi:10.1111/1467-954X.12220

Molesworth, M., Nixon, E., & Scullion, E. (2009). Having, being and higher education: the marketization of the university and the transformation of the student into consumer. *Teaching in Higher Education* 14:3, 277–287. doi:10.1080/1356251090289884.

Moore, T., & Morton, J. (2017). The myth of job readiness? Written communication, employability, and the 'skills gap' in higher education. *Studies in Higher Education* 42:3, 501–609. doi:10.1080/03075079.2015.1067602.

Moreau, M.P., & Leathwood, C. (2006). Balancing paid work and studies: working (-class) students in higher education. *Journal of Education Policy* 31:1, 23–42. doi:10.1080/03075070500340135.

Moutsios, S. (2013). The de-Europeanization of the university under the Bologna Process. *Thesis Eleven* 119:1, 22–46. doi:10.1177%2F0725513613512198.

Naidoo, R., Shankar, A., & Veer, E. (2011). The consumerist turn in higher education: policy aspirations and outcomes. *Journal of Marketing Management* 27:11–12, 1142–1162. doi:10.1080/0267257X.2011.609135.

Neill, C. (2015). Rising student employment: the role of tuition fees. *Education Economics* 23:1, 101–121. doi:10.1080/09645292.2013.818104.

Nissen, S., & Hayward, B. (2017). Students' associations: The New Zealand experience, in: Brooks, R. (ed). *Student Politics and Protest: International Perspectives.* London: Routledge.

Nixon, J. (2011) *Higher Education and the Public Good. Imagining the University.* London: Continuum.

Olcese, C., Saunders, S., & Tzavidis, N. (2014). In the streets with a degree: how political generations, educational attainment and student status affect engagement in protest politics, *International Sociology* 29:6, 525–545. doi:10.1177%2F0268580914551305

O'Shea, S. & Delahunty, J. (2018). Getting through the day and still having a smile on my face! How do students define success in the university learning environment? *Higher Education Research and Development* 37:5, 1062–1075. doi:10.1080/07294360.2018.1463973

Reay, D., Crozier, G., & Clayton, J. (2010). 'Fitting in' or 'standing out': working class students in UK higher education. *British Educational Research Journal* 36:1, 107–124. doi:10.1080/01411920902878925.

Rochford, F. (2014) Bringing them into the tent – student association and the neutered academy. *Studies in Higher Education* 39:3, 485–499. doi:10.1080/03075079.2014.896184.

Sarauw, L.L. & Madsen, S.R. (2020). Higher education in the paradigm of speed. Student perspectives on the risks of fast-track degree completion. *Learning and Teaching* 13:1, 1–23. doi:10.3167/latiss.2020.130102.

Sukarieh, M. & Tannock, S. (2015). *Youth Rising? The Politics of Youth in the Global Economy.* London: Routledge.

Tomlinson, M. (2017). Student perceptions of themselves as 'consumers' of higher education. *British Journal of Sociology of Education* 38:4, 450–467. doi:10.1080/01425692.2015.1113856.

Ulriksen, L. (2020). Balancing times – a study of how students spend their study time and why. *Sociological Research Online.* doi:10.1177%2F1360780420957036

Waters, J. (2009). In pursuit of scarcity: transnational students, 'employability' and the MBA. *Environment and Planning A* 41:8, 1865–1883. doi:10.1068%2Fa40319.

Williams, J. (2013). *Consuming Higher Education. Why Learning Can't Be Bought.* London: Bloomsbury.

Chapter 2

On becoming a university student

Young people and the 'illusio' of higher education

Sally Patfield, Jennifer Gore and Leanne Fray

Introduction

In Australia, the contemporary higher education landscape is characterised by two pervasive, but closely related, discourses. First, access to higher education is a significant commodity, with the economic importance of a university education for the individual strategically intertwined with the federal government's own pecuniary ambitions for the nation (Commonwealth of Australia, 2016; Pitman, 2012). Second, universities provide a significant social justice apparatus, giving rise to the idea of a 'fair chance for all', whereby the spoils of a university education can supposedly be enjoyed by a more diverse range of Australians (Department of Employment, Education and Training, 1990). Together, these discourses foreground what Gale and Hodge (2014) call the new 'higher education imaginary', in which economic and social agendas coalesce as the government jostles for position in the global knowledge economy. Arguably, then, the macro-level role of universities has shifted in recent decades, with higher education becoming 'less about what students learn and more about what students are worth' (Blackmore, 2003, p. 2).

Against this backdrop, the dominant relationship of students to higher education has come to be constructed through a 'customer' or 'consumer' metaphor. That is, universities are now 'business enterprises' and students are informed and rational beings entering a 'marketplace' (Marginson, 2013; Pitman, 2016). The rise of this metaphor has been well-researched both in Australia (Baldwin & James, 2000; Onsman, 2008; Pitman, 2016) and in other countries where a similar view of university students has emerged (Naidoo, Shankar, & Veer, 2011; Saunders, 2015). Scholars largely attribute this phenomenon to the introduction of quasi-market mechanisms in higher education and particularly to the movement of governments towards neoliberalism, taken here to mean the promotion of free markets, privatisation and competition (Connell, 2019).

As a case in point, Australian market-based reforms to universities have included the following: the reintroduction of tuition fees; the uncapping of undergraduate places through the demand-driven funding system; the establishment of a national body to regulate quality assurance; and the development of websites which allow prospective applicants to compare data from student satisfaction and graduate employment surveys. Inherent in these reforms is the ideology that universities must now answer to students, who not only have 'consumer rights' but can reward or penalise institutions at various points along the student life cycle (Naidoo et al., 2011), from initially choosing where to attend to the views they express as alumni.

Recently, however, this conceptualisation of university students as 'customers' of higher education has been called into question. Critics maintain that just because the field of higher education is now constructed as a marketplace, students do not automatically behave in ways consistent with consumerism (Brooks, 2018a; Pitman, 2016). Indeed, little empirical evidence in Australia actually points to the truth of this metaphor, with one study finding university applicants are unsure about specific degrees and institutions (James, Baldwin, & McInnis, 1999), despite market reforms ostensibly giving prospective students *more* and *better quality* information to inform their decision-making. Other Australian scholars who claim university students think of themselves as customers do so often without widespread empirical evidence (Onsman, 2008; White, 2007). For example, in White's (2007) study of undergraduate students at one Australian institution, all kinds of pedagogic behaviours, such as student laziness and questioning unfair grades, are characterised by the author as indicative of consumerist discourse, yet few students in the sample actually use the term 'customer' to describe their experience.

This chapter engages with the 'student-as-customer' metaphor from a different angle – with empirical evidence sourced from *prospective* university students; that is, young people enrolled in primary and secondary school who have not yet entered university. By turning our attention towards how the 'university student' is understood outside of the academy (Pitman, 2016), we offer a fresh perspective to the hegemonic view, teasing out what becoming a university student actually means to young Australians as they form and articulate their aspirations for higher education. Given the intensity of consumerist discourse in the sector, we might expect young people to seek university because they merely want to 'have a degree' (Molesworth, Nixon, & Scullion, 2009), thus valuing economic success (Lolich, 2011) and seeing intellectual scholarship as a secondary pursuit (Gottschall & Saltmarsh, 2017). However, few Australian studies have examined how university students articulate their relationship to higher education (White, 2007) and none that we are aware of have considered the views of the next generation of applicants – the very individuals the sector is hoping to attract. By shifting the focus to the outlooks and values of young Australians, our study makes a unique contribution to this limited body of research, challenging common assumptions bound up in the idea of what it means to be a university student.

Forming an interest in the field: The 'illusio' of higher education

In our study of young people, we draw on the Bourdieusian concept of *illusio* to help unpack what becoming a university student essentially means *to them*, well before the point of enrolment. *Illusio* is an oft-ignored component of Bourdieu's oeuvre but has recently gained traction among educational researchers and sociologists as a productive analytic lens in much the same way as his customary 'thinking tools' of habitus, capital and field. Indeed, there is growing agreement that *illusio* should be considered a core relational component of Bourdieu's framework (Colley & Guéry, 2015; Threadgold, 2017). Accordingly, we tease out our use of the concept within the broader domain of Bourdieu's work.

Broadly speaking, we interpret *illusio* as an individual's interest in a specific field. With *field* understood as a spatial metaphor to elucidate a distinct arena of social action, such as the higher education sector, we understand *illusio* as one's interest in the 'game' that takes place within, and in relation to, this field. Bourdieu often refers to everyday social practices as a 'game', drawing attention to underlying dimensions of power as individuals engage in a struggle for distinction. As such, if one has an *illusio*, they are 'caught up in and by the game' (Bourdieu, 1998, p. 76); that is, they believe that the game is worth their time and energy, and therefore worth participating in or 'playing' (Bourdieu & Wacquant, 1992). What is at stake within the game is *capital* – to conserve or accumulate symbolically legitimised economic, cultural and social resources. However, it is important to highlight here that this competition is far from a level playing field, as the volume and structure of one's capital also acts as a form of currency – that is, 'players' come to the game from very different social positions, shaped by their *habitus*, or dispositions – while simultaneously, and perhaps paradoxically, the value of capital hinges on the very existence of the game.

Conceptually, then, we see *illusio* as a fundamental component of the perpetuation of a field. Although fields are dynamic entities that change over time, it is *illusio* that continues to reinforce the unquestioned shared beliefs of the game and, motivated by its practices, social actors can be seen as having a shared interest that it is something worthwhile (Bourdieu & Wacquant, 1992). An important caveat here is that individuals do not have to agree with the overall game itself; rather, they only have to see it as sufficiently important to pursue and struggle over (Threadgold, 2017). This point is particularly relevant to the field of higher education where, on the one hand, a degree is almost a prerequisite for gaining access to a professional career, yet, on the other hand, it provides no guarantee of securing a job – even more so in the context of credential inflation (Brown, Power, Tholen, & Allouch, 2016). In this way, *illusio* is dialectically related to Bourdieu's notion of *indifference*, which he uses to capture the way some social actors are 'unmoved' by the game (Bourdieu & Wacquant, 1992); such as those who do not accept – or even actively reject – the value placed on higher education.

Key to an understanding of *illusio* is that different kinds of interest exist in relation to the same field. At the macro-level, there is the *grand illusio* of governments and institutions (Colley, 2012) – the *illusio* that social actors are urged or expected to adopt (Threadgold, 2017). In the field of Australian higher education, we see this as the coupling of personal and national investment (that is, constructing university as both a private good *and* public good), and therefore a fundamentally economic interest. Arguably, in Bourdieu's framework, all 'games' have a core economic grounding. However, individuals also develop their own *illusio* in the same field, which 'ultimately have economic consequences, but are not always expressed in overt economic terms' (Grenfell, 2014, p. 156).

For young people, in particular, *illusio* is manifest in seeing university as a field worth aspiring to (Threadgold, 2019). For this reason, our analysis concentrates on young people who articulate a desire to go to university in the future. But, *illusio* can be expressed in different ways depending on how and why they see higher education as desirable *to them*. Our concern, therefore, is to understand the ways in which young people are 'taken in by the game', and the extent to which their outlooks and values align with the official rhetoric that has come to characterise university students as 'customers' or 'consumers'.

Research design

In this chapter, we draw on data from a larger project (2012–2015) that examined the formation of educational and occupational aspirations among young people in the state of New South Wales (NSW), Australia. The project employed both quantitative (surveys) and qualitative (focus groups) methods, sampling students enrolled in Years 3–12 (approximately aged 8–18 years) at government schools, along with their parents/carers and teachers. Findings from the quantitative strand, which involved 6,492 students, have been reported in a number of publications (see, for example, Gore et al., 2017). Here, we concentrate exclusively on the student focus group data, given our aim to explore the perspectives of young people in relation to higher education as a future educational trajectory.

The focus group data are drawn from 30 schools in NSW. Two levels of sampling were employed in order to recruit young people from a diverse range of backgrounds. First, schools were recruited in partnership with the NSW Department of Education (DoE), taking into account geographic location (categorised as metropolitan or provincial, according to definitions provided by the Australian Curriculum, Assessment and Reporting Authority) and school-level socio-educational advantage (a numerical value publicly available on the *MySchool* website). Second, students at each school were purposively recruited using a sampling frame developed by the research team, which included within-strata variance by: (1) individual-level socio-economic status (SES), categorised as low, low-mid, mid-high and high SES derived from parental education and occupation from school enrolment records; (2) prior academic achievement, based on data from a student's most recent National Assessment Program – Literacy and Numeracy (NAPLAN) results, categorised as low achieving, mid achieving and high achieving; and (3) desired occupational aspirations, stated by students in the first wave of the survey.

Overall, 553 students participated in focus groups, which were held at two time-points during the final three years of the study. Focus groups were held on school grounds during normal school hours. The discussions centred around the broad themes of schooling; educational and occupational aspirations; careers activities in school and perceptions of, and experiences with, university and vocational education. Of particular importance for the analysis presented in this chapter, the final theme included questions prompting young people to reflect on their understandings of higher education and university life. All focus groups were digitally audio-recorded, with recordings transcribed verbatim and students allocated pseudonyms to protect anonymity.

Narrowing our sample to those students who expressed interest during the focus groups in pursuing university (n = 310), we looked for patterns in the way these young people talked about their aspirations for higher education, and thus the different forms of *illusio* evident in their talk. Coding of the data was undertaken by the lead author using the NVivo™ software program and discussed by all authors in an iterative process of refinement. First-level inductive coding was used to capture emergent nodes based on a careful reading of students' talk, followed by a more theory-driven approach to analysis which was used to group nodes at higher levels of abstraction. Due to the semi-structured nature of the focus groups, not all students were asked the exact same probing questions about their university aspirations, limiting the depth of the data in some instances.

In this chapter, we detail five broad forms of *illusio* we characterised through our analysis: the *work-oriented illusio*; the *scholastic illusio*; the *social illusio*; the *emancipatory illusio* and the *quixotic illusio*. Our specific purpose here is to provide a rich description of each characterisation, as a means to juxtapose the aspirations of young Australians against the prevailing 'student-as-customer' metaphor. These characterisations are not discrete analytical categories but, rather, overlap in complex ways given that multiple forms of *illusio* could be expressed by the same student. In light of the economic *and* social justice discourses that underpin the contemporary higher education imaginary, we note salient characteristics of the young people within each category; a brief summary of this information is provided in Table 2.1. Variables available for consideration were SES, prior academic achievement, Indigenous status, language background, gender and Year level (a proxy for age). However, as indicated in Table 2.1, no clear patterns were identified for any form of *illusio* in relation to Indigenous status, language background or gender.

Table 2.1 Forms of illusio mapped to salient student characteristics

Form of illusio	Espoused by
Work-oriented illusio	Mostly young people from higher SES backgrounds; predominantly mid-high levels of academic achievement
Scholastic illusio	Young people from a range of SES backgrounds; predominantly mid-high levels of academic achievement
Social illusio	Mostly young people from lower socio-economic backgrounds; predominantly mid-high levels of academic achievement
Emancipatory illusio	Young people from a wide range of socio-demographic backgrounds (no clear patterns)
Quixotic illusio	Mostly young people enrolled in primary school and the early years of secondary school

Work-oriented illusio

The *work-oriented illusio* characterises the way young people position employment as the ultimate goal of higher education. Specifically, the students in this analytic category see university as an 'investment' in their career, drawing parallels with Brooks' (2018a) description of university students as 'future workers'. Consequently, we see this form of *illusio* as being most closely aligned with consumerist discourse, as students' talk largely centred on 'having' the object of a degree (Molesworth et al., 2009) rather than on what they thought it might be like to be *at* university. As identified in Table 2.1, these young people are predominantly from higher SES backgrounds, with mid-high levels of academic achievement; a socio-demographic that most closely aligns with the so-called 'traditional' university applicant (Burke, 2012).

The young people in our study who embraced a *work-oriented illusio* saw higher education as almost being mandatory for employment:

> I would definitely go to uni because you can't really get a job without a piece of paper. Most jobs require having a qualification so I would definitely go and get some sort of qualification in design or something.
>
> (Ashlee, Year 9, high SES, high achievement)

Here, higher education has instrumental rather than intrinsic value, assisting students like Ashlee to achieve the desired goal of a job. In particular, Ashlee's focus on the labour market and explicit reference to a *piece of paper* reduces the whole experience of being a university student to the credential awarded at the very end, prioritising the outcome or 'product' of higher education. Such a view evokes Connell's (2019) description of credentialism, wherein the *qualification* represents all that is seen as being valued in society, symbolising a person's ability and worth. While at this point in time Ashlee may be unsure of the specific degree she wants to pursue (*design or something*), higher education is a certainty in her life (*definitely go to uni… definitely go*), believing that an academic qualification is a tangible asset of great importance to her future.

The *work-oriented illusio* also shapes how young people see university relative to other kinds of educational pathways. Luna's choice to pursue university, for example, is fundamentally linked to what others think; that is, the professed value in society:

> Well I haven't really thought about it, but I think I will go to university. I don't know what I'll study but I think I'll go. Because, like, it just looks good. Like someone who's like, 'Oh, I just went to school and dropped out in Year 10'. And someone who's like, 'Oh, I finished university'. It's like, who's going to be hired?
>
> (Luna, Year 9, high SES, high achievement)

Starkly, Luna positions university students as better than those who *drop out* of school, a colloquialism used to refer to leaving secondary school prior to graduation. In her opinion, university not only *looks good* but is a comparatively superior pathway to take due to the competitive nature of the labour market. In this light, Luna's use of the question *who's going to be hired?* can be read as rhetorical, helping to make her point about the normative hierarchy that exists in the education system (Burke, 2012). As such, higher education is conceived as a positional good (Marginson, 2011), a form of capital that confers advantage to those who possess a degree. While Luna may not feel that higher education is something that she has *really thought about* in any depth, it is certainly embodied as important for one's social position, perhaps even more so for young people from relatively advantaged backgrounds who must maintain and even extend their position in society.

Scholastic illusio

The *scholastic illusio* represents a disposition towards higher education explicitly focused on learning. Brooks (2018b) describes such a view as a 'common sense' understanding of the university student, particularly linked to the historical positioning of universities as sites of intellectual thought and enquiry. Although some scholars have argued that the marketisation of higher education has led to students being disinclined to 'be' learners (Molesworth et al., 2009), we found quite the opposite among young people who embraced a *scholastic illusio*. Indeed, their focus is on the virtue of learning and personal fulfilment, with absolutely no reference in their talk of future employment. The young people in this analytic category predominantly have mid-high levels of academic achievement, but come from a range of SES backgrounds.

In many cases, young people with a *scholastic illusio* explicitly focused their attention on the pursuit of knowledge, underpinned by the mantra 'learning for the sake of learning':

> I'll definitely go to university, that's the thing – the top of the list. And that's the thing with university, since there's so much that's being offered to attract more students, it ticks all your interests. I especially have a lot of them since I adore history and geography, and all sorts of things that are not going to be focused on my career, but I'll still do them anyway.
> (Hugo, Year 9, low-mid SES, mid achievement)

A number of features stand out in Hugo's account. First, the desire to learn about a specific subject or discipline is spoken of with great energy. No practical justification is given; rather, Hugo unambiguously embraces the idea of studying subjects that he *adores* and that are definitely *not* required for employment. Elsewhere in the focus group Hugo indicates he wants to pursue a career in business – the epitome of consumerism – yet his heart is set on doing *other subjects anyway*. In this manner, higher education is about expanding knowledge and curiosity, not simply a product to be bought and consumed in order to get a job (Saltmarsh, 2011). Second, and relatedly, Hugo is essentially drawn towards a university trajectory by the wide array of options he will have the chance to study (*it ticks all your interests*). Here, he alludes to the massification of higher education – *so much being offered* – clearly aware that the deliberate goal of universities is to *attract more students*. It is particularly noteworthy, therefore, that while massification is associated with the emergence of consumerist discourse (Pitman, 2016), young people like Hugo do not simply focus on the economic 'game' that has been fashioned around university.

Young people in our study with a *scholastic illusio* also associated higher education with a sense of enjoyment, spurred on by their love of learning:

> I think that I would enjoy it, getting to learn new things.
> (Amanda, Year 6, high SES, mid achievement)

> I think it would be quite enjoyable and – because I always love learning new things because it just makes me feel good because then I've learnt something each day.
> (Maria, Year 6, high SES, mid achievement)

The language used by Amanda and Maria emphasises the affective dimensions of the *scholastic illusio*. Being a university student is all about intrinsic value and positivity – *love, enjoyment,* and feeling *good* – emotions these students associate with acquiring new knowledge. Unlike the assumptions bound up in the 'student-as-customer' metaphor, there is no indication that they 'tether' education and economic participation (Saltmarsh, 2011), or that they see learning as a commercial transaction (Naidoo et al., 2011). It is perhaps surprising, then, that a *scholastic illusio* has often been disregarded in the ascendency of market rhetoric, such that higher education has been repositioned as, above all, having economic exchange-value rather than any inherent worth (Biesta, 2007).

Social illusio

Closely aligned with the *scholastic illusio* is what we have termed the *social illusio*. While these students also make specific reference to the learning that takes place at university and do not associate learning with employment, their emphasis is on the social dimensions of learning (Christie, Tett, Cree, Hounsell, & McCune, 2008) rather than learning *per se*. In particular, university symbolises an opportunity to meet people who share similar interests and passions, as well as a desire to form new relationships. This analytic category mostly comprises young people from lower SES backgrounds who have mid-high levels of academic achievement.

Here, students like Krystal and Levi who embrace a *social illusio* discuss the kinds of people they envision meeting at university:

> It's going to be a lot of learning opportunities with like-minded people that are open-minded and aren't just going to not care about their education. Like, they care and they want to do something, not be with people that don't care and don't want to do anything. Like, I want to go and meet people that are like-minded and open-minded.
>
> (Krystal, Year 6, low SES, mid achievement)

> [You're with] people that actually want to learn. There's none of those jerkoff kids that just will sit in the corner playing on their iPhones and that.
>
> (Levi, Year 7, low-mid SES, mid achievement)

As they think about university, Krystal and Levi anticipate interacting with a cohort of peers who will be *like-minded*, receptive to different ideas (*open-minded*) and, above all, share the desire to learn. Consequently, the value of higher education is not attached to the credential (Connell, 2019) but is inherent in the experience of being *at* university. In their account, a stark binary is created between their imagined future as a university student and their current experience of formal schooling – a place where they feel students *don't want to do anything*. Attending relatively disadvantaged schools in the same metropolitan area, both Krystal and Levi mobilise a language of negativity to characterise their peers as passive learners invested neither in their education nor in the same kind of *illusio* about university: they merely *sit in the corner* and *don't care*.

For such students, becoming a university student subsequently revolves around forming relationships with new and 'different' kinds of people:

> It's just being in a place, being in, like, a dorm with a lot of people who want to learn just like you. Here there's a lot of people who I know don't want to go. They're probably going to drop out or something. But in university everyone wants to learn. And you meet really cool people; different people. So, yeah, I'm really excited for that aspect of university.
>
> (Suzette, Year 9, low SES, high achievement)

Although notions of 'cool' can often be attached to consumer culture – such as what products to buy and where to hang out (Kenway & Hickey-Moody, 2011) – Suzette equates *coolness* with learning. She even sees university students as the epitome of 'cool' because they have a strong disposition towards learning. Much like Krystal and Levi, a powerful contrast is drawn between her current circumstances and her desires for university life. While at Suzette's school, *a lot* of people want to *drop out*, she expects that literally *everyone* at university will share her mentality and outlook about education, instilling a sense of excitement. In this light, what stands out here is Suzette's reference to *difference*, foregrounding two important aspects of the *social illusio*. First, that university represents a platform for opening up a new realm of social capital for young people from relatively disadvantaged backgrounds. Second, that university is a significant period in life during which one can build a sense of belonging with others *just like them*.

Emancipatory illusio

The *emancipatory illusio* represents a hoped-for space of independence and freedom. Given that our research focuses on young people yet to enter university, it is not surprising that higher education is often viewed as a stepping stone to becoming – and being seen as – an adult, and being able to gain real maturity and responsibility. This form of *illusio* provides a counterpoint to policy that constructs university students through notions of juvenility, as still children (Brooks, 2018a). Specifically, there is no sense here of young people still picturing themselves as children after becoming university students; on the contrary, they conveyed a strong belief that they will no longer be children. This analytic category comprises young people from a wide range of socio-demographic backgrounds, with no clear patterns in student characteristics being evident in our analysis.

In speaking about their aspirations for university, young people who we characterise as having an *emancipatory illusio* often foregrounded the absence of parents and teachers:

I think it would be a really good experience. Like, living without your parents on site. And you would, like – there wouldn't be people telling you what to do as much.

(Liana, Year 7, high SES, high achievement,
non-English speaking background)

[Because] it's different to school as in, like, from Year 7, 8, 9 and 10 you're pretty much babysitted [sic] at school. Then Year 11 and 12 it's more self-directed. But then uni is all yourself.

(Shian, Year 11, high SES, high achievement)

As Liana and Shian think about their future selves at university, they imagine a world of greater control over their lives. Higher education becomes a proving ground for adulthood – a significant transition from childhood – from dependence to independence (Christie, 2009). Liana not only thinks it will be *good* to be *without her parents*, but believes this change will lead to a greater capacity to make her own decisions. While Shian's reference to being *all by yourself* could be interpreted as individualised self-sufficiency (Nixon, Scullion, & Hearn, 2018), we propose that her description signals a desire to move beyond the watchful eye of adults – no longer infantilised and *babysat*. While the final years of schooling provide structured opportunities to become more independent, it is the move into university which fuels the biggest leap to becoming oneself.

In drawing comparisons between university life and formal schooling, the idea of emancipation also emerges strongly in many student accounts:

It's a more independent style of learning rather than sort of just having – it's not as rigid a structure as school classes and things like that. It's really up to you. You're responsible for being at a lecture. You're responsible for taking the notes and getting things in and sort of the lecturer is just there to give you the information and you can ask them questions or whatever but it's really you're responsible for your own learning and your own style of learning, which is nice.

(Destiny, Year 11, low-mid SES, high achievement)

Destiny's repeated emphasis is on the level of responsibility one has as a university student – being accountable for turning up, taking notes, submitting assessments and, in fact, the whole learning process. In this way, she contrasts the rigidity of schooling with the autonomy of university; no longer will she have the guidance of a teacher or a fixed structure – instead, *it's really up to you*. Destiny clearly recognises that participation in university will require new ways of learning (Christie et al., 2008), or what others have termed 'lean and mean' pedagogies wherein academics spend considerably less time with students than in formal schooling (Scanlon, Rowling, & Weber, 2007). However, she is not daunted by this prospect. Instead, it is a feature of university life that attracts her, enabling her to figure out her own learning style for herself.

Quixotic illusio

Finally, the *quixotic illusio* captures an idealised version of university life. In talking about their aspirations for higher education, students focused their talk on the lifestyle university affords, often in ways that romanticise or even glorify the life of a university student. From the perspective of young people yet to enter higher education, this idealistic view can be seen as reflecting the normative student-subject historically associated with higher education (Burke, 2012), of a young, able-bodied person leaving the family nest to pursue university in a linear fashion (Christie, 2009), free of any kind of domestic responsibilities and financial constraints (Leathwood & O'Connell, 2003). This analytic category mostly comprises students enrolled in primary school and the early years of secondary school.

The young people in our study who held a *quixotic illusio* imagine their future selves at university in ways that symbolise youthfulness and dynamism:

> I have my headphones on, my MP3 in my pocket, have my laptop, have my bags, looking at the place, it's big, everybody's walking in. …And then when I walk in the door I will see everybody going up the stairs, getting their room keys, going to their rooms, popping their bags down and, like, when I get into my room I have a roommate, setup all my stuff and get ready for my first class. And I'm happy to be in uni and I walk in with my MP3.
>
> (Vanessa, Year 5, mid-high SES, high achievement,
> non-English speaking background)

Vanessa's strikingly specific imagery epitomises what Gottschall and Saltmarsh (2017) refer to as 'the good life'. In their work analysing the promotional videos of Australian universities, they found that student subjectivities are constructed through the privileging of a 'leisure and pleasure' lifestyle, rather than academic or intellectual pursuits. Such a perspective is tangible in Vanessa's account: she walks around campus, well-equipped with the right technology – her MP3 player and laptop – surrounded by others who are active and busy just like her, all the while imbibing the excitement of moving into independent, on-campus accommodation. Collectively, these visions of 'the good life' constitute a whimsical *illusio* of a youthful transition to university (Brooks, 2018b), forming a powerful affective connection between becoming a university student and the lure of happiness and excitement.

Media and pop culture also feature strongly within the *quixotic illusio*, projecting idealised notions of university life in a more fantastical way:

> It's like in this movie 'Transformers Number 2' how he goes and has a roommate and you study a lot in halls and stuff. Yeah. It looks pretty cool in that.
>
> (Jace, Year 7, mid-high SES, low achievement)

> In this movie that I saw it was kind of about university and how they will actually teach you how to drive a car... [And] in 'Monsters University' some people have rooms in the university and some people stay out at night and get jobs or go to football.
>
> (Theodore, Year 5, low SES, low achievement, Indigenous)

Like Vanessa, Jace and Theodore construct university life in terms of coolness and vitality. While *studying* and *teaching* are briefly hinted at, it is the archetype that movies like 'Transformers 2' and 'Monsters University' project which shape Jace's and Theodore's imaginings of their own educational futures. Normative representations of youth feature in both accounts: living on-campus, learning to drive, partying, fitting in paid work and watching sports games, thus shaping a fantasy image of the university student (Leathwood & O'Connell, 2003). Although a somewhat fictitious understanding – even inspired by a movie where monsters, rather than humans, go to university – the *quixotic illusio* should be taken seriously as a compelling force moulding young people's thoughts about university.

Conclusion

In the current moment, the 'student-as-customer' metaphor has come to characterise a multitude of pedagogic behaviours and experiences relative to the contemporary, marketised university. This study joins an emerging body of research that challenges this totalising view (Brooks, 2018a; Saunders, 2015; Tomlinson, 2017), disrupting widely held perceptions that university students adopt consumerist-style behaviours simply because the higher education sector is now considered a marketplace. By shifting the focus to young people who aspire to university, and exploring the multiplicity of *illusio* they start to form in relation to this field, our study finds little empirical evidence to suggest that early interest in university – well before the point of entry – is articulated through a consumerist orientation.

Using a Bourdieusian lens, we characterised five key ways that young people express their interest, or *illusio*, in higher education as a future educational trajectory. Of these five, only one potentially aligns with market-based rhetoric: the *work-oriented illusio*. This *illusio* certainly has undertones of consumerist discourse, wherein higher education is essentially a 'product' or 'investment' – even reduced to a credential – that one needs in the context of the current labour market. However, only rarely did the young people in our research explicitly mention the economic value of university, which arguably lies at the heart of consumerism. Unlike other studies which focus on the experience of university students (Tomlinson, 2017) or interrogate policy rhetoric (Brooks, 2018a), we found no underlying connotations of 'buying a degree' in young people's talk, or of universities merely being seen as service providers that must deliver 'value for money'.

Certainly, this absence may be explained by the age of our sample, a group of young people still enrolled in primary and secondary school. Indeed, their dispositions towards university are likely shaped by the fact that they are *aspiring* towards higher education and are yet to experience some of the concerns that confront university students. As such, an important caveat here is that their relationship to higher education might change as they move closer to the so-called 'marketplace'; through applying to, and eventually entering, university. Nonetheless, it is here that our findings provide important insight into the enduring use of the 'student-as-customer' metaphor, illuminating the extent to which this ideology extends outside of the higher education sector. As Pitman (2016) succinctly explains, 'in developed, democratic nation states, it is these wider perceptions that [can] influence public policy; more so than advocates within the sector itself' (p. 346).

In this way, the other four forms of *illusio* we have identified – *scholastic, social, emancipatory,* and *quixotic* – demonstrate a wide gamut of university aspirations that have largely been disregarded because of the ubiquitous nature of the 'student-as-customer' metaphor. The young people who embrace these forms of *illusio* desire to go to university for a multitude of reasons: to be a learner, form relationships with other learners, become an adult and even just to enjoy the imagined pleasures of university life. Collectively, these subjectivities signal a desire for an 'experience' rather than to merely have the 'object' of a degree (Molesworth et al., 2009), all of which are tied to different stakes in the practices of the field. Some scholars argue that a field subsumed by consumerist discourse will attract students with the same orientation (Molesworth et al., 2009). However, this is clearly not the case among these young people, who have begun to form their own beliefs that higher education is 'worth the candle', as Bourdieu and Wacquant (1992, p. 98) would say, although it is clearly worthwhile for different kinds of reasons. Consequently, these forms of *illusio* help to counter the view that marketisation has altered the nature of the rewards that social actors believe can be derived from higher education (Naidoo et al., 2011), revealing a powerful disconnect between the grand *illusio* fashioned by government and the way young people articulate their own interest in the field.

Despite university students now widely positioned as 'consumers' or 'customers', we argue, therefore, that this metaphor is vastly out of step with the way young people envisage their future selves in relation to higher education – particularly so for those from under-represented equity groups. In Australia, specifically, the macro-level discourse of higher education remains firmly grounded in a fundamentally economic *illusio*, even when the explicit objective of higher education policy is motivated by concerns for social justice (Commonwealth of Australia, 2016; Department of Employment, Education and Training, 1990). And yet, our analysis suggests that young people from disadvantaged backgrounds in particular are not taken in by this economic 'game'; they are much more likely to fall into the four analytic categories furthest removed from consumerist discourse. While previous research suggests that higher education can involve considerable economic risks for students from low SES backgrounds (Burke, 2012), it is noteworthy that we found that these young people are actually interested in the cultural and social capitals tied up in university study. Starkly, the *work-oriented illusio* is shaped primarily by a habitus aligned with that of the traditional university applicant – high SES and high achieving – the only characterisation of *illusio* that has any signs of consumerism. Arguably, higher education represents a tool for social reproduction for those from relatively advantaged backgrounds, evident in the symbolic value placed on university in our findings.

If higher education is to continue to appeal to young people – and especially to a more diverse range of young people – policy must therefore take heed of other forms of *illusio* that have been shrouded in the new 'higher education imaginary' (Gale & Hodge, 2014). In particular, if part of the aim of higher education policy is to genuinely attract a broader representation of students and alter the social composition of universities (Pitman, 2016), then the different kinds of aspirations we have identified should not be dismissed as childish. Rather, we see this research as a timely reminder of what higher education *can be*, challenging the sector to think carefully about the future of universities and the narrow way students are constructed as 'customers' or 'consumers'. Reframing this metaphor through the outlooks and values of young Australians – our next generation of potential applicants – provides a much-needed step in reimagining this outdated and over-used conceptualisation of the higher education student.

References

Baldwin, G., & James, R. (2000). The market in Australian higher education and the concept of student as informed consumer. *Journal of Higher Education Policy and Management* 22: 139–148. doi:10.1080/713678146

Biesta, G. (2007). Towards the knowledge democracy? Knowledge production and the civic role of the university *Studies in Philosophy & Education* 26: 467–479. doi:10.1007/s11217-007-9056-0

Blackmore, J. (2003). Tracking the nomadic life of the educational researcher: What future for feminist public intellectuals and the performative university? *The Australian Educational Researcher* 30: 1–24. doi:10.1007/bf03216795

Bourdieu, P. (1998). *Practical reason: On the theory of action* (R. Johnson, Trans.). Stanford, CA: Stanford University Press.

Bourdieu, P., & Wacquant, L. J. D. (1992). *An invitation to reflexive sociology*. Chicago, IL: University of Chicago Press.

Brooks, R. (2018a). The construction of higher education students in English policy documents. *British Journal of Sociology of Education* 39: 745–761. doi:10.1080/0 1425692.2017.1406339

Brooks, R. (2018b). Understanding the higher education student in Europe: A comparative analysis. *Compare: A Journal of Comparative and International Education* 48: 500–517. doi:10.1080/03057925.2017.1318047

Brown, P., Power, S., Tholen, G., & Allouch, A. (2016). Credentials, talent and cultural capital: A comparative study of educational elites in England and France. *British Journal of Sociology of Education* 37: 191–211. doi:10.1080/01425692.2014.920247

Burke, P. J. (2012). *The right to higher education: Beyond widening participation.* Milton Park, UK: Routledge.

Christie, H. (2009). Emotional journeys: Young people and transitions to university. *British Journal of Sociology of Education* 30: 123–136. doi:10.1080/01425690802700123

Christie, H., Tett, L., Cree, V. E., Hounsell, J., & McCune, V. (2008). 'A real rollercoaster of confidence and emotions': Learning to be a university student. *Studies in Higher Education* 33: 567–581. doi:10.1080/03075070802373040

Colley, H. (2012). Not learning in the workplace: Austerity and the shattering of illusio in public service work. *Journal of Workplace Learning* 24: 317–337. doi:10.1108/13665621211239868

Colley, H., & Guéry, F. (2015). Understanding new hybrid professions: Bourdieu, illusio and the case of public service interpreters. *Cambridge Journal of Education* 45: 113–131. doi:10.1080/0305764X.2014.991277

Commonwealth of Australia. (2016). *Driving innovation, fairness and excellence in Australian higher education.* Canberra, Australia: Department of Education and Training. Retrieved from https://docs.education.gov.au.

Connell, R. (2019). *The good university: What universities actually do and why its time for radical change.* London, UK: Zed Books.

Department of Employment, Education and Training. (1990). *A fair chance for all. National and institutional planning for equity in higher education: A discussion paper.* Canberra, Australia: Australian Government Publishing Service. Retrieved from http://hdl.voced.edu.au/10707/152620.

Gale, T., & Hodge, S. (2014). Just imaginary: Delimiting social inclusion in higher education. *British Journal of Sociology of Education* 35: 688–709. doi:10.1080/01425692.2014.919841

Gore, J., Patfield, S., Holmes, K., Smith, M., Lloyd, A., Gruppetta, M., ... Fray, L. (2017). When higher education is possible but not desirable: Widening participation and the aspirations of Australian Indigenous school students. *Australian Journal of Education* 61: 164–183. doi:10.1177/0004944117710841

Gottschall, K., & Saltmarsh, S.. (2017). You're not just learning it, you're living it!: Constructing the 'good life' in Australian university online promotional videos. *Discourse: Studies in the Cultural Politics of Education* 38: 768–781. doi:10.1080/01596306.2016.1158155

Grenfell, M. (2014). Interest. In M. Grenfell (Ed.), *Pierre Bourdieu: Key concepts* (2nd ed., pp. 151–168). Abingdon, UK: Routledge.

James, R., Baldwin, G., & McInnis, C. (1999). *Which university?: The factors influencing the choices of prospective undergraduates.* Canberra, Australia: Department of Education, Training and Youth Affairs. Retrieved from https://www.voced.edu.au.

Kenway, J., & Hickey-Moody, A. (2011). Life chances, lifestyle and everyday aspirational strategies and tactics. *Critical Studies in Education* 52: 151–163. doi:10.1080/17508487.2011.572828

Leathwood, C., & O'Connell, P. (2003). 'It's a struggle': The construction of the 'new student' in higher education. *Journal of Education Policy* 18: 597–615. doi:10.1080/0268093032000145863

Lolich, L. (2011). …and the market created the student to its image and likening. Neo-liberal governmentality and its effects on higher education in Ireland. *Irish Educational Studies* 30: 271–284. doi:10.1080/03323315.2011.569145

Marginson, S. (2011). Higher education and the public good. *Higher Education Quarterly* 65: 411–433. doi:10.1111/j.1468-2273.2011.00496.x

Marginson, S. (2013). The impossibility of capitalist markets in higher education. *Journal of Education Policy* 28: 353–370. doi:10.1080/02680939.2012.747109

Molesworth, M., Nixon, E., & Scullion, R. (2009). Having, being and higher education: The marketisation of the university and the transformation of the student into consumer. *Teaching in Higher Education* 14: 277–287. doi:10.1080/13562510902898841

Naidoo, R., Shankar, A., & Veer, E. (2011). The consumerist turn in higher education: Policy aspirations and outcomes. *Journal of Marketing Management* 27: 1142–1162. doi:10.1080/0267257X.2011.609135

Nixon, E., Scullion, R., & Hearn, R. (2018). Her majesty the student: Marketised higher education and the narcissistic (dis)satisfactions of the student-consumer. *Studies in Higher Education* 43: 927–943. doi:10.1080/03075079.2016.1196353

Onsman, A. (2008). Tempering universities' marketing rhetoric: A strategic protection against litigation or an admission of failure? *Journal of Higher Education Policy & Management* 30: 77–85. doi:10.1080/13600800701745077

Pitman, T. (2012). Selling visions for education: What do Australian politicians believe in, who are they trying to convince and how? *Australian Journal of Education* 56: 226–240. doi:10.1177/000494411205600303

Pitman, T. (2016). The evolution of the student as customer in Australian higher education: A policy perspective. *The Australian Educational Researcher* 43: 345–359. doi:10.1007/s13384-016-0204-9

Saltmarsh, S. (2011). Economic subjectivities in higher education: Self, policy and practice in the knowledge economy. *Cultural Studies Review* 17: 115–139. doi:10.5130/csr.v17i2.2007

Saunders, D. B. (2015). They do not buy it: Exploring the extent to which entering first-year students view themselves as customers. *Journal of Marketing for Higher Education* 25: 5–28. doi:10.1080/08841241.2014.969798

Scanlon, L., Rowling, L., & Weber, Z. (2007). 'You don't have like an identity… you are just lost in a crowd': Forming a student identity in the first-year transition to university. *Journal of Youth Studies* 10: 223–241. doi:10.1080/13676260600983684

Threadgold, S. (2017). *Youth, class and everyday struggles* London: Routledge.

Threadgold, S. (2019). Bourdieu is not a determinist: Illusio, aspiration, reflexivity and affect. In G. Stahl, D. Wallace, C. Burke, & S. Theadgold (Eds.), *International perspectives on theorizing aspirations* (pp. 36–50). London, UK: Bloomsbury Academic.

Tomlinson, M. (2017). Student perceptions of themselves as 'consumers' of higher education. *British Journal of Sociology of Education* 38: 450–467. doi:10.1080/01425692.2015.1113856

White, N. R. (2007). 'The customer is always right?': Student discourse about higher education in Australia. *Higher Education* 54: 593–604. doi:10.1007/s10734-006-9012-x

Chapter 3

'She's like, "you're a uni student now"'

The influence of mother–daughter relationships on the constructions of learner identities of first-in-family girls

Sarah McDonald

Introduction

Wider life trajectories, including educational journeys, are influenced by both social class and gender. Within Australia, the *Review of Australian Higher Education* (Bradley, Noonan, Nugent, & Scales, 2008) initiated by the Australian government has become the catalyst for federal aims to widen participation in higher education. According to the Bradley Review, there is a commitment in Australia to improve the educational outcomes of students who have a disability, who are Indigenous, female (in non-traditional degrees), from non-English-speaking backgrounds, from rural areas or who are from low-socio-economic backgrounds to attend higher education. However, despite policies to widen participation in education for students from disadvantaged backgrounds, the take-up of university places for girls with low socio-economic status (SES)[1] remains below that of girls from other socio-economic cohorts in Australia (National Centre for Vocational Education Research, 2018). Research continues to illustrate the variety of barriers which impede efforts to widen participation. Social class is a contested term in Australia and is routinely misrecognised, and yet it is a determining factor in the lives of young Australians (Kenway, 2013). Working-class students may hold an attitude that university is not for them due to lacking knowledge of the 'system' (Archer & Yamashita, 2003; Reay, Crozier, & Clayton, 2009; Smith, 2011). O'Shea (2014), a leader in the study of first-in-family (FIF) experience in Australia, argues that FIF students often hold specific cultural ideals and understandings of the self which may not seem compatible with the cultural and learning environments of universities. This chapter seeks to explore this phenomenon and make a contribution to working-class girlhood, intergenerational relationships and the FIF experience.

Research on young women has emphasised the way they seek to position themselves as without the gendered barriers of the past (Baker, 2010; Harris, 2010). Bowers-Brown (2019) has written about the 'supergirl' who is acutely aware of the 'high' aspirations expected for the upwardly socially mobile. In her more recent work on working-class girls' aspirations,

Bowers-Brown (2019) suggests that the 'expectation that all girls will embody supergirl aspirations misrecognises the differences in privilege that create an uneven platform to achieve this subjectivity and for many this may involve self-adaptation' (p. 157). Researching in Australia, McLeod and Yates (2006) found that young Australian women feel a certain responsibility to succeed by comparing and contrasting their own experiences with that of their mothers. They assert that the 'association of femininity with success destabilises understandings of the conventional successes expected to flow to men, but also raises questions about how young women will themselves negotiate the imperatives to be successful, to be their own person' (p. 107). Keeping in mind both class and gender, what remains largely unexplored is the extent to which girls in Australia, who would be considered FIF, experience education and futures differently from previous generations. Such an exploration involves consideration of significant changes regarding what higher education has come to be in Australia today as well as how the gendering of aspiration both advances and remains the same.

Drawing on feminist scholarship (Skeggs, 1997, 2004; Reay, 2018b; McLeod & Yates, 2006; Walkerdine, Lucey, & Melody, 2001) regarding the lived experience of class, this chapter explores how two FIF young women incorporate the classed and gendered experiences of their mothers into their subjectivities as they transition from secondary school into their first year of university. The experiences of working-class girls, intergenerational relationships and aspirations have received limited attention in studies of widening participation; rather, dominant constructions of girls position them as the success story of a 'feminised' education system. An important factor in how FIF girls construct their learner identities in higher education is the mother–daughter relationship, specifically the mother's unrealised aspirations which are placed upon their daughters. The chapter begins with a brief outline of working-class experiences of education with a focus on the Australian context. This is followed by a consideration of the importance of family as a site of meaning-making and fostering aspirations where the focus is on motherhood, specifically working-class motherhood and education. The chapter then presents its theoretical tools before recounting the research methodology. Then the stories of two FIF young women, Chloe and Ella, are presented. The aim of the comparative case study is to further an understanding of the mother–daughter relationship which contributes significantly to how both these young women make sense of their subjective and social positionings as they become consumers of, and performers within, the future-focused space of universities.

Working-class transitions to higher education

When considering working-class families and education, research has tended to document the way working-class families are less able to create middle-class capital for young people to draw on in education settings. For instance,

Connell (2003) discusses how working-class parents are less likely to show active involvement in their children's schooling, often due to a lack of familiarity with more recent curriculums. In terms of working-class transitions into higher education, the literature consistently highlights feelings of ambivalence, disorientation, marginalisation and shame (Reay, 2001; Sellar & Gale, 2011), where the educational experience is fraught with judgements and negative emotions for socially mobile students. A lack of economic resources means working-class students are more likely to engage in paid employment during their time at university (France & Roberts, 2017), while middle-class students often rely on family contributions in terms of financial help. These studies focus on how young people draw on middle-class capitals in order to experience success within middle-class educational structures. For example, it is suggested that working-class young people independently researching their post-secondary school options strongly rely on the academic capital they have acquired in school, rather than on familial capital (Bowers-Brown, 2015; Smith, 2011). This can create a gap in the information and guidance received about pathways into university, where middle-class girls are more able to draw on multiple sources of capital in their decision-making (Bowers-Brown, 2015). Furthermore, working-class young people are less likely to consider elite universities when making choices about higher education institutions and, if they do enrol, can experience dislocation of 'disquiet, ambivalence, insecurity and uncertainty' (Reay et al., 2009, p. 1105).

In Australia, the existence of social class is routinely denied and yet it remains a determining factor in people's lives (Kenway, 2013). Youth studies in Australia have maintained a consistent focus on how young people negotiate social class (Pini & Previte, 2013; Threadgold & Nilan, 2009; Woodman & Wyn, 2015). Overall, these studies have sought to understand how social structures contribute to or reproduce particular patterns of outcomes. McLeod and Yates (2006) suggest that while young people in Australia do not think about themselves in terms of class, there remains a strong relationship between socio-economic status and long-term outcomes in terms of what people can obtain. Furthermore, research suggests young people *do* recognise social class in others as part of a continual process of internalising class within their subjectivities (McLeod & Yates, 2006). Additionally, Australia's education system is socially stratified with a mix of government, catholic and independent schools, where 'educational and social segregating undermine the educational performance of lower achievers and of socially disadvantaged students' (Kenway, 2013, p. 289). Researching widening participation in Australia, Southgate et al. (2017) state that 'Patterns of social mobility are linked to economic inequality as family background plays a bigger role in determining adult outcomes than individual characteristics such as ability, talent and effort' (p. 244). Class as a predictor of academic success plays out across multiple educational fields within Australia, including compulsory schooling and higher education.

Families, working-class motherhood and education

In terms of the familial aspect of working-class transitions, Rondini (2016), in her work on FIF college students and their parents in the United States, highlights how working-class parents are active participants in the meaning-making which happens in connection to educational mobility. She speaks of the way in which parents of FIF students 'constructed narratives regarding their children's educational trajectories that served to lighten the burden of such injuries' (Rondini, 2016, p. 101). Similarly, Gofen (2009) writes about how some working-class young people attribute their social mobility to their parents, suggesting that despite economic challenges, 'the families of first-generation students are often a key resource rather than a constraint' (Gofen, 2009, p. 114). Gofen (2009) suggests that it is significant aspects of family life – attitudes towards education, interpersonal relationships and family values – which create the necessary circumstances which lead towards higher education for working-class young people.

In terms of motherhood in fostering aspirations, Cooper (2017) highlights how middle-class mothers 'gift' their daughters opportunities in the way of the economic, cultural and social capital needed to be successful at university. The 'gift' of capital is in the form of the mothers 'assertively engaging in material, financial and knowledge-based support' (p. 337) where there is 'an explicit and open belief that their behaviour is normative mothering support and practice in a competitive educational marketplace' (p. 337). Middle-class mothers, drawing on their cultural capital, are becoming increasingly involved in 'co-constructing' the decisions and experiences of their daughters' higher education (Cooper, 2017). In contrast, Reay (2004) notes the difficulties for some working-class mothers to 'generate the same levels of academic confidence and enthusiasm among their children as their middle-class counterparts' (p. 577). It has been argued that these difficulties may be due to the normalising of middle-class mothering practices (Reay, 2004; Walkerdine et al., 2001).

While research has documented the way that middle-class mothers work to reproduce privilege in their daughters (Cooper, 2017; Walkerdine et al., 2001), Reay (2004) reports that mothers across classes are expected to take on the task of encouraging and motivating their children in terms of academic progress. However, it is middle-class practices which often structure the working-class experience of education as much as individual working-class dispositions (Reay, 2018a), so that working-class experiences of transitions into middle-class education fields are relational and collective as opposed to individualised. In this way, the social and relational aspect of shaping and constructing working-class transitions includes not only family but also those within middle-class fields (Reay, 2018a). Examining mother–daughter relationships in Australia, McLeod (2015) argues that girls will often look to their mothers in terms of their aspirations or hopes for something different. For the girls in McLeod's research, they discuss staying on at school in order to escape what they view as the 'drudgery' of their mothers' lives which suggests that in some ways, 'the daughters inherit some of their mothers' own memories, taking traces of them into who they are and who they would like to become' (p. 323). Young women today do not necessarily experience the same gendered limits that affected their mothers' educational and employment experiences. Yet, for some working-class girls, their mothers' experiences play a significant role in structuring their constructions of higher education futures. What remains largely unexplored is how girls in Australia today experience education and futures differently from previous generations. For girls who are the first-in-their-family to attend university, they have formed very different identities in comparison to their mothers, thus influencing their aspirations.

Working-class feminine subjectivities

The feminist scholarship used to inform this chapter is based on theories of feminine subjectivities and notions of the 'supergirl'. Skeggs (1997) argues that gendered social discourses specify what is legitimate, where femininity is theorised as a process 'through which women are gendered and become specific sorts of women' (p. 98). Working-class femininities are juxtaposed against middle-class femininities in terms of what they are not, where the 'positioning, codification and valuing of women as "different" establishes limits on the amounts and forms of capital that are available and can be generated from a particular position' (Skeggs, 1997, p. 101). Renold and Allan (2006) suggest normative and idealised performances of gender – for example, those that are white, heterosexual and middle-class – *rely on* the existence of non-normative gender performances in order to exist and hold power. In this way, they speak to the proposed powerlessness of working-class gendered performances within educational contexts.

Stemming in part from various policies working to widen the participation of girls in the education system (Lingard & Douglas, 1999), girls and young women in contemporary westernised contexts are 'frequently represented as the new success story, the bearers of academic excellence, the overachievers at school, and the beneficiaries of feminism who can have it all' (McLeod & Yates, 2006, p. 106). The success of girls has been aligned with neoliberal notions of meritocracy which often ignore the nuances of girls' experiences in terms of their academic achievements (Harris, 2010; McLeod & Yates, 2006; Ringrose & Renold, 2012). Conceptions of the 'successful girl' are problematic because they privilege a form of femininity which is white, heterosexual, female and middle-class (Archer, Halsall & Hollingworth, 2007). Furthermore, McLeod and Yates (2006) and Bowers-Brown (2019) criticise the girls' success discourse for ignoring the way the different experiences and futures enjoyed by modern girls in the education system are not equally available to all girls. It is argued that high-achieving working-class girls may perform a middle-class 'supergirl' femininity which they equate with educational achievement (Allen, 2016; Bowers-Brown, 2019; Renold & Allan, 2006). Walkerdine et al. (2001) suggest that the identity work undertaken by many working-class young women – referred to as a 'different and hybrid subjectivity' (p. 142) – is imbued with anxieties about potential failure. At the same time, working-class women contend with a 'girl power' narrative that 'cruelly sets limits on any ambition, together with an education system that classifies them as fit for certain kinds of work depending on their academic capabilities' (Walkerdine et al., 2001, p. 21). The way that working-class women are positioned as 'other' against idealised middle-class gendered performances suggests the significance of a recognition of classed identities in the positioning and experience of educational institutions including that of secondary and higher education.

Methodology

The research project examined the experiences of 22 FIF girls from diverse schooling sectors in Adelaide, Australia, as they transitioned from secondary school into their first year of university. For the purposes of this chapter, FIF students are defined as those who do not have immediate family members who have attended university (O'Shea, May, Stone, & Delahunty, 2017; Southgate, Kelly, & Symonds, 2015).

The participants were recruited through school-leaders, social media and in-school presentations during their final year of schooling. The majority of participants (n = 18) live in the southern suburbs of Adelaide, Australia. 13.5% of people living in this region have attended university, in comparison to the national average of 22% (Australian Bureau of Statistics, 2016). Data collection took place through multiple one-on-one semi-structured interviews. The first round of interviews took place in the weeks after the participants graduated from high school, with subsequent interviews occurring during the first university year. Interviews took place at times negotiated with the young women and most often at their universities or community libraries. Interviews investigated participant relationships with their school and university sites and focused on how participants make meaning and negotiate gender relations in the context of these sites. The interviews were digitally recorded, transcribed and then coded using the NVivo computer-aided qualitative data analysis package. By constructing semi-structured interview protocols, analysis focused initially on themes which were decided on before interviews took place, along with an emergence of themes. Coding was primarily used as a way to 'cluster' data thematically so that sections of answers to specific questions could be read and understood within the larger cohort. At the same time, moving away from coded data and onto reading the interviews as narratives became important in building an overall picture of participant experiences (Denzin, 2013).

During interviews and thematic analysis, the way that some participants positioned university and social mobility as meaningful against specific classed and gendered experiences became evident. The two young women discussed here, Chloe and Ella, are illustrative of narratives which highlight a nuance within the successful but at times precarious natures of their university transition experiences. Reay (2018b) emphasises the importance of case studies for bringing 'working-class young people's narratives to life' through devoting 'time and reflexivity in order to develop in-depth case studies' (p. 18). Chloe and Ella were specifically chosen for this chapter because they both grew up in low-income single-mother households, attended middle-class schools and incorporated their mothers' experiences of education and work into narratives constructing their higher education futures. It is important to note that all discussion of the mothers within this chapter is from the perspective of their daughters, as the mothers were not interviewed.

Findings

Case Study 1 – Chloe

I first met Chloe at her school in the same week she finished her final Year 12 exams. Chloe, a twin, described her mother as working long hours in her job at a funeral home. She spoke about having moved multiple times during her high school years, depending on her mother's romantic relationships, and how they had mostly lived in 'really tiny and quite nasty' rental properties close to public transport. Illustrating her experiences with class, Chloe recounted the excitement she and her sister felt when one boyfriend owned his own home, as it was the first time they had lived in what she described as a 'massive house where we had our own rooms and everything'. Overall, Chloe's descriptions of their housing situation suggested it was generally precarious, whereby at one point during her final school year, her mother was given two weeks to find new accommodation after a relationship with a boyfriend suddenly finished.

Despite the precarious nature of housing, Chloe was able to consistently attend a government school in a middle-class area with an enforced school zone[2]. The school offered music scholarships to high-achieving students, which is how Chloe and her sister, who lived out of the zone, were able to enrol. Auditioning for a music scholarship resulted in an early pressure on Chloe to be successful in order for both her *and* her sister to attend Reed High School:

> I wasn't in the zone for this high school, so the only way that I was going to get into the school was through the music program. So, I auditioned and I obviously got in, and that's how my sister got in as well because there was still a sibling rule at that stage, but

> if I didn't get in through music, then I would have had to go to another high school.

Bourdieu highlights middle-class strategising to reproduce class privilege; for families, this often takes the form of private school, tutors, buying houses within specific school zones, extra-curricular activities and choosing specific universities (Connell, 2003; Waters & Brooks, 2010). Chloe successfully securing a position at Reed High School suggests a degree of strategising on the part of her mother since Chloe was only 12 when she auditioned.

Chloe started working at 13, and at various points during her schooling, she held down two to three part-time jobs in the service sector. These forms of employment allowed her to purchase facets of a middle-class childhood. During Chloe's high school years, she was able to buy her own cello, extra-curricular dance lessons as well as multiple inter-state and overseas school trips.

> I think I felt really lucky with what I've achieved, like I feel like I've made the most out of it, like that was always my goal, that I was going to come to high school and I was going to make the most out of everything. So, I went on the ski trip to Victoria, I've been to Scandinavia, I went to Sydney on a music trip. And I paid for them all myself.
>
> But I worked really hard to get the most out of all the opportunities I could, and I joined every possible group at the school. So, I think I'm successful, and I got really good grades mostly, except for the last part of the year, but they were still good grades, just not straight As. But I would definitely say my high school career's been really successful.

The language Chloe used to describe her high school years shows how she defined herself through the performance of the successful middle-class girl (Bowers-Brown, 2019), where her long hours of precarious service sector work provided her with the economic resources for such performances. Bathmaker et al. (2016) suggest that working-class childhoods developed around self-sufficiency may be common, where educationally successful students in particular 'develop an orientation towards thinking outside of the family habitus' (Bathmaker et al., 2016, p. 57). However, Chloe specifically positioned her independence as inculcated by her mother's experiences and disposition:

> She said that she likes how independent that we are. She knows lots of other people that are our age and are still so reliant on being

at home and often I won't talk to her for a few days and she'll just call up and be like, 'Hi, you wanna come home any time soon?' (laughs) and I'm like, yeah, I will… but she likes the fact that, because that's what she did when she was younger.

Chloe also explained that her mother dreamed of going to university to study nursing but could not afford the time off work to study while supporting two daughters: 'She never went to uni, so she's never been able to get the job she really wants to 'cos obviously she's up against people that have uni degrees and stuff.' This aligns with Hinton-Smith's (2016) research showing how access to higher education can be imbued with risk for working-class single mothers managing low economic capital and sole parenting. Furthermore, Reay et al. (2009) note that stoicism and resilience are commonly understood as working-class attributes, and we see how Chloe embodied the independence and resilience so valued by her mother.

In terms of her transition beyond secondary school, Chloe was surprised to receive a very high ATAR (Australian Tertiary Admission Rank) and so changed her university trajectory from a Bachelor of Music to a Bachelor of Psychology with Honours. Chloe described her mother as supportive of her ability to make this difficult decision alone: 'My mum was supportive though, she was like, "Just do whatever you wanna do. Whatever will make you happy"'. There is evidence here of the way that working-class parents are less able to guide their children's choices in higher education due to having less of a 'feel for the game' so that the process is a solitary one for working-class young people (Bathmaker et al., 2016). As a result, working-class students 'develop skills of self-reliance and resilience that aid their progress through university' (Bathmaker et al., 2016, p. 57). Certainly, while not offered specific guidance by her mother, the choice-making process imbued Chloe with confidence, bolstering her higher education identity: 'I think that I see myself more as capable of making decisions, like I said, I'm in charge of my future and what I feel that I love.'

Furthermore, building on Rondini's (2016) suggestion that some parents will construct their FIF children's success as a redemption, when asked about her motivations for being at university, Chloe stated:

I'm really glad I'm here. Like I feel like I'm really proud to be here in ways. Especially since my mum never got here either so it's good that she's sort of… it's weird, she's living it through me, hearing about all the stuff that I'm doing.

Chloe extended the pride she felt in becoming a university student to include her mother; instead of viewing her success as something Chloe was doing *for* her mother, she symbolically took her mother along *with* her. Limited experience with higher education meant Chloe's mother was only able to offer implicit guidance (Reay et al., 2009). Yet, her experience with education and work was positioned as a powerful narrative by Chloe, who drew on it in constructing her subjectivity as an independent and resilient FIF student.

Case Study 2 – Ella

Ella had also been raised by a single mother, and she and her mother worked at different retail stores in the same local shopping centre. Ella spoke about how her mother had started an early childhood degree at a vocational education and training provider, which was put on hold when Ella was born, and never returned to. Similar to Chloe, Ella spoke of her mother as a positive influence in her life:

> Probably my mum [has influenced me the most] still even though she didn't go on to doing further studies. She kind of put everything on hold when she had me. And then now – well, then having my sister as well. But I think how she still works and pays the bills and stuff like that and she still gives the best for me and my sister. So, you don't – I guess, you don't have to go – have a uni education to be successful, I guess. I feel like she wanted more of a family than to have a career.

Unlike Chloe's intensive self-investment in her skills as a musician, Ella spoke more casually regarding being part of her local netball team and going to football games with her mother. She enjoyed spending time with her friends in the local beachside towns in her area and in her spare time caught the train into the city to go 'window-shopping' because she never had much money.

When I first spoke to Ella, she was planning to study teaching and disability studies at university. However, the 'supergirl' narrative was not evident when Ella discussed her plans. Instead, her commitment to university was precarious, and she mainly intended to go because it was what her mother wanted: '[My mother's] reason is that she doesn't want me just to work in a store like she does. She wants to me actually have, I guess, kind of a career. She says it's my decision, but she would like me to go.' Ella spoke multiple times through the initial interview about how important it was to her mother that Ella have a 'career' – a lifestyle Ella compared on multiple occasions to the kind of work her mother did, aligning with gendered social discourses which legitimise social status (Skeggs, 1997). While both teaching or retail work may be understood as typically feminine employment, for Ella and her mother, there was a positioning of working-class and middle-class femininities in terms of what they are not – a middle-class 'career' or a working-class 'job' – and the forms of legitimised (cultural) and real (economic) capital available to them as a result (Skeggs, 1997). Furthermore, it appeared it was largely Ella's mother, rather than Ella's inner desires, which inspired her towards a 'respectable career'.

In terms of her aspirations, Ella found it difficult to imagine herself as a university student though she could see herself working in retail like her mother, supporting Bowers-Brown's suggestion that working-class young people's 'future choices may be limited to what appears probable if the options that are considered are determined by their familiarity' (Bowers-Brown, 2019, p. 149). This identity was bolstered when she was offered a full-time salaried position in her retail job – a form of employment which can be difficult to access for young people. Furthermore, securing a place at university did not happen as easily as Ella had hoped. She had applied for a double degree in a Bachelor of Education and Bachelor of Disability but was disappointed to find that her ATAR was too low for admission by at least 20 points. However, Ella was relieved to be offered a place on a Pathways course [3]:

SARAH: So, when you got your ATAR, at that point, were you worried about what was going to happen?
ELLA: Um, a little bit because I did know the ATAR for the disability one was an 80, so I was like, oh no. But I kind of thought about it like if I have to do the extra pathways bit, it's still getting me to where I want to go…then the main round, I got an email saying I got into that one, so yeah.
SARAH: And so how did you feel at that point?
ELLA: It was a kind of relief because, like leading up to it, I was like oh no, am I even going to get in? But it was kind of like a wave of relief over me when I got the email.

As Ella made the decision to attend university, she incorporated into her sense of self the narrative of her mother's experiences of not being able to finish her education and 'have a career', so that part of Ella's subjectivity became made up of the experiences her mother missed out on. However, once Ella began university, her identity as a university student and motivations for attending began to change.

Um, well at the start, as I kind of said in the last interview, it was kind of mum that I was going to go to uni and stuff like that, but now that I'm there, I feel like I want to be there. Like, I see some of my friends now who aren't doing anything good, just kind of sitting around, and I guess I'm being more proactive and actually doing something.

Ella began to incorporate the future-oriented culture of the university into her subjectivity, where she began to position herself against those who did not go. By referring to her friends as not 'doing anything good', Ella constructed university as a 'good,' as a place where she could progress. There is a sense here of what Skeggs (2004) highlights as a need for working-class young women to dis-identify with a particular social positioning or as Reay (2013) writes, of social mobility as 'a wrenching process' (p. 667).

I think still with like my mum as well, she's like, you're a uni student now kind of thing. And I try to always like, I think my family's kind of, has more pride in saying it. Like, I know when I went to Queensland and like my dad and my nanna would be with their friends and be like she's a uni student now kind of thing, you know?

While Ella had seriously considered going into retail work and could see herself enjoying that as a career, she was ultimately motivated to attend university by her mother. Although Ella began university with a degree of uncertainty, she did eventually come to feel a sense of belonging there. Throughout this period of transition in Ella's life, her mother continued to ask about her university experiences and the homework she had, much as she had while Ella was in high school. Furthermore, Ella was particularly positive about her pathways course, speaking about how she felt it would better prepare for the rigour of the rest of her degree.

Discussion

While the discourse around successful girls remains pervasive and grounded in a notion of femininity which is largely white and middle-class, this chapter has focused on how two working-class young women experience the transition into university in different ways. Part of the way they negotiate the demands of performing feminine identities is encapsulated in their relationship with their mothers and – more specifically – with their mothers' unrealised aspirations.

In terms of their classed identities, Chloe and Ella negotiate the period leading up to beginning university in differing ways. Chloe focusses strongly on the accrual of capital and, with an awareness of her mother's stagnation, she is definitive about her goal to 'make the most out of everything.' For Chloe, making the most out of everything means consistently striving for and engaging in middle-class pursuits. Chloe incorporates her classed positioning into her subjectivity, feeling a strong sense of pride and accomplishment in striving for and receiving the things she wants through independence, sheer determination and hard work – working-class values her mother expresses with particular pride (Reay et al., 2009). Chloe draws on these values to reimagine a different trajectory for herself – one which denies her social origin and is more aligned with her middle-class schooling context. However, while Chloe attends an elite university, there is no evidence that notions of symbolic capital of the institution or employability beyond the degree – key aspects of middle-class strategising – have played a significant role. Research has suggested that working-class young people are highly intentional in the way they approach higher education, in contrast to middle-class students who may have a more internalised sense of 'playing the game' (Bathmaker, Ingram, & Waller, 2013). Yet, Chloe, who continually strived throughout her secondary school years in the lead up to university, does not exhibit purposeful strategising in terms of the institution and degree itself. Rather, Chloe has reached her goal of becoming a university student. In contrast, Ella does not embody the 'supergirl' identity and, at least initially, appears less driven to move beyond her class status. Yet, Ella's juxtapositioning in terms of working-class and middle-class work is suggestive of a weighing-up of options. As she comes to university, with the intensive urging of her mother, she finds it enjoyable and, through her family, feels a sense of pride in being able to call herself a university student. Skeggs (1997) argues that, while the middle-class may show ambivalence about class, working-class women require an awareness of class positioning to position themselves outside of it. Certainly, there is evidence of this awareness of class positioning in the way that Chloe invests in herself to not end up in the same position as her mother, while Ella's mother helps her to re-imagine herself, not as a retail worker, but as a university student. This re-imagining, supported by the mother–daughter relationship, builds on Reay et al.'s (2009) observations of the reinvention which takes place for working-class students at university. Both mothers appear to be mostly concerned with their daughters' future happiness, ultimately allowing Chloe and Ella to make their own decisions. While evidence suggests that students from low-SES backgrounds may desire occupations that provide financial security (Gore, Holmes, Smith, Southgate, & Albright, 2015), neither Chloe or Ella appear driven by financial rewards but instead fulfilment and pride.

Rondini (2016) speaks of the way that the parents of FIF students are active in creating narratives regarding their children's social mobility. Furthermore, the parents in her study engage in their own identity-work where, through co-creation of social mobility narratives, they see their own identities positively reflected in and informed by the successes of their children. In terms of working-class motherhood, both Chloe and Ella's mothers appear to have an acute awareness of class positioning (Skeggs, 1997) which contributes significantly to how they foster the aspirations in their daughters. Rondini (2016) refers to this identity work as a 'narrative of redemption' where parents position what they see as shortcomings as redeemed by the success of their children. Indeed, there is evidence within both Chloe and Ella's stories that their mothers, and wider families, feel a sense of pride regarding their daughters' status as university students. This sense of pride extends to Chloe and Ella themselves, so that pride, success, excitement and pleasure becomes a shared experience between mother and daughter. Chloe and Ella do not see their mothers' past experiences as failures – instead, Chloe and Ella position their status as university students as a shared success, where their mothers having 'missed out' on higher education is redeemed through entering and experiencing university *along with* their daughters.

Conclusion

This chapter contributes to understanding nuances in the ways that young FIF women experience university transitions, despite narrow, idealised discourses around successful girls. Furthermore, Rondini (2016) highlights the way that research on FIF students experiencing social mobility has 'tended to focus on evidence of adversarial dynamics between low-income parents and their upwardly mobile children, implying intergenerational conflict as a singular foregone conclusion' (p. 100). Chloe and Ella's narratives give insight into the way that working-class experiences of the transition into university can be different, where the relationship between mother and daughter can positively influence the construction of higher education identities. Across the larger cohort of participants in this study, a third of the girls spoke specifically about their mothers as having encouraged or urged them to attend university, with some mothers making concerted efforts to support their daughters either financially, emotionally or academically. One third of the girls, with some overlap, discussed the way they were inspired by their mothers' experiences to enroll in higher education. While for middle-class girls, university is often the next logical step after compulsory education, working-class young women in Australia often make a concerted choice to attend university, and this in part may be motivated or supported by the experiences of their mothers. However, it was evident through the narratives of Chloe and Ella that while both mothers were supportive of their daughters going to university, this support was not imbued with the cultural capital to further their daughters' futures in terms of advancement and social mobility, but rather was focused on future happiness. Yet, it is clear that during the transition to becoming university students, both Chloe and Ella were able to positively draw on different aspects of their mothers' support and experiences in re-imagining and constructing higher education futures. What remains unexplored is whether, in the context of classed and gendered experiences, the mother–daughter relationship has a more lasting impact on the higher education experience of FIF students.

Notes

1 It is important here to note that the use of socio-economic status is problematic because it is not class but has often been used to reduce class struggles to economics.
2 Most government schools in the state of South Australia manage enrolments by accepting their core student cohort from a defined area around the school.
3 Some universities in Australia offer pathway programs which can help students gain entry into their preferred degree.

References

Allen, K. (2016). Top girls navigating austere times: Interrogating youth transitions since the 'crisis'. *Journal of Youth Studies* 19:6, 805–820. doi:10.1080/13676261. 2015.1112885

Archer, L., Halsall, A., & Hollingworth, S. (2007). Inner-city femininities and education:'race', class, gender and schooling in young women's lives. *Gender and Education*, 19:5, 549–568. doi:10.1080/09540250701535568

Archer, L., & Yamashita, H. (2003). 'Knowing their limits'? Identities, inequalities and inner city school leavers' post-16 aspirations. *Journal of Education Policy* 18:1, 53–69. doi:10.1080/0268093032000042209

Australian Bureau of Statistics 2016, *Themes: Onkaparinga community profile*, Retrieved from <http://quickstats.censusdata.abs.gov.au/census_services/get-product/census/2016/quickstat/40304?opendocument>

Baker, J. (2010). Great expectations and post-feminist accountability: Young women living up to the 'successful girls' discourse. *Gender and Education* 22:1, 1–15. doi:10.1080/09540250802612696

Bathmaker, A. M., Ingram, N., & Waller, R. (2013). Higher education, social class and the mobilisation of capitals: Recognising and playing the game. *British Journal of Sociology of Education* 34: 5–6, 723–743. doi:10.1080/01425692.2013.816041

Bathmaker, A. M., Ingram, N., Abrahams, J., Hoare, A., Waller, R., & Bradley, H. (2016). *Higher education, social class and social mobility: The degree generation*. Springer. doi:10.1057/978-1-137-53481-1_1

Bradley, D., Noonan, P., Nugent, H., & Scales, B. (2008). *Review of higher education in Australia, final report*. Canberra: Australian Government, Retrieved from <http://hdl.voced.edu.au/10707/44384>

Bowers-Brown, T. (2019). 'It was noticeable so I changed': Supergirls, aspirations and Bourdieu', in G Stahl, D Wallace, C Burke & S Threadgold (eds), *International perspectives on theorizing aspiration: Applying Bourdieu's tools*, Bloomsbury, London, pp. 145–160. doi:10.5040/9781350040359.0021

Bowers-Brown, T. (2015). 'It's like if you don't go to uni you fail in life': The relationship between girls' educational choices, habitus and the forms of capital, in J Thatcher, N Ingram, C Burke & J Abrahams (eds), *Bourdieu: The next generation: The development of Bourdieu's intellectual heritage in contemporary UK sociology*, Routledge, UK, pp. 55–72. doi:10.4324/9781315693415-5

Connell, R. (2003). Working-class families and the new secondary education. *Australian Journal of Education* 47:3, 235–250. doi:10.1177/000494410304700304

Cooper, L. (2017) The maternal gift: mothers' investment in their daughters' higher education. *Journal of Further and Higher Education* 41:3, 328–339. doi:10.1080/0309877x.2015.1100716

Denzin, N. (2013). The death of data? *Cultural Studies, Critical Methodologies* 13:4, 353–356. doi:10.1177/1532708613487882

France, A., & Roberts, S. (2017). *Youth and social class: Enduring inequality in the United Kingdom, Australia and New Zealand.* Springer: UK. doi:10.1057/978-1-137-57829-7

Gofen, A. (2009). Family capital: How first-generation higher education students break the intergenerational cycle. *Family Relations* 58:1, 104–120. doi:10.1111/j.1741-3729.2008.00538.x

Gore, J., Holmes, K., Smith, M., Southgate, E., and Albright, J. (2015). Socioeconomic status and the career aspirations of Australian school students: Testing enduring assumptions. *Australian Educational Researcher* 42:2, 155–177. doi:10.1007/s13384-015-0172-5

Harris, A. (2010). Mind the gap: Attitudes and emergent feminist politics since the third wave. *Australian Feminist Studies* 25:66, 475–484. doi:10.1080/08164649.2010.520684

Hinton-Smith, T. (2016) Negotiating the risk of debt-financed higher education: The experience of lone parent students. *British Educational Research Journal* 42:2, 207–222. doi:10.1002/berj.3201

Kenway, K. (2013) Challenging inequality in Australian schools: Gonski and beyond. *Discourse: Studies in the Cultural Politics of Education* 34:2, 286–308. doi:10.1080/01596306.2013.770254

Lingard, B., & Douglas, P. (1999). *Men engaging feminisms pro-feminism, backlashes and schooling.*

McLeod, J., & Yates, L. (2006). *Making modern lives: Subjectivity, schooling, and social change.* State University of New York Press: Albany, NY.

McLeod, J. (2015). Gender identity, intergenerational dynamics, and educational aspirations: Young women's hopes for the future, in J Wyn & H Cahill (eds), *Handbook of children and youth studies*, pp. 315–327. doi:10.1007/978-981-4451-15-4_6

National Centre for Vocational Education Research (2018). *Longitudal surveys of Australian youth*, Retrieved from <https://www.lsay.edu.au/>

O'Shea, S. (2014) Transitions and turning points: Exploring how first-in-family female students story their transition to university and student identity formation. *International Journal of Qualitative Studies in Education* 27:2, 135–158. doi:10.1080/09518398.2013.771226

O'Shea, S., May, J., Stone, C., & Delahunty, J. (2017). *First-in-family students, university experience and family life motivations, transitions and participation.* Palgrave Macmillan: London. doi:10.1057/978-1-137-58284-3

Pini, B., & Previte, J. (2013). Gender, class and sexuality in contemporary Australia, *Australian Feminist Studies.* 28:78, 348–363. doi:10.1080/08164649.2013.857385

Reay, D. (2001). 'Finding or losing yourself?: Working-class relationships to education. *Journal of Education Policy* 16:4, 333–346. doi:10.1080/02680930110054335

Reay, D. (2004). Gendering Bourdieu's concepts of capitals? Emotional capital, women and social class. *The Sociological Review* 52:2, 568–585. doi:10.1111/j.1467-954x.2005.00524.x

Reay, D., Crozier, G., & Clayton, J. (2009). 'Strangers in Paradise'? Working-class students in elite universities *Sociology* 43:6, 1103–1121. doi:10.1177/0038038509345700

Reay, D. (2013). Social mobility, a panacea for austere times: Tales of emperors, frogs, and tadpoles. *British Journal of Sociology of Education* 34:5–6, 660–677. doi:10.1080/01425692.2013.816035.

Reay, D. (2018a). Working class educational transitions to university: The limits of success. *European Journal of Education* 53:4, 528–540. doi:10.1111/ejed.12298

Reay, D. (2018b). Working-class educational failure: Theoretical perspectives, discursive concerns, and methodological approaches, in A. Tarabini & N. Ingram (eds), *Educational choices, transitions and aspirations in Europe* (pp. 15–31). doi:10.4324/9781315102368-2

Renold, E., & Allan, A. (2006). Bright and beautiful: High achieving girls, ambivalent femininities, and the feminisation of success in the primary school. *Discourse: Studies in the Cultural Politics of Education* 27:4, 457–473. doi:10.1080/01596300600988606

Ringrose, J., & Renold, E. (2012). Teen girls, working-class femininity and resistance: retheorising fantasy and desire in educational contexts of heterosexualised violence. *International Journal of Inclusive Education* 16:4, 461–477. doi:10.1080/13603116.2011.555099

Rondini, A. (2016). Healing the hidden injuries of class? Redemption narratives, aspirational proxies, and parents of low-income, first-generation college students. *Sociological Forum* 31:1, 96–116. doi:10.1111/socf.12228

Sellar, S., & Gale, T. (2011). Mobility, aspiration, voice: A new structure of feeling for student equity in higher education, *Critical Studies in Education* 52:2, 115–134. doi:10.1080/17508487.2011.572826

Skeggs, B. (1997). *Formations of class and gender: Becoming respectable.* SAGE: London and Thousand Oaks, CA. doi:10.4135/9781446217597

Skeggs, B. (2004). Context and background: Pierre Bourdieu's analysis of class, gender and sexuality, *The Sociological Review* 52:2, 19–33. doi:10.1111/j.1467-954x.2005.00522.x

Smith, L. (2011). Experiential 'hot' knowledge and its influence on low-SES students' capacities to aspire to higher education. *Critical Studies in Education* 52: 2, 165–177. doi:10.1080/17508487.2011.572829

Southgate, E., Kelly, B., & Symonds, I. (2015). Disadvantage and the 'capacity to aspire' to medical school. *Medical Education* 49:1, 73–83. doi:10.1111/medu.12540

Southgate, E., Brosnan, C., Lempp, H., Kelly, B., Wright, S., Outram, S., & Bennett, A. (2017). Travels in extreme social mobility: How first-in-family students find their way into and through medical education. *Critical Studies in Education* 58:2, 242–260. doi:10.1080/17508487.2016.1263223

Threadgold, S., & Nilan, P. (2009). Reflexivity of contemporary youth, risk and cultural capital, *Current Sociology* 57:1, 47–68. doi:10.1177/0011392108097452

Walkerdine, V., Lucey, H., & Melody, J. (2001). *Growing up girl: Psychosocial explorations of gender and class.* Palgrave Macmillan: Hampshire.

Waters, J., & Brooks, R. (2010). Accidental achievers? International higher education, class reproduction and privilege in the experiences of UK students overseas. *British Journal of Sociology of Education* 31:2, 217–228. doi:10.1080/01425690903539164

Woodman, D., & Wyn, J. (2015). *Youth and generation: Rethinking change and inequality in the lives of young people*. London. doi:10.4135/9781473910591

Chapter 4

Constructions of *nákseuk-săa*

Tracing contested imaginings of the Thai university student

Thornchanok Uerpairojkit and James Burford

Introduction: *Dèk sà-măi née* (young people these days)

Thai policymakers have identified higher education (HE) as an important mechanism for addressing a range of social, economic and cultural ills that beset the nation (OHEC, 2013). HE appears to promise a host of desirable outcomes: sustainable economic development, international competitiveness, a resilient knowledge society and political stability (OHEC, 2008). Due to such recognition, and relatively high resource allocation to the sector, Thai university students are a common site of public consternation. Yet the worries articulated about *nákseuk-săa*[1] (Thai university students) are diverse and often conflicting. This raises questions about *which* university student is configured in debates at any given time. This complexity is compounded by the fact that scholarly accounts addressing *nákseuk-săa* are currently dispersed, and where students do appear they are infrequently the central subject of investigation. By writing this chapter we hope to demonstrate that 'the *nákseuk-săa*' is an important educational subject worthy of detailed consideration.

Given the absence of focused scholarly commentary about the discursive construction of *nákseuk-săa*, we began our research by investigating how Thai university students are represented on popular Thai websites. In our various engagements online, we had noticed that discussions have increasingly configured *nákseuk-săa*, and the associated figure *dèk sà-măi née*, rather negatively. In general, we observed descriptions of students as increasingly individualistic, materialistic, instrumentalist and too readily taking on 'foreign' values. We found such descriptions in *pantip.com* (literally translated as 'a thousand tips'), a popular Thai language website where users discuss topics ranging from cosmetics to health, relationships to national politics across 38 topic boards (at the time of writing). The website draws users of all ages and is ranked as Thailand's fifth most visited website (Alexa, 2020). On *pantip.com*, there were frequent criticisms of young people (including university students) suggesting that they lack manners and are spoilt and selfish. For example, *dèk sà-măi née* were said to 'demand that their own rights are respected but aren't considerate of others'. They were also said to lack charitableness ('they grow up as receivers; they have never been taught to give') and to have limited patience and organisational loyalty. Other users positioned students more positively, perceiving today's *nákseuk-săa* as a sub-group of *kon rûn mài* (the new generation), and celebrating young people for discovering themselves and doing what makes them – rather than neces-sarily their parents or 'the nation' – happy.

Following these emerging constructions we observed on *pantip.com*, we also undertook a search of the term #นักศึกษา (*#nákseuk-săa*) on Twitter and Facebook. Rather than discovering critiques of the work ethic and selfishness of *nákseuk-săa*, to our surprise, the vast majority of 'student' content on Thai social media platforms was highly sexualised. Many posts using the hashtag featured young women in either university uniforms[2], in underwear, or with-out clothing, and appeared to be advertising sex work. In these postings, often the university uniform itself seemed to feature as an object of sexual interest. While it is impossible to know if the young people on social media advertising sex work or seeking sexual partners are in fact university students, this search reveals that meanings about *nákseuk-săa* are both in flux and situ-ated to particular kinds of discourse communities. These constructions of the university student as a sexual subject stand in stark contrast to idealised notions of the *nákseuk-săa* as chaste and intently focused on their education. As these two brief examples (*pantip.com* and social media) demonstrate, the picture of *nákseuk-săa* is clearly a complex and contested one; even within two popular kinds of online space, there is no ready coherence to the idea of the *nákseuk-săa* that is easy to grasp.

While public portrayals surface particular meanings of *nákseuk-săa,* in this chapter, we are interested in tracking policy visions of this figure. We have elected to focus on policy documents because they arguably portray desired constructions of the university student to their enactors: higher education institutions (HEIs) and educators. To undertake our study, we explore long-range HE policy documents because they provide overarching directions for smaller policies – national and institutional – of desirable constructions of *nákseuk-săa* (from the perspective of Thai governments). While as Brooks (2018) notes, 'educational policies do not determine student subjectivities in any direct and straightforward sense' (p. 746), policy influence is often sig-nificant. Therefore, exploring representations of *nákseuk-săa* in policy is valuable because they are likely to shape the responses of various stakehold-ers, including HEIs.

By focusing on how university students are constituted in the context of Thailand, this chapter also contributes to a growing body of international research on the idea of the university student (Brooks, 2018, 2019; Leathwood & Read, 2009). Scholars, mostly writing from the Global North, have offered constructions of students as learners, consumers, workers, fam-ily members and political actors (Brooks, 2018), among other possible figu-rations. Our contribution extends this research by exploring the construction of a culturally distinct figure: *nákseuk-săa*. By focusing our analysis on an under-considered global context, such as Thailand, we hope to (albeit momentarily) shift attention to the Global South, which remains marginal in these debates. Speaking from a different location does not only fill gaps in the global picture; it also offers a valuable foundation for cross-country comparison with regard to continuities and change in imaginings (and 'realities') of studenthood.

The remainder of this chapter is structured as follows. In the next section, we offer a background discussion of constructions of *náksèuk-săa* throughout history, connecting together a dispersed literature to provide the foundations for understanding contemporary ideas of the Thai university student. Then, we outline the methods for this chapter and introduce our corpus of policy texts, which span a period of approximately 30 years. Following this, we discuss key ways in which *náksèuk-săa* are constructed in these texts. We conclude by situating these constructions in their broader socio-economic and geopolitical context. Across this chapter, we develop richer understandings about the discursive construction of *náksèuk-săa* in order to invite reflection about what these various constructions make im/possible within Thai HE.

Historical review: Shifting constructions of the *náksèuk-săa*

In this section, we situate our study within the wider arc of the history of Thai HE, exploring how *máhăawíttáyaalai* (university) and *náksèuk-săa* have been constructed across various time periods[3]. We offer this historical review to provide a foundation for tracking ideas of *náksèuk-săa*. Historical context is crucial because many constructions of *náksèuk-săa* have a long 'tail', continuing forward across time. At the outset, it is also important to note that scholarship on the construction of Thai HE students is limited (with the notable exception of: Bovonsiri, Uampuang, & Fry, 1996; Crocco, 2018), and existing analyses are largely disconnected from each other. Our task in this section is to read across a variety of scholarly texts in order to join together the constructions of *náksèuk-săa* that we can identify.

Early historical period (pre-1889)

While many accounts identify the establishment of Chulalongkorn University in 1917 as the origin of Thai HE, this remains a contested starting point. Eaksittipong (2018), for instance, argues that this is a state-centric view which assumes state-level initiatives to be effective changes, whereas it actually took another decade for the university to offer undergraduate courses. In contrast to these debates about the establishment of the first institution recognisable as a 'university', we believe it is useful to offer a more expansive view of the history of *advanced knowledge production* in Thailand. For example, as Wyatt (1969) notes, like the old church universities of Europe, 'at least some monasteries in Sukhothai Siam [Early 13th century BCE] must have functioned as the academies and universities of their day' (p. 6). This is further complicated by the founding of various institutes for higher learning under the 1868–1910 reign of King Chulalongkorn (Bovonsiri et al., 1996; Crocco, 2018). For the purposes of this chapter, we acknowledge the significance of traditions of accumulating and passing advanced knowledge in Thailand, and the ways that learners have been constructed in these exchanges. Beginning the review prior to the establishment of formal institutions called 'universities' therefore matters because some educational practices present in contemporary Thai education can be traced back to earlier histories of teaching, learning and knowledge production.

Within this early historical period, various constructions of learners are discernible. For example, Giordano (2011) describes Thailand's traditional conception of teacher-student relations as one where learners are viewed as new links in sacred chains of knowledge transmitted by generations of teachers before them. Given that in much of the country formal study was conducted in monasteries, this arguably produced 'passive and respectful' constructions of learners where the learner was idealised as a 'pure receptacle' (Giordano, 2011, p. 126). Students (here constructed as boys and young men) were expected to provide respectful service to monks and to abide by an elaborate code of regulations which emphasised 'respect for their teachers and for learning, and on complete obedience as well as good manners' (Wyatt, 1969, p. 11–12). Arguably, these ideas continue to shape social expectations of teaching and learning, where students may be discouraged from challenging the ideas of their teachers (Bovonsiri et al., 1996). The dynamics of gratitude within this relationship are perhaps symbolised in the *wâai kroo* (teacher reverence) ceremony, a widespread ritual carried out annually across Thai schools and universities. Passive and respectful constructions of learners also sit in tension with current policy aspirations to produce 'active learners' who engage, participate and collaborate. Building on previous feminist analyses of the changing constructions of the university student (Leathwood & Read, 2009), we can see that during this historical period 'the learner' of higher knowledge was also positioned as a masculine subject (with the exception of royals and noblewomen who could access certain learning opportunities in the palace, for example). This construction remained throughout much of early Thai history, with the first women being admitted to Chulalongkorn in 1927, some ten years after its establishment (Bovonsiri et al., 1996).

Early modernisation period and the post-revolution period (1889–1949)

During the early modernisation period, Siam (the former name of the Kingdom of Thailand) was under considerable threat from imperial powers spreading throughout Southeast Asia (Winichakul, 2000). HE emerged as an important investment designed to both build a fledgling nation and position the country 'as a civilized land unsuitable for colonisation' (Rhein, 2016, p. 262). The most prominent construction of *náksèuk-sǎa* during this period was as civil servants and nation builders. According to Sinlarat (2005), the early Thai universities, like Chulalongkorn, aimed 'to produce graduates to serve as government officials, rather than intellectuals or researchers' (p. 265). Later in the period, following the Siamese revolution (1932), further institutions were founded, sometimes drawing upon quite different nation-building ideologies. This can be seen in the case of Thammasat University (1934) which focused on law and politics with the aim of democratising access to HE and contributing to the formation of a new democratic political system. Later in the period Mahidol University, Kasetsart University and Silpakorn University (1943) were founded, focusing on medicine, agriculture and fine arts, respectively, as these were national development priorities. From the location of these institutions, all in Bangkok, it is also apparent that the university student was someone based in the capital city. Additionally, for much of this period, *náksèuk-sǎa* were constructed as social elites (Rhein, 2016). For example, Chulalongkorn University's curriculum was oriented towards serving noble and aristocratic families, with the expectation that graduates would go on to work as civil servants.

Development planning period (1950–present)

Thailand, like Hong Kong, Taiwan, Singapore and South Korea – also known as 'the Four Tiger economies' (Ashton, Green, James, & Sung, 2005) – has used skill formation as an economic tool of the state. During the early years of this period, Thailand received significant support from Western powers following World War II (e.g. via USAID and The Colombo Plan), to help educate citizens and produce future academics. Much of this funding was related to Western concerns about the spread of communism throughout Asia (Eaksittipong, 2018). These influences shaped the organisational and administrative structures of Thai universities, as well as the pedagogical practices and curricula that were set. The 1960s goal of decentralising development also saw the spread of HE to regions outside of Bangkok (Bovonsiri et al., 1996). Yet during this period 'higher education was still a one-tier system with limited access for the non-elite' (Rhein, 2016, p. 264). From the 1980s, this developed further into a massified system, which addressed some challenges in access, such as enabling much higher participation of women. However, other access issues remain, with HE spending concentrated in Bangkok and disproportionately benefitting wealthier Thai people, for example.

While previously identified constructions arguably continue throughout this period, two new prominent constructions arise. At times during this period, *náksèuk-sǎa* were also constructed as political radicals. Mass student protests against the authoritarian rule of the military government occurred in

1973, with hundreds of thousands of students calling for a new constitution and the release of political prisoners. In 1976, the return of military rule again brought students out in protest. On October 6, 1976, state forces and right-wing paramilitaries attacked students gathered at Thammasat University. While the death toll remains disputed, unarmed students were beaten, raped and murdered, with some students lynched from nearby trees. Thousands of students were subsequently arrested.

Another key construction of *náksèuk-săa* emerged following the 1997 Asian financial crisis. Thai HE underwent significant neoliberal reform as a condition of World Bank and IMF 'rescue packages', including privatisation, decentralisation and practices of autonomisation (Burford & Mulya, 2019). Tuition fees and private provision have increased, leading to HE being increasingly framed as a private good, and students and families as paying customers investing in their social capital and labour mobility. According to Sinlarat (2005), Thai students have increasingly become viewed as 'consumers' (p. 265), a construction also identified by Ma Rhea (2017). In line with international trends (e.g. Brooks, Byford, & Sela, 2016), increasingly Thai students are said to focus on outcomes (e.g. having a degree) rather than subjectivity (e.g. being a learner). This sits in direct contrast to earlier constructions of the learner as one who is involved in a sacred exchange. As our analysis will demonstrate, this construction of the *náksèuk-săa* appears more prominent over time, particularly in the most recent HE development plan.

Methods: Analysing Thai HE policies

In this chapter, we track the figure of the *náksèuk-săa* in Thai HE policy documents across history (1990–2019). We draw on texts produced by a particular policy actor: the Office of the Higher Education Commission (OHEC)[4], a government department concerned with Thailand's HE policy. Four documents were selected for analysis. Two documents are 15-year HE plans (1990–2004; 2008–2022), one is a 20-year HE plan (2018–2033), and the other is a 5-year HE student development strategy (2017–2021)[5] (see Table 4.1 for details). The 5-year HE student development strategy is the first of its kind to be separated from the long-range HE plans. The selected texts are the primary documents translating national development objectives to the HE sector and are operationalised via shorter-range plans. They have been selected because they offer a high-level overview of proposed developments in Thai HE.

Across our analysis, we closely attended to prominent discursive constructions of *náksèuk-săa* that were identifiable within our corpus. Following Brooks (2018), we explored how 'students are represented and the conceptualisations of them that underpin the various policy measures' (p. 747). In terms of the analytic procedure, a process of close reading was undertaken. While our analysis was primarily concerned with the idea of *náksèuk-săa*, each of these texts was read in detail in order to discern particular ways that

Table 4.1 List of policy texts

Identifier	Period	Full title
First Plan	1990–2004	Objectives, Policies, Measures and Goals of the Long-Range Higher Education Plan (B.E. 2533–2447) (MUA, 1990).
Second Plan	2008–2022	The 15-Year Higher Education Plan (B.E. 2551–2565) (OHEC, 2008).
Third Plan	2018–2037	The 20-Year Higher Education Plan (B.E. 2561–2580) (OHEC, 2018a).
Student Strategy	2017–2021	Higher Education Student Development Strategy (B.E. 2560–2564) (OHEC, 2018b).

náksèuk-săa are constructed in discourse. Initially, the documents were coded inductively. Following this coding process, a thematic analysis was undertaken (Braun & Clarke, 2006) to identify dominant themes and to consider changes in constructions of *náksèuk-săa* across time. As we present these constructions, it is important to remember that none of these ways of figuring *náksèuk-săa* are separate from each other, nor are they necessarily coherent positions (Ball, 1993). Instead, constructions are often layered within texts that have no shortage of ambiguity, inconsistency and doubt as to their intended meaning. While the four constructions that we present are those which we judge to be 'prominent', within the texts there were other distinguishable constructions that we have either subsumed within a broader category or excluded because they appeared to be minor constructions.

Analysis: Dominant constructions of *náksèuk-săa*

Background

Across the three long-range plans, the primary stated purpose of HE is identified as 'national development'. Where students are concerned, HE is primarily positioned as a mechanism which supplies various sectors with necessary 'human capital'. Each of the three long-range plans identifies four key functions of HE: instruction, research, academic service and preservation of arts and culture.

Across these documents, national development priorities appear to shift, as does how the state views HE's national development function. The First Plan, situated within Thailand's policy shift towards globalisation and HE massification, aims to produce graduates who both contribute to 'national development and international economic competition' (p. 2) while at the same time maintain local communities and cultural heritage. In the Second Plan, HE is identified as a mechanism to remedy social ills (environmental damage, conflict and violence, population change, labour market changes, energy dependency) as well as to promote the economic competitiveness of the nation within a globalised economy (via technological development, economic reform, decentralisation initiatives). The Third Plan focuses national development on driving Thailand out of the 'middle-income trap' (p. 8) and into the status of a high-income economy. This also informs a shift in the instruments of change, where HEIs are expected to prioritise research and innovation, as well as produce graduates who meet the needs of the labour market.

Some other trends are worth noting. Across the plans, there is a shift in the actor who defines how graduates ought to develop. In the First Plan, this is primarily the state, which identifies needs across sectors relevant to national development. By the Third Plan, while state priorities are noted, employers' needs are equally pronounced. Over time, the rationale for change also appears to shift: from meeting the needs of local communities, 'Thai society' and national-level industries in the First Plan, to employers' satisfaction, global rankings and global measures of economic competitiveness in the Third. Arguably, this also sets other changes in motion, such as shifts in the desirability of various disciplines: from sciences alongside social sciences and humanities in the First Plan, to a prioritisation of the sciences in the Third. And while in the First Plan, HE has a role in cultivating the knowledge, skills and ethics for students, by the Third Plan the key concepts framing student development are 'competencies' and 'soft skills'.

Across each of the three plans, there is also a shift in the level of explicit focus on *nákseuk-săa*. While the First and Second Plans generally focus on how HEIs ought to adjust to meet policy goals, in the Third Plan, there is much greater emphasis on what university graduates should be like, what qualities they should have and what expectations they need to meet. The Third Plan has an accompanying document, the Student Strategy, which offers greater detail about how the development of future graduates ought to align with wider national policies. This Student Strategy document is the first of its kind, demonstrating a growing interest in how students are developing and indeed the imagined purpose of university students vis-a-vis the nation. This shift towards a greater focus on how the *nákseuk-săa* is being constructed by policymakers provides the impetus for our analysis.

Nákseuk-săa *as future workers (who contribute to national development)*

Across the four policy documents, the most prevalent construction of *nákseuk-săa* is as future workers who contribute to Thailand's national development. Arguably, this configuration provides the core rationale for all four texts: it is in the national interest to be strategic in preparing a workforce appropriate for Thailand's development goals. Perhaps, the prevalence of this construction is not surprising, given that since the Early Modernisation period of Thai HE (see historical review) graduates have been expected to contribute to national development, particularly in the civil service. This construction also resonates with regional development approaches, such as those of the Asian Tigers (Singapore, Hong Kong, South Korea and Singapore) who connected skills formation policies to the figure of 'the student' in pursuit of nation-building (Ashton et al., 2005).

In the First Plan, the construction of students as the country's future workforce is evident: graduates are tasked with 'responding to local problems and the needs of the production sector' (p. 3). In the Second Plan, the *student as future worker* is again tasked with solving national problems, from economic changes to environmental concerns; HEIs are expected to provide a well-prepared and knowledgeable workforce to deal with these challenges. However, the Second Plan also notes a 'mismatch' (p. 20) between students' subject selection and occupational skills that are needed, presenting extra-curricular activities as a solution for equipping students with competencies 'beyond academic skills' (p. 20). The notion of skills and competencies is increasingly emphasised in the Third Plan and Student Strategy, which present the gap between graduate skills and those required by employers as a core challenge. The education of graduates is to be adjusted 'to the appropriate needs' (Third Plan, p. 81) of human resource planning, with graduates' ability to transition into work comprising one of the 14 key performance indicators (KPIs) of the plan. Although the Student Strategy document does foreground more individual-level goals, such as graduates thriving in the 21st century world of work, these are tied very closely to national-level objectives of a competent workforce contributing to international economic competitiveness. The document encourages HEIs to prioritise 'soft skills', to 'enable students to use hard skills in leading a good life as well as create their own futures and benefit society' (p. 4).

The *student as future worker* construction is also evident when we examine anticipated career pathways. The metaphor used to describe students' social role is that they are 'products' supplied to various 'users'. Interestingly, the description of these 'users' ranges across the plans, from predominantly the 'government and various production sectors' (First Plan), to 'the private sector' (Second Plan) and 'employers' (Third Plan). Throughout each of the plans, these 'users' are presented as central to determining areas of student development to be prioritised. In the First Plan, for example, the idea of 'the expert, the well-rounded, and the socially responsible and dutiful [student]' (p. 3) is introduced as the desirable graduate to fulfil nation-building roles, led by government priorities. The Second Plan and particularly the Third Plan, in contrast, highlight how 'graduates' weaknesses' (Second Plan, p. 43) in essential non-academic skills demonstrate how 'HEIs have yet to adequately prioritise preparing graduates for the labour market' (Third Plan, p. 67). Indeed, in the Third Plan, employers' 100% satisfaction rate towards graduates is listed as another KPI, responding to complaints that graduate qualities do not match labour market expectations.

By contrast, the Student Strategy does not pinpoint particular stakeholders as 'end goals' to the same extent. While it maintains the *student as future worker* discourse by stating that graduates are 'key drivers in national development' (p. 13), it is much more focused on individual outcomes. The primary desired outcome of the Student Strategy is graduates surviving and thriving in the 21ˢᵗ century, with students' skills and character presented as the main targets of investment. Students' anticipated contribution to national development also differs in this document, described as those who 'are change leaders, respond to society and exhibit good morality with their knowledge' (p. 13). Also noteworthy are the different foci in the Third Plan and the Student Strategy: while in the former HEIs produce graduates for employers and the nation, in the latter graduates are expected to lead change and build their own futures. This may be considered an example of parallel policy texts offering slightly different spins to the *student as future worker* construction.

Náksèuk-sǎa *as preservers of Thai culture*

While the *student as future worker* construction pushes the country forward, the *student as cultural preserver* traces back in an effort to maintain national values and heritage. This construction is especially pronounced in the First Plan, which recognises the impetus for Thailand to engage internationally while also emphasising '[building] preparedness and social recognition of the values and national cultural heritage' to enable participation 'with pride and dignity' (p. 9). Indeed, the First Plan is also the only document that considers the arts and culture function of universities at any length. The construction of *náksèuk-sǎa as preservers of Thai culture* is closely related to the idea of 'the good citizen', who, through education, has a 'broad worldview' and 'good social conscience' (p. 3). This construction calls graduates to strike the 'right' balance between external knowledge and local cultural responsibilities – between looking outward to the world and staying connected to Thai values. The First Plan urges HEIs to support students in achieving cultural preservation through 'fostering desirable cultural attributes in students' (p. 9), '[increasing] and [focusing] on heritage-based curricula' (p. 10), and '[developing] curricula that are problem-based, community-based, and cultural and ethical conscience-based' (p. 3).

Despite its visible absence, this construction does surface in all three other documents, albeit more subtly. The Second Plan, in recognising the new challenges Thailand was facing at the turn of the century, identifies a 'social values crisis as a result of the diffusion of outside cultures' (p. 1) that the HE sector needs to respond to. In particular, it states: 'What society should be able to expect from universities are graduates who are knowledgeable, able to transition into work, and able to *abide by social and cultural expectations of proper conduct*' (p. 1, emphasis added). The Student Strategy and the Third Plan, while sharing a more 'global' outlook, still stress the importance of cultural preservation and striking the 'right' balance. In the Third Plan, it is desirable for graduates to 'exhibit values according to good societal norms'

(p. 107) while conducting themselves as 'members of a multicultural society' (p. 109). Similarly, the Student Strategy notes that the ability to maintain cultural identity is vital. Arguably, recent policy orientations towards 'active learners' who engage, participate and collaborate that emerge from a *future worker* construction sit uneasily in relation to ideas of preserving Thai culture; traditional constructions of the Thai learner position this subject as passive, obedient and respectful. In sum, even though the *student as cultural preserver* sits in the shadows of the larger construction of the *student as future worker*, it is present in all policy texts.

Náksèuk-săa *as customers*

In line with many other HE systems that have introduced neoliberal reforms (Brooks et al., 2016), *náksèuk-săa* were positioned as *customers* within the documents we analysed. Although not a strong construction, increasingly *náksèuk-săa* appear to be constructed as 'customers' alongside, and sometimes in opposition to, their construction as 'learners'. This figure surfaces in the Third Plan especially, where goals are set for HEIs to increase opportunities for students (herein defined as *pôo ráp bor-rí-gaan:* service users). HEIs are also asked to 'compete more in terms of quality' (p. 70) in order to appeal to prospective student-customers. While the term *pôo ráp bor-rí-gaan* is primarily translated as service users, it is our interpretation that such a positioning of the student in relation to the university also positions them as potential customers. Indeed, this construction operates against the backdrop of emerging neoliberal, economistic and metricised discourses operating in Thai HE policy, traceable in various instances throughout the document. Examples include (a) redefining HEIs as 'providers' and OHEC as a 'regulator' (p. 64), thus re-imagining the relationship between HEIs and the state; (b) promoting knowledge and research that can 'create added value' (p. 8) and may be converted 'into intellectual property' (p. 61), in turn re-framing research via its potential economic impact; (c) incorporating 'international rankings' (p. 67) and 'top 200 global university ranking' (p. 11), operationalising global rankings as indicators of quality and (d) emphasising 'graduate competencies' (p. 31) for employability in contrast to conceptions of knowledge and academic skills.

The *students as customers* construction has important implications for what it means to be a *náksèuk-săa*. Although it does not contradict the figure of *the future worker*, the two constructions do not layer together in the smoothest way. Where the *student as customer* is ascribed the power to choose an education they desire, the *student as future worker* is guided by national development targets informing resource mobilisation supporting their education. More fundamentally, while the *customer–student* appears to have the autonomy to make decisions about educational investments, the *student as future worker* is instead deemed a 'product' groomed for purposes pre-determined by national priorities and supplied to various sectors as employees.

Additionally, the *student as customer* places greater emphasis on the wants of the student and financial decision-makers (e.g. families) rather than positioning the *náksèuk-săa* as a 'pure receptacle' for knowledge or a link in a sacred chain of knowledge transmission. The *student as customer* construction may therefore deeply challenge traditional notions of the teacher–student relationship in Thailand that we traced earlier.

The 'new gen' náksèuk-săa

The construction of the 'new gen[eration]' *náksèuk-săa* emerges as a temporally distinct position in the more recent policy documents, namely the Third Plan and the Student Strategy. While *dèk sà-măi née* is an expression commonly used to express anxiety and disappointment with young people, the 'new gen' configuration constructs today's *náksèuk-săa* as fundamentally different from previous generations in terms of learning style, motivation and values. This has been reflected in calls for HE systems, curricula and pedagogies to respond to changes in student subjectivity. Indeed, the Third Plan makes it clear that, because '*kon rûn mài* (Gen-Z) constantly desire to develop new skills and knowledge' (p. 77), HEIs should support academics so that 'pedagogies may be updated to suit the times' (p. 91). This development ties in with the endorsement in both policy texts for extra-curricular activities to be further supported, which is deemed crucial for students developing 'holistically' and thriving in the 21st century as mentioned above. Although the *'new gen' student* is not explicitly discussed in earlier documents, the Second Plan does recognise emerging signs of shifts in the working lives of future graduates, including multiple jobs, freelance work, income uncertainties and shifting teams of colleagues. In light of this, it also pushes for HEIs to focus on skills 'beyond disciplinary expertise' (p. 20), what is later termed 'soft skills' in the Third Plan and Student Strategy.

At the same time, however, we also notice more disapproving ways that the *'new gen' student* surfaces in the two recent policy texts, echoing the public sentiment that initially prompted our desire to write this chapter. In the Third Plan, *'new gen' students* are configured as degree-seekers, viewed to be instrumental, self-centred and neglectful of their duty to others: 'There is a need to change [students'] attitudes in pursuing HE, from seeking degrees to seeking to improve their own learning potential, to be independent, and to contribute to society' (p. 70). From a different angle, the Student Strategy notes 'worsening cultural decline and changing social values' (p. 17). It identifies students' materialism and consumerism as a result of 'the influx of foreign cultures' (p. 16) on the one hand, and their 'inappropriate behaviour' on the other. Thus, the 'new gen' construction of the student is a two-sided coin, offering promise for the future while also being a risky figure who may not contribute to national development or cultural preservation in an orderly way.

Discussion and conclusion: *náksèuk-săa* as a complex figure worthy of consideration

Across this chapter, we have advanced our position that *náksèuk-săa* are important educational subjects worthy of detailed consideration. While they have been the feature of much public commentary, there have been few attempts to piece together who exactly *náksèuk-săa* should be in the eyes of Thailand's policymakers. We have read across scholarly literature and analysed policy documents in order to contribute to ongoing debates about Thai HE, its students and the wider global literature on university studenthood. Drawing these texts together has allowed us to trace continuities and change in the development of the Thai HE system and has revealed various discursive constructions of *náksèuk-săa* situated within a broader socio-historical context.

The predominant construction that we identified across the dataset was *náksèuk-săa* as future worker and developer of the nation. This was the most prominent theme across all four policy texts and informs all of the policy strategies articulated. As we identified in the historical review, the idea of the *náksèuk-săa* as future worker is traceable to the late 19th century origins of the formal Thai HE system. HE in Thailand arose out of desires among elites to produce future civil servants to build and administer a fledgling nation. In this sense, the *náksèuk-săa as future worker* is a bedrock construction that has been re-animated throughout Thailand's modern history. However, through our analysis, we have tracked the changing orientations of the future worker: from government service to employment in the private sector and as entrepreneurs.

Another construction visible from the origins of Thai HE is *náksèuk-săa* as preservers of Thai culture and heritage. Maintaining moral and social values, and preserving cultural practices, runs in parallel with developing the nation – arguably in order to both protect and construct what is unique about 'Thai-ness'. *Náksèuk-săa* are again called upon to fulfil a national duty of upholding social values under threat because of imperialism, internationalisation and more recently globalisation. While constructions of *náksèuk-săa as future worker* often call upon *kwaam-róo jàak paai-nôk* (outsider knowledge), particularly *kwaam-róo pí-pát-tá-naa-gaan* (development knowledge) (Ma Rhea, 2017), the *náksèuk-săa as preserver of culture* calls upon local knowledge systems. Thus, these twin constructions are set up as counterweights in order to steer the nation on the right course. The relationship between them is perhaps captured in a popular idiom, *kwaam-róo kôo kun-ná-tam*, which translates to 'knowledge with virtue' – this happens to be the motto of Thailand's first university, Chulalongkorn.

A less prevalent theme, the *náksèuk-săa as customer*, is both a more individualistic orientation towards student subjectivity and a manifestation of the fact that the state will not provide HE for all on the public purse; it makes an assumption that students and their families ought to share the cost.

This stance is connected to the rise of autonomous universities in particular, and growing neoliberalism in the Thai HE system more broadly (Burford & Mulya, 2019). Indeed, this is highly troubling for idealised notions of the teacher–learner relationship in Thailand, historically configured as a moral exchange with ensuing duties. Constructing students as customers – purchasing educational services – has profound impacts on curricula, pedagogies, the idea of the *aa-jaan* (academic) and the idea of the *máhǎawíttáyaalai* (university) itself. The *student as customer* construction is one that has been identified internationally (Brooks et al., 2016) and our study demonstrates the connection between the Thai HE system and others around the world. However, through a nationally distinct angle, we are able to demonstrate how policy ideas arriving in Thailand are met with different kinds of resistance: logics grounded in Thai cultural values and historical characteristics.

In the last two documents, *dèk sà-mǎi née* constructions produce the figure of the *'new gen' university student* who is fundamentally different from previous generations of *náksèuk-sǎa*. The texts portray a sea change in the world of work, with more freelancing and entrepreneurialism and less job stability, accompanied by growing globalisation and rapid technological advances. The *'new gen' náksèuk-sǎa* is visible in the policy documents via calls for academics to teach differently, as well as the new domains of competencies identified as necessary. Indeed, 'new gen' students are even marked in policy, described as a 'New Breed of Graduates'. While one possible explanation is that policymakers are embracing change and recognising the different needs and aspirations of today's *náksèuk-sǎa*, another interpretation is that these new policy constructions arise out of anxiety that university students are increasingly difficult to understand and control, and that new ways of categorising, understanding and addressing them ought to be found. In many ways the *'new gen' student* construction has a complex relationship with other constructions we have identified. It differs from the *future worker* construction precisely because the future of work has become disrupted, leaving the government uncertain to what ends they are developing students for. It also sits in contrast with the *student as cultural preserver*, with materialism and consumerism identified as forms of 'cultural decline' rather than maintenance and preservation. Clearly, this discursive landscape is a complex and incoherent one; for example, while the *'new gen' student* as 'degree seeker' is commonly positioned pejoratively, as though 'all they want is a qualification', HE students are also defined by the government as 'service users' and called into 'customer' constructions, as noted above.

Of note in our analysis is that 'political radical' constructions that erupted through student activism of the 1950–1970s have remained inhabitable positions. While this construction was not addressed in any of the policy documents we analysed, it is important to investigate the absence of discussion about students' political agency. Arguably, Thai governments of various hues have not sought to encourage student political activity, with recent governments clamping down on this quite explicitly. However, this has not stopped students from organising to oppose unelected governments, or refusing to prostrate themselves in oath-taking ceremonies (see Burford, Uerpairojkit, Eppolite, & Vachananda, 2019), for example. Indeed, as we were putting our final touches to this chapter, *náksèuk-săa* across numerous HEIs held unprecedented mass demonstrations against the Prayuth administration in response to the dissolution of a 'new gen' political party 'Future Forward'. Adulyanon and Wongpanya (2020) have described these political activities as a 'phenomenon' in Thai politics, with recent *náksèuk-săa* demonstrations being animated via social media but without any formal coordination. Some commentators have even described them as 'evocative of the Oct 14, 1973, popular uprising launched by university students' (Chetchotiros, 2020, n.p.). This recent case surely demonstrates that ideas of *náksèuk-săa* are in tension; student subjectivities may be at once shifting, unpredictable and unplanned, while also possibly linked to historical figurations preceding them. Equally, policymakers may set out to 'curate' student constructions, whereas others may effloresce and veer wildly 'off plan'.

This chapter has contributed to the wider project of tracing possible understandings of *náksèuk-săa* circulating in policy texts and across social debates about Thai HE. It is our contention that throughout Thailand's modern history, the *náksèuk-săa* has been positioned as essential for the development and preservation of the nation. Within this framing, a number of constructions have co-existed over time, fading in and out of view, layering onto each other, and sometimes conflicting with each other. Thus, in concluding this chapter, we find that *náksèuk-săa* often sit right in the middle of paradoxes. The current period sees Thailand aspiring to compete internationally and participate in the global community on the one hand, and striving to preserve its cultural heritage against globalising forces on the other. The 'right' place for the contemporary *náksèuk-săa* is thus a deep and complex question, set against the historical backdrop of unsettled politics and underlain with conflicting aspirations of the nation, the community and the self.

We have sought to home in on these contradictory imaginings of *náksèuk-săa* with the hope of contributing to a richer understanding of the construction of HE students in an under-considered context such as Thailand. By drawing attention to how constructions of Thai students can inform our understandings of university students on a global scale, we offer a platform for cross-country conversations about continuities and change in imaginings of studenthood. We invite readers to consider what might be done with these student constructions, all of which have the capacity to enable and constrain. The next task is to consider how to use these ideas, how they are entangled with our routine practices and where they are submerged within our own habits of thinking. Knowing that ideas of *náksèuk-săa* are fractured and contested might encourage further debate: How might these various constructions be animated to advocate for ideals of studenthood we desire? Indeed, they might remind us that ideas of *náksèuk-săa* have been, and may still be, imagined otherwise.

Notes

1 In the Thai language, there is no plural form. Therefore the noun *nákseuk-săa* can be used in both plural and singular modes.
2 In Thailand all undergraduate university students wear university uniforms. Thai university uniforms have been a site of much debate, which extends beyond the scope of this chapter (see for example: Bunyawanich, Järvelä, & Ghaffar, 2018).
3 The historical periods we use in this paper correlate with those used by the Office of the Higher Education Commission (OHEC, 2014) (cited in Crocco, 2018).
4 One included document was from the Ministry of University Affairs, which later became OHEC as part of the Ministry of Education.
5 The 20-year plan and the 5-year student development strategy were completed and disseminated for use prior to the restructuring of OHEC, which saw it moved from the Ministry of Education to the Ministry of Higher Education, Science and Innovation.

References

Adulyanon, S. & Wongpanya, T. (Presenters) (2020, February 27). แสงดาวแห่ง ศรัทธา *VS* 'จันทร์โอชา' และพวก [The starlight of faith VS 'Chan-ocha' and allies]. The Standard. https://thestandard.co/podcast/thepowergame43/

Alexa, (2020). *Top site in Thailand.* https://www.alexa.com/topsites/countries/TH

Ashton, D., Green, F., James, D., & Sung, J. (2005). *Education and Training for Development in East Asia: The Political Economy of Skill Formation in Newly Industrialised Economies.* Routledge.

Ball, S. (1993). What is policy? Texts, trajectories and toolboxes. *Discourse: Studies in the Cultural Politics of Education* 13:2, 10–17. doi:10.1080/0159630930130203

Bovonsiri, V., Uampuang, P., & Fry, G. (1996). Cultural influences on higher education in Thailand. In K. Kempner & W. Tierney (Eds.) *The Social Role of Higher Education: Comparative Perspectives*, 55–78. Garland Publishing.

Braun, V. & Clarke, V. (2006). Using thematic analysis in psychology. *Qualitative Research in Psychology* 3: 77–101. doi:10.1191/1478088706qp063oa

Brooks, R. (2018). The construction of higher education students in English policy documents. *British Journal of Sociology of Education* 39:6, 745–761. doi:10.1080/01425692.2017.1406339

Brooks, R. (2019). The construction of higher education students within national policy: A cross-European comparison. *Compare* doi:10.1080/03057925.2019.1604118.

Brooks, R., Byford, K. & Sela, K. (2016). Students' unions, consumerism and the neo-liberal university. *British Journal of Sociology of Education* 37:8, 1211–1228. doi:10.1080/01425692.2015.1042150

Bunyawanich, S., Järvelä, M. & Ghaffar, A. (2018). The influence of uniform in establishing unity, hierarchy, and conformity at Thai universities. *Journal of Education and Training Studies* 6:7, 28–37. doi:10.11114/jets.v6i7.3151

Burford, J. & Mulya, T.W. (2019). Neoliberalism in Thai and Indonesian universities: Using photo-elicitation methods to picture space for possibility. In C. Manathunga & D. Bottrell (eds.), *Resisting Neoliberalism in Higher Education Volume II*, 219–245. Palgrave.

Burford, J., Uerpairojkit, T., Eppolite, M. & Vachananda, T. (2019). Analysing the national and institutional policy landscape for foreign academics in Thailand: Opportunity, ambivalence and threat. *Journal of Higher Education Policy and Management* 41:4, 416–429. doi:10.1080/1360080X.2019.1606881

Chetchotiros, N. (2020, March 1). *Students vent their fury: Experts weigh in on recent reignition of student activism across country.* Bangkok Post https://www.bangkok-post.com/thailand/special-reports/1868549/students-vent-their-fury

Crocco, O.S. (2018). Thai higher education: Privatization and massification. In G. Fry (ed.) *Education in Thailand: An Old Elephant in Search of a New Mahout,* 223–255. Springer.

Eaksittipong, S. (2018). A preliminary studies on the development of Thai higher education in the Cold War context: The rise of Thai academia, nationalist scholars and intellectual nationalism under the Eagle's Shadow. *Inthaninthaksin Journal* 13:2, 59–87.

Giordano, J. (2011). Teacher's heads. *Prajna Vihara* 12:2, 123–142.

Leathwood, C. & Read, B. (2009). *Gender and the Changing Face of Higher Education: A Feminized Future?* Open University Press.

Ma Rhea, Z. (2017). *Wisdom, Knowledge, and the Postcolonial University in Thailand.* Palgrave Macmillan.

Ministry of University Affairs. (1990). *Objectives, Policies, Measures and Goals of the Long-Range Higher Education Plan (B.E. 2533–2547).* MUA.

Office of the Higher Education Commission. (2008). *The 15-Year Higher Education Plan (B.E. 2551–2565).* OHEC.

Office of the Higher Education Commission. (2013). *The Eleventh Higher Education Development Plan (B.E. 2555–2559).* OHEC.

Office of the Higher Education Commission. (2018a). *The 20-Year Higher Education Plan (B.E. 2561–2580).* OHEC.

Office of the Higher Education Commission. (2018b). *Higher Education Student Development Strategy (B.E. 2560–2564).* OHEC.

Rhein, D. (2016). Westernisation and the Thai higher education system: Past and present. *Journal of Educational Administration and History* 48:3, 261–274. doi:1 0.1080/00220620.2016.1184133

Sinlarat, P. (2005). Changing the culture of education in Thai universities. *Higher Education Policy* 18, 265–269. doi:10.1057/palgrave.hep.8300088

Winichakul, T. (2000). The quest for "Siwilai": A geographical discourse of civilizational thinking in the late nineteenth and early twentieth-century Siam. *The Journal of Asian Studies* 59:3, 528–549. doi:10.1017/S0021911800014327

Wyatt, D. (1969). *The Politics of Reform in Thailand: Education in the Reign of King Chulalongkorn.* New Haven: Yale University Press.

Chapter 5

The shifting subjectification of the 'widening participation' student

The affective world of the 'deserving' consumer

Emily Danvers and Tamsin Hinton-Smith

Introduction

Access to becoming a higher education (HE) student in the UK is increasingly mediated through an outreach industry in which the academy's opportunities are communicated and distributed *from* education providers *to* prospective applicants and their communities. These outreach practices are traditionally ordered though foci on particular elements of disadvantage including lower socio-economic status, those who are first in their families to go to university, ethnicity, disability and age, with the intention of widening access to these previously under-represented groups. This chapter draws from our experience of Phase 1 of the Office for Students[1]-funded UK-wide National Collaborative Outreach Programme (NCOP)[2], which ran from January 2017 to July 2019. Both authors were seconded from academic education roles with a focus on HE participation and inequalities, to lead regional research and evaluation of this £60 million per year funding initiative in England. NCOP was established to support the UK government's social mobility goals by rapidly increasing the number of young people from under-represented groups who go into HE. NCOP does not include any targeted focus on older learners, although in Phase 2 providers are able to work with this group but without any incentive to do so. In practice, this severely limits opportunity for outreach professionals to work with older learners.

NCOP's focus is on university progression 'cold spots', postcode areas where HE participation is lower than might be expected among young people who choose not to go to university despite achieving or being on track to achieve the entry requirements. Phase 1, which completed in June 2019, included particular focus on the target groups of young men from disadvantaged backgrounds and BAME (Black and Minority Ethnic) learners, who have been identified as much less likely to progress to HE (Boliver, 2013). NCOP has since been extended with a second phase to run until July 2021.

Widening participation – what, why and with whom?

HE inequalities are the outcomes of educational gaps that start early and open up as people move through their education journeys (Crozier, 2005). This necessitates the development of deep and wide understanding into the relevant factors at play. The mechanisms that inform progression pathways are a complex constellation of individuals' own contextualised decision-making, and that of other decision-making gatekeepers in their educational trajectories, including school and university teachers as well as outreach professionals. These influential others are invariably well intentioned and committed to supporting equity in educational progression, often informed by coming from widening participation (WP) backgrounds themselves. There is a need to develop greater understanding of the complex confidence growing and decision-making processes that take place between individuals, their families and key education professionals in their lives, within the surrounding nexus of wider social context and trends.

What constitutes WP activity aimed at encouraging students into HE comprises a variable set of practices – from outreach work in the community to specialist summer schools or mentoring programmes. Traditionally, this agenda has appeared to be directed from HE institutions themselves in specialist outreach departments, yet with concurrent pressures on schools to demonstrate progression and further education colleges providing HE programmes, the sector has proliferated. Elsewhere we have noted that 'there is seldom guidance on good practice for academics' (Johnson et al., 2019, p. 3) engaged in outreach work. Indeed, there remains a lack of compelling evidence either produced by or to guide this diversified outreach sector. This includes paucity of information around what activity constitutes effective WP, as well as which groups it should be aimed at and how it should be delivered.

The UK has traditionally been perceived as leading the agenda to widen participation in HE (Burke, 2013), and successive governments have been keen to emphasise their success in both increasing HE participation and closing the gap in participation between rich and poor. There have been undoubted substantial gains both in actual participation and in wider cultures of understanding and commitment in the half century of successive British governments' WP agendas (Hinton-Smith, 2012). However, it is important that growing participation does not necessarily negate the persistence of inequalities.

Persistent gaps in HE participation are not only the residue of stubborn past inequalities, but can be seen as mapping to new and emergent insecurities. In the UK, this includes the introduction of tuition fees in 2010 and ensuing concerns around the perceived balance of costs and returns of investing in HE moving from the tax payer on to the individual student (Hinton-Smith, 2016). It also includes the end of the Aimhigher[3] WP Programme, the demise of which effectively ended universities' external accountability for the success of their WP activities. Further, the replacement of universal Educational Maintenance Allowance (EMA) with the National Bursary Programme ended universal entitlement to financial support for further education students aged 16–18 from poorer families while they studied, closing the gateway into HE for many whose parents could not afford for them to remain at home without a financial contribution (Hinton-Smith, 2012). Sitting within the wider context of welfare reform, austerity, and wider instability such as the protracted unsureness around Brexit, these developments have raised the challenge for the UK HE sector as it works to increase participation from socially disadvantaged backgrounds. The combination of influencing factors in mediating the HE progression journeys of those from the most financially vulnerable backgrounds has been referred to as a 'toxic mix' (Finlay, 2014), and the stresses suffered by students can be seen reflected in rising mental health problems, including anxiety, loneliness and substance misuse (Insight Network, 2019).

NCOP draws together attainment and geography as proxies of disadvantage represented by a postcode indicator. Yet we argue that this particular targeting, and the surrounding socio-economic and policy climate, has shifted the imaginary of how these 'WP' students are understood within the UK context. Within this discourse, prospective students become positioned as agentic choosers who need only to be persuaded to take up the opportunities open to them. This can inform approaches to WP that focus on telling rather than guiding decision-making and alter conceptions of those who fail to capitalise on the opportunities presented as being available to all. The potential for disjuncture between education market agendas and the anxieties of prospective students is exacerbated within the context of increasingly marketing and recruitment approaches to WP, set against legitimate fears of prospective students and their families around uncertain futures in terms of the job market and potential gains of making what has become an individual investment in HE (Brown, 2013; Crawford & Van der Erve, 2015; Crawford, Gregg, Macmillan, Vignoles, & Wyness, 2016). It is argued that the UK student loan system has become increasingly regressive, with the highest costs being paid by those who get the least return from their participation (Johnston & Barr, 2013), and that increased costs have encouraged those from less advantaged backgrounds to become more strategic university decision-makers (Clark, Mountford-Zimdars, & Francis, 2015). An awareness that the risks of university are not distributed evenly has led to HE funding policies being identified as a contributory factor in widening inequalities (Callender & Mason, 2017). Further, an approach to WP that has such a specific agenda is seen as out of sync with supporting individual choice. It also implies an increased responsibility for universities to interrogate the targeting and impact of their institutional policies to both widen access and increase student numbers.

Theorisation

The theoretical context for our conceptualisation of the responsibilities of WP is, as we have discussed elsewhere, informed by the principle that this form of participation ought not to be reduced to recruitment (Johnson et al., 2019, p. 7). There is a need for collectively developing more nuanced conceptualisations of the intricate web of individuals' lives as they interact with education and a limited definition of 'value' that rarely moves beyond quantitative measures.

The perceived importance of aspiration and individual responsibility for academic success or failure arguably problematises the marginalised for their own exclusion, resonating with criticisms of much of the wider discourse of WP in HE over recent decades (Hinton-Smith, 2012). This emphasis on individual aspiration intersects with identification that without targeted parental investment of the economic and cultural valued in education, less privileged students have to struggle to get to university, requiring a strong self-reliance (Reay, Crozier, & Clayton, 2010). In contrast, it is suggested that universities frequently position marginalised students negatively as deficit in capitals as a result of their background (O'Shea, 2015); this includes lacking the right kinds of knowledge, experience and social networks (Bathmaker, Ingram, & Waller, 2013). Furthermore, working-class parents are frequently perceived as deficit in providing the 'right' kinds of support (Gazeley, 2012; Gewirtz, 2001).

The repositioning of responsibility for the cost of participating in HE in England reflects changing deeper assumptions around the positioning of its value, centred around a growing consumerist model built on the assumption that it is an individual good that can be relied upon to deliver individual benefits (Clark et al., 2015; Callender & Mason, 2017), so long as people make informed choices. Widening conceptions of the individual and collective value of and responsibility for successful HE engagement is essential to acknowledging the unsureness of individual instrumental returns. Theoretical insights around the identified risks of HE participation for all, but particularly less advantaged students, have been central to informing our approach to developing understanding of the complexities of progression decision-making that deviate far from depoliticised and emotionally neutral assumptions around information, opportunities and choice.

HE participation is an investment, but a risky one because of the uncertainties of securing a well enough paid job to make the financial investment worthwhile (Dwyer, Hodson, & McCloud, 2013). The extent to which fear of debt influences decision-making is debated (Harrison, 2019). There is an argument that young people as a whole are more accepting of debt now given that it is so often unavoidable; yet also identification of a widening gap in attitudes according to family background, with those on lower incomes becoming more debt averse (Callender & Mason, 2017). Low-income students have been shown to more often perceive university costs as debt rather than investment compared with wealthier peers (Callender & Jackson, 2008), with it being suggested that increased debt aversion among those with fewest financial resources is better understood as aversion to the increased *risk* of debt rather than direct aversion to debt itself (see Barr, 2012). More widely, this links to sociological perspectives on risk that have increasingly acknowledged the significance of socio-demographic factors in influencing individuals' apprehension of and responses to risk (Taylor-Gooby & Zinn, 2006). Rather than chastising less advantaged students for failing to grasp the promised opportunities of HE, we suggest the need for more respectful and emotionally aware approaches to WP. These approaches should legitimate the astute appraisals of HE's precarities by prospective students and their parents and engage with these in direct and honest ways rather than seeking to brush them aside in pursuit of student numbers. This theoretical underpinning informs our methodological approach to developing, evaluating, researching and capacity-building within outreach, including in this work as explored further in our methodological discussion below.

Given the critiques above around the failure to socially contextualise individual experiences of educational marginalisation, we draw theoretically on Gordon's (2008, 2011) work on 'haunting' to argue that perceptions around the 'deserving consumer' of WP outreach are deeply linked to the affective pasts, presents and futures of individuals. By affect, we refer to a broad range of intensities of emotion that are constructed, re-produced and performed within and through the social world. This includes reflections on self-confidence and striving to succeed which emerge from participant histories and reveal themselves in everyday feelings of being, for example, deserving/ undeserving. These 'feelings' that punctuate a learner journey into, through and beyond HE may emerge in the individual but, we argue, are revealing of social, historical and political constructions of the WP student.

Methods

The data we draw on in this chapter were collected between October 2017 and December 2018 as part of regional research and evaluation of Phase 1 of NCOP. It forms part of a larger data set that included participant evaluation of funded outreach activities (1150 responses), a learner survey (1258 responses) and a staff survey that included teachers and WP practitioners (38 responses). These data generated important insights into experienced and perceived benefits of measured gains including knowledge, self-confidence, aspiration and ability.

Our qualitative research data were smaller in scale, yet provided some important areas of deeper insight into the contribution and challenges of this programme and outreach provision more widely. Developing insight into the complexity of individual journeys and the nuancing of success can be challenging and requires more in-depth understanding than that provided by standard tracking requirements. Indeed, there is a complex mix of reasons for why this might be the case, most notably the challenges in attributing a 'decision' to a specific moment or activity provided. Our qualitative data collection engaged with 108 participants representing diverse key stakeholder groups within the region. This included focus group interviews with 76 young people aged between 14 and 19 years old drawn from four 11–16 schools selected to capture diversity within the region, in terms of school profile, locality and opportunities, and 7 'walking interviews' with NCOP learners that took place within their further education colleges of study. Alongside learner interviews, we carried out 25 interviews with key adults that included education and outreach practitioners, careers advisors and parents.

In this chapter, we draw predominantly on insights from the qualitative learner data generated through the individual and group interviews with a total of 83 NCOP learners aged between 11 and 18 years. Participants were spread across four schools in one region, and we also accounted for gender and ethnicity distribution and attempted to present a range of pathways and experiences. Within these schools, we ran two separate focus groups each for Year 9 and Year 12 NCOP pupils. This reached approximately 39 Year 9 learners and 37 Year 12s. The first focus group asked about some of the challenges young people face in thinking about their progression into HE, as well as some of the opportunities HE might provide, with responses noted in a poster and through verbal feedback. In the second focus group, we asked young people to design an outreach activity using a worksheet. These focus groups were digitally recorded and we kept copies of the worksheets and posters.

Our role in these focus groups was to listen and to gently guide, informed by Kvale's (1996) metaphor of the researcher as 'traveller', 'wandering together with' their participant in the process of arriving at insight (p. 4). As researchers, we were informed by principles of social justice, in playing close attention to how data get collected, produced and interpreted. This provoked a desire to rethink the impacts and 'value' of outreach beyond quantitative measures as well as consider broader contextual issues that shape how outreach might be received, understood and valued. It also included awareness of the need to utilise and empower the voices and expertise of multiple stakeholders as partners in our research. For example, we were mindful of the dynamics of academic researchers entering classrooms as 'transient' strangers asking young people to give experiences and perspectives with us. Our approach to interrogating and developing the success of WP work has been guided by work theorising the value of more participatory forms of research relationships that seek to dissolve distinctions between researcher and researched (Pain, Whitman, & Milledge, 2011).We wanted to set up opportunities for young people to tell adults engaged in WP what they think rather than the other way round, being guided in our approach to the research by the principle of speaking 'next to' rather than for (Trinh, cited in Chen, 1992). Consequently, we ensured these focus groups were led by their voices and ideas for what they would like to see in future outreach activity, rather than us priming them for what we wanted to hear, at the expense of articulations of experience (Tremlett, 2015).

The research data were coded using NVivo software which generated a series of common or significant themes. In this chapter, we focus on an emergent theme, broadly defined as 'affect' which we explored in light of our theoretical understandings of consumerism, debt and educational inequalities. In offering a critique of some elements of NCOP, we explore both the state of the 'WP market', and the potential 'students' it imagines.

Discussion

The affective worlds 'behind' postcode data

A static reading of space and place using target postcodes within NCOP resulted in scant attention being paid to the affective dimensions of transitioning into HE, specifically how does it *feel* to be positioned as a recipient of outreach and to negotiate the progression journey in the context of wider complex life stories? Young people were acutely aware of being 'more than' their WP selection criterion. In our discussions, they revealed experiences of affect in terms of their excitements and anxieties about their possible educational futures and how this related to them being targeted for specific opportunities and interventions because of their home postcode.

As a proxy measure of educational disadvantage, the use of postcode was felt by young people to be too blunt and did not enable attention to other relevant aspects of identity and experiences. One learner described it as a 'bit of a stereotype' in that:

> I come from a poor estate and I want to go to university. But there are people on rich estates who don't want to go to university.
>
> (Year 9[4], Beach Green[5])

The quote describes the simple fact that postcode reveals something, but not everything, about educational trajectories and obfuscates other factors such as ethnicity, gender and the complex other economic, social and material factors informing socio-economic class. Importantly, this person did not *feel* defined or determined by place. He was keen to state how he was more than his estate but, at the same time, by contrasting his experience with the 'people on rich estates' as being exceptional he indicated the presence of place as a limiting of possibilities. Using Gordon (2008), place and its concurrent histories and connections to formations of class, becomes a malevolent spectre in that it 'emerges uninvited...to mess up boundaries and protocols' (p. 148). For the young person exemplified above, postcode should not matter and yet something remained as mattering significantly and inescapably. Similarly, in a focus group with Year 9s in Townside, one girl said she would be nervous of stating where she lived on her UCAS form in case this might put universities off in positioning her as being someone 'like them'. This prompted further discussion within their small group about why they had been selected to take part in the focus group which was revealing for some – 'Oh I didn't realise you were from there'. For others, shared post-code was a clearer categorisation. As we asked Year 12s in Church School why they thought they were here, the group laughed, echoing 'it's because we're from a shit area'. While place clearly played a part in perceptions of possible futures, postcode did not accurately define what place represented. Indeed, a discussion with Year 12s in Townside focused on the nuances of selection:

> In a deprived area, it's difficult to, sort of, know where that area starts and finishes, difficult to pick out which areas are less well-off and which areas are more well off. And sometimes that will go wrong, and people who are already quite well off will end up getting resources that could be going to someone who's not so well off.
>
> (Year 12[6], Townside)

In echoing a discourse of deservedness, young people were clearly aware of the WP selection game and how postcode shaped the allocation of opportunities. The use of 'well off' and 'resource' in this quote reveals how postcode alone provides scant information about current economic realities of young people and their families. Waller, Harrison, and Last (2015) interviewed regional directors of one of the most substantial programmes to widen access to HE in the UK – Aim Higher (2004–2011). Their analysis found that the use of geo-demographic markers like postcodes for targeting offered a quick measure where other data were lacking but equally they caution that 'uncritical or mechanistic' (p. 2) applications could offer limited information about young people's lives. Within our study, postcode was seen to be too blunt in both not providing enough information about lives and experiences, as well as not accurately representing what might be the educational disadvantages these learners faced in their future HE participation.

Indeed, what we were struck by in our data was the emotional intensity of our conversations with young people and how this co-existed alongside the reductive postcode measure. Indeed, words such as worry, risk, pressure, fear, unclear and overwhelmed arose as significant themes in our data. This was most often presented in terms of whether the financial, social and emotional investment in HE would offer a meaningful return. This risky payoff was described predominantly in financial terms set against fears of loans and debt:

> We are going to need degrees to get most jobs, so it's going to benefit you in the way of, you're going to get a better paying job. But also it's a huge risk, like it's such a gamble because if you go there for four years

and then at the end you pass or you don't pass or you just go back to the job you had before, then was it worth it?

(Year 12, Townside)

Young people struggle to get jobs nowadays so you might have the qualification just working or you might as well just go into a job straight away because then you'll get money and you can actually pay for your apartment and stuff. In the sense like, it's not qualifications that make the world go round. It's money that does. So what's the point?

(Year 12, Church View)

In these discussions, debt was not an abstract concept but an embodied worry as both a risky undertaking but also shaping everyday practicalities such as living at home or the opportunities to find part-time work easily. This supports Barr (2012) who described how it was the *risk* of debt and concern whether it would prove worth it, rather than the debt itself, that was of most concern, particularly for those from low incomes. Importantly, risk was described as a 'gamble' that was to some extent out of their control and this was connected to other worries and fears around a lack of agency in terms of their education and life transitions.

For example, participants described HE as a further pressure to perform and succeed, layering on top of the demands expected to achieve GCSEs at age 16, and then progressing on to succeed at A-Levels by age 18:

A level is such a jump and it's just like, so stressful and with university it's another jump and like, I'm a bit scared.

(Year 12, Townside)

It's more of a mental effect, like university has more, like, pressure and it's rushed. They make you want to grow up faster than you are so they're like hurry up and get the grades... So a lot of people are rushing into it [uni]...And you have so many tests and it's like stress.

(Year 9, Beachside)

As soon as they get to that point where they want to pick it [university], some people may go, I don't know, it's too scary, I don't want to do that.

(Year 9, Townside)

In the first quote, the educational 'treadmill' was experienced as highly problematic. The thought of HE was fraught with concerns around whether young people could sustain the levels of pressure they were experiencing in their current schooling contexts. In the second quote, this young person was almost breathless as they described how university might represent even more stress on top of what they were facing as they approached the start of their GCSEs and their desire to slow down and feel in control of their future choices. The third quote echoes similar themes of worry and fear. Stress was conceptualised as a barrier for educational progression and yet this was rarely explicitly addressed within WP initiatives that these young people had taken part in or within the broader discourse we were aware of as researchers and practitioners.

What these data excerpts suggest to us is the importance of paying attention to the considerable emotional terrain of HE decision-making. The use of postcode within the NCOP programme offered very limited data or concurrent measures of 'success' around young people's thoughts and feelings as they negotiated whether or not HE was a possibility for them, although there was a connection between place and its relationship to complex classed formations of possibility. In addition, risk and uncertainty, worry and stress were normalised within the lives of young people we spoke to as they contemplated HE yet these 'affective worlds' (and the policy landscapes that shaped their emergence) were rarely addressed in WP interventions they had experienced or we had observed in our wider study.

The positivity industry of WP

Our data suggested that, where emotions were addressed within WP discourse, this operated under individualised discourses of young people needing to be more resilient or to upskill their coping mechanisms. For example, our regional NCOP funded a number of interventions focused on 'Grit and Resilience'. These took the form of confidence-raising activities, often linked to an extra-curricular task such as sport or music, in which young people were supported to challenge their attitudes and perceptions towards their existing capabilities and future possibilities. The underlying philosophy was of a growth mindset which argues that you can improve intelligence, ability and performance through cognitive and psychological work (Dweck, 2017). Such initiatives were very popular among young people in our region and had benefits in terms of improved self-confidence in the short-term. However, much like the concept of aspiration in WP work, growth mindset narratives can serve to apportion 'blame' at an individual level (Sellar & Storan, 2013) and suggest that educational disadvantage can predominantly be 'thought away' through cultivating the correct, positive frame of mind around one's individual circumstances and opportunities. This starkly contrasted with our data, particularly around the financial fears of HE, which felt insurmountable for those in our study.

For example, we interviewed one young woman, Karli, about her views on HE and she described how involvement in confidence building opportunities had increased her self-belief that she might 'fit' at university. Here she describes her feelings about attending a university open day talk:

> I went along and I went, oh, I don't think I want to go to university. It proper scares me. I don't think I'm educated enough. But, you are.

> ...It doesn't matter how academic you are, as long as you have the mindset to want to achieve and do well, and to persevere and to actually work your butt off, then you're going to achieve, I think.

These quotes attest to the success of the event in raising her self-confidence, as well as her echoing the growth mindset discourse that she had been exposed to. However, the defining factor shaping her decision not to go to university was that she saw it to be less risky to continue in her part-time work as a personal trainer and build a career for herself by taking on short courses at college. Even as she contemplated university in the future, she continually repeated the need to be working:

> You've always got to have a back-up plan. So, I could do personal training as a part-time job, as well as studying in university, if I wanted...to help pay and live comfortably... Being in part-time work to help support my parents as well as myself, that would really help.

This is not to suggest a lack of value in confidence-raising work for Karli, but that it seemed to offer a limited understanding of the 'spectre' (Gordon, 2008) of the emotional, socio-political and financial barriers of HE that shaped her need to have a 'back-up plan' that could not simply be gotten over through positive psychological thinking.

This reductive psychologising of barriers to further study was linked to a broader trend of positivity within the WP industry in which HE was seen as an unproblematised part of the 'good life'. For example, young people described how HE was almost always sold to them in highly positive and idealised ways and that this felt at odds with their current experiences of study. They also felt that HE's benefits were universally lauded with little attention to how their specific circumstances would enable/disable them from capitalising on their earned qualifications compared to those who were more socially privileged. This is illustrated by the following discussion between two Year 12s at Academy School:

A: You deal with stress here, you've dealt with stress during your GCSEs. College isn't perfect, but I enjoy college. I enjoy going to school here. And that was stressful. I don't see the point in saying, oh yes, uni is perfect...Just don't tell us what we want to hear, tell us what we need to hear. Because otherwise we're going to be in for a big shock.

B: Yeah...they try and make you feel like everyone's always there to help you when that's not the case, I know it's not the case.

A: We're not stupid. We know there's going to be issues. ..they can't just try and sit there and say, oh yes, it's going to be all smooth, it's going to be all happy days. It's not... They just try and make it seem so much better than it is. We want to know the bad as well as the good bits...But we just want, I feel like realisation rather than just a smack in the face when we get there.

In this discussion, 'stress' was so normalised in these young people's lives that they found it unusual that this was not something talked about often in outreach work. Moreover, awareness of what university is like from older friends or siblings made them hyper-aware of what messages were silenced, particularly around the 'struggles' such as the pressures of independent working or the cost of living. They knew that studying at university can be challenging and that people drop out for a variety of reasons. These nuanced understandings contrasted sharply with anxieties sometimes present in WP around perceived lack of aspiration to be corrected through outreach. Instead they conveyed an ability to decode dominant narratives of promised gain. These young people showed a sophisticated grasp of the precarity of promises around graduate outcomes, that is in line with the analyses of expert commentators (e.g. Shildrick, MacDonald, Webster, & Garthwaite, 2012). However, the vision they were presented with was hyper-positive, potentially leading to a sense of being unprepared for what might be to come or to being suspicious of such 'marketing hyperbole'. Shortly after attending this focus group, we went to a national training for WP practitioners in which we were encouraged to loudly chant 'outreach works', suggesting that critical messages around both university and the success of WP did not fit with current narratives. This likely reflects the shifting agendas of the WP sector which has blurred the lines between outreach and recruitment (Johnson et al., 2019), with the consequence that a key performance indicator of outreach is return on investment in student numbers.

Grit and resilience work enabled 'fixing' the emotional concerns of the applicant but there was little WP practice that sought to question the affective challenges of the institution and, in its slide to recruitment, it risked becoming a 'positivity industry'. While there is considerable work being done to address the mental health concerns of young people in schools and for university students, there is a potential 'transition' gap in outreach work that could better recognise that making choices around higher education is a deeply emotional, not just a strategic, process.

Complex lives/idealised targets

In our focus groups, we found that the most marginalised young people experienced chaotic lives and engaged in complex decision-making, with few support structures. The strategic, well-informed student, making 'logical' choices from a plethora of HE products, supported by an educationally rich family was atypical for many NCOP learners. This was highlighted most strikingly in a discussion with Clara, in Year 12 in Academy school. We asked her, what she'd like to do when she leaves her sixth form and she responded:

> I've always wanted to be a primary school teacher. My whole life. And so I'm definitely going to university. I'll need to do some sort of teaching degree because I don't want to be a teaching assistant... I think I'm going

to stick around Sussex because I'm living with my Dad now. But I'm not sure whether I'm going to go to the MET [Local FE college] to do Hair and Beauty first. So once I have finished that course, I can then go to university and have a job as a hairdresser whilst I am at uni.... I thought I'd get it to be a fall back whilst I'm at uni to earn money ....I've always been quite interested to go somewhere I've never been before. I haven't really looked at it because obviously I'm not going to go there anymore. I just thought it would be nice to go somewhere else away from where I'm used to, but I think I'll be a bit more comfortable sticking with where I am.

On one hand, it could be interpreted as highly strategic for Clara to gather a qualification that might secure a regular income to support future studies. On the other hand, while we do not have reliable data on those who enter HE directly after studying vocational courses in further education, this 'extended' route is likely to be atypical of those she would meet on the highly competitive teaching courses offered at the local universities. In addition, her decision-making around HE took place against a dominant concern about staying local to live with and support her family. Moreover, as Clara contemplates a move away, she is 'haunted' (Gordon, 2008) by associations of place drawing her back to where she feels she belongs. The complex factors at play in her decision-making stood at odds with policy constructions of the strategic consumer of an educational product. For example, the underpinning narrative of the NCOP initiative is to understand which WP activities have the greatest 'impact' and, crucially here, impact is measured in terms of an individual's likelihood of becoming a future student. In such recruitment and marketing dominated provision, WP becomes an input/output educational process, which is out of sync with supporting young people's own choices as agentic decision-makers in highly complex lives.

A further possible outcome of such an input/output WP model is an opportunity marketplace in which *some* and not others could thrive as idealised 'targeted' learners. This could occur at a targeting/policy level within universities, schools and colleges. For example, the marketisation of WP as described by commentators (Johnson et al., 2019) creates a 'safe' approach to WP practice that discourages working with those young people and staff who need it most. Instead WP practitioners can avoid risking investing in those for whom they do not feel confident that their efforts will translate into acceptance of a place and success at their institution. NCOP used the terminology of 'quick wins' for those learners who were likely to attend and who required only minimal intervention to produce this return on investment. These young people become idealised subjects of WP, the ones for whom the work 'pays off', rather than the more complicated cases, lives and experiences of those such as Clara. As WP becomes increasingly about measurability, it is seen as important that identifying value and success needs not to become buried only in measurable targets, with a concurrent risk that social justice agendas get left behind (Harrison & Waller, 2017).

Conclusion

In this chapter, we have argued that the particular targeting employed by NCOP of geo-demographic measures, and the surrounding socio-economic and policy climate, has shifted the imaginary of how these WP students are understood. The provision of targeted outreach that identifies and focuses on how intersections of geography and demography impact distance from HE can suggest that the problem has been addressed. Such an approach risks obscuring the persistence of more pervasive forces against HE progression beyond the individual or community levels, in our wider socio-economic and policy contexts. We have argued specifically that such a static reading of space and place using target postcodes results in scant attention being paid to the affective dimensions of transitioning into HE. Alongside more commonly understood concerns around debt and future employability, participants in our research, astutely expressed more affective anxieties around 'risk', 'pressure' and 'fear' as they narrated their educational decision-making. These insights presented pictures of challenges to mental health and well-being. While outreach activities focused on grit and resilience ostensibly speak to recognition of this affective dimension to HE decision-making, they can be seen as effectively undermining the legitimacy of such responses, through positioning the 'good' subject of outreach who demonstrates aspiration, grit and resilience in the face of adversity. The seemingly positive and empowering outreach message that everyone is capable of succeeding if they believe and apply themselves, overlooks that capabilities are a complex mix of external as well as internally composed resources, and that they are not evenly distributed (O'Shea, 2019). In contrast to dominant constructions of motivation and achievement within outreach discourse, we argue for a persistent and powerful place for 'affect' as politically and socially located and experienced as embodied feeling and, consequently, something that cannot be reduced to an individualised and psychologised barrier that can simply be 'thought away'. Finally, our readings of students' affective worlds and complex lives stood at odds with policy constructions of the strategic consumer of an educational product. This created a context in which outreach opportunities similarly became an opportunity marketplace, where *some* and not others could thrive as 'targeted' learners, but with little space for concern to understand or address the complex structural barriers that prevent some from embracing and thriving in response to the educational opportunities on offer.

With this in mind, we assert a pressing need for a new approach to outreach to more explicitly and sympathetically acknowledge and speak to the emotional realities of HE decision-making. This involves attending to the complex interplay between structure, agency and serendipity in individual lives, forcing more sophisticated understandings of the potential of outreach, that redistributes responsibility for success and failure more equitably across stakeholders more widely from parents to policy makers, beyond polarised assumptions of students as agentic choosers decision-making within a vacuum in response to outreach advice. Such an assertion is far from value-free; rather it is politically loaded in tapping into the ever bubbling but often obscured rub in WP between social justice and neo-liberal agendas. While we may strive to work together across stakeholder groups, the challenge remains to continue to search for creative and collaborative new practical approaches to bridge different aims and understandings, to work effectively within the context of such diametrically informed agendas.

Notes

1 The regulatory body for higher education in the UK.
2 https://www.officeforstudents.org.uk/publications/ncop-two-years-on/
3 A UK Government initiative providing investment in UK widening participation between 2004-11.
4 This is the year of UK schooling in which pupils are normally between 13-14 years old. It is also significant in being the time they choose which subjects to focus on in their GCSEs, which are exams taken at the end of secondary school, aged 15–16.
5 Our four schools, Townside, Church School, Beach Green and Academy schools were spread across the Sussex region, a county in the South East of the UK. Schools were a mix of faith, academy and local authority funding models and were from different geographic locations e.g. coastal and city.
6 This is the year of UK schooling in which pupils are normally between 16 and 17 years old and studying qualifications in a school or a sixth form college. The January of this academic year is the normal deadline for applying for university and we conducted the majority of our focus groups in the preceding October and November.

References

Barr, N. (2012). The Higher Education White Paper: The good, the bad, the unspeakable—and the next White Paper. *Social Policy and Administration* 46:5, 483–508. doi:10.1111/j.1467-9515.2012.00852.x

Bathmaker, A.M., Ingram, N. & Waller, R. (2013). Higher education, social class and the mobilisation of capitals: Recognising and playing the game. *British Journal of Sociology of Education* 34:5–6, 723–743. doi:10.1080/01425692.2013.816041

Boliver, V. (2013). How fair is access to more prestigious UK Universities? *British Journal of Sociology* 64:2, 344-364. doi:10.1111/1468-4446.12021

Brown, P. (2013). Education, opportunity and the prospects for social mobility. *British Journal of Sociology of Education* 3:5–6, 678-700. doi:10.1080/01425692.2013.816036

Burke P.J. (2013). The right to higher education: neoliberalism, gender and professional mis/recognitions. *International Studies in Sociology of Education* 23, 107–126. doi:10.1080/09620214.2013.790660

Callender, C. & Jackson, J. (2008) Does the fear of debt constrain choice of university and subject of study? *Studies in Higher Education* 33(4): 405–429.

Callender, C. & Mason, G. (2017). Does student loan debt deter higher education participation? New evidence from England *Annals of American Political and Social Science* 671:1, 20-48, doi: 10.1177/0002716217696041

Chen, N. (1992). Speaking nearby: A conversation with Trinh T. Minh-ha. *Visual Anthropology Review* 8:1, 82–91. doi:10.1525/var.1992.8.1.82

Clark, S. Mountford-Zimdars, A., & Francis, B. (2015). Risk, choice and social disadvantage: Young people's decision-making in a marketised higher education system. *Sociological Research Online* 20:3, 9. doi:10.5153/sro.3727

Crawford, C., & Van der Erve, L. (2015). Does higher education level the playing field? Socio-Economic differences in graduate earnings *Education Sciences* 5, 380–412. doi:10.3390/educsci5040380

Crawford, C., Gregg, P., Macmillan, L. Vignoles, A., & Wyness, G. (2016). Higher education, career opportunities, and intergenerational inequality. *Oxford Review of Economic Policy* 32:4, 553–575. doi:10.1093/oxrep/grw030

Crozier, G. (2005) 'There's a war against our children': black educational underachievement revisited. *British Journal of Sociology of Education* 26:5, 585-598, doi:10.1080/01425690500293520

Dweck, C. (2017). *Mindset: Changing The Way You think To Fulfil Your Potential.* 6th edition. New York: Robinson.

Dwyer, R. E., Hodson, R., & McCloud, L. (2013) Gender, debt, and dropping out of college, *Gender and Society* 27:1, 30-55. doi:10.1177/0891243212464906

Finlay, H. (2014). A toxic mix ... the demise of a widening participation Outreach programme for low-income parents. (Blogpost), Birkbeck, University of London. http://blogs.bbk.ac.uk/george/2014/09/23/a-toxic-mix-the-demise-of-a-widening-participation-outreach-programme-for-low-income-parents/ (Accessed November 20 2019).

Gordon, A. (2011). Some thoughts on haunting and futurity. *Borderlands.* 10:2, 1-21.

Gordon, A. (2008). *Ghostly Matters: Haunting and the Sociological Imagination.* 2nd edition. Minnesota: University of Minnesota Press.

Gazeley, L. (2012). The impact of social class on parent–professional interaction in school exclusion processes: deficit or disadvantage? *International Journal of Inclusive Education* 16:3, 297-311. doi:10.1080/13603116.2010.489121

Gewirtz, S. (2001). Cloning the Blairs: New Labour's programme for the re-socialization of working class parents. *Journal of Education Policy* 16:4, 365–378. doi:10.1080/02680930110054353

Harrison, N. (2019). Students-as-insurers: rethinking 'risk' for disadvantaged young people considering higher education in England. *Journal of Youth Studies* 22:6, 752-771. doi:10.1080/13676261.2018.1535174

Harrison N., & Waller. R. (2017). Evaluating outreach activities: overcoming challenges through a realist 'small steps' approach. *Perspectives: Policy and Practice in Higher Education* 21:2-3, 81-87. doi:10.1080/13603108.2016.1256353

Hinton-Smith, T. (2016). Negotiating the risk of debt-financed higher education: The experience of lone parent students. *British Educational Research Journal* 42:2, 207-222. doi:10.1002/berj.3201

Hinton-Smith, T. (2012). *Widening Participation in Higher Education.* London: Palgrave.

Insight Network (2019). *University Student Mental Health Survey.* https://www.theinsightnetwork.co.uk/uncategorized/university-student-mental-health-survey-2018/ (Accessed 20/11/19).

Johnson, M., Danvers, E., Hinton-Smith, T., Atkinson, K., Bowden, G., Foster, J., Garner, K., Garrud, P., Greaves, S., Harris, P., Hejmadi, M., Hill, D., Hughes, G., Jackson, L., O'Sullivan, A., ÓTuama, S., Perez Brown, P., Philipson, P., Ravenscroft, S., Rhys, M., Ritchie, T., Talbot, J., Walker, D., Watson, J., Williams, M., & Williams, S. (2019). Higher education outreach: Examining key challenges for academics. *British Journal of Educational Studies* 67:4, 469-491. doi:10.1080/00071005.2019.1572101

Johnston, A. & Barr, N. (2013) Student loan reform, interest subsidies and costly technicalities: lessons from the UK experience. *Journal of Higher Education Policy and Management* 35:2, 167-178. doi:10.1080/1360080X.2013.775925

Kvale, S. (1996). *An Introduction to Qualitative Research Interviewing*. London: Sage.

Pain, R., Whitman, G.. and Milledge, D. (2011). *Participatory Action Research Toolkit* . Durham: Durham University Press.

O'Shea, S. (2019). *Creating a capabilities-based persistence framework (or matrix) on university student persistence*. A Framing Paper. https://arcdiscoveryproject.files.wordpress.com/2019/06/final-capabilities-document-060619.pdf (Accessed 20/11/19).

O'Shea, S. (2015). Avoiding the manufacture of 'sameness': First-in-Family students, cultural capital and the higher education environment. *Higher Education* 72:1, 59–78. doi:10.1007/s10734-015-9938-y

Reay, D., Crozier, G., & Clayton, J. (2010). 'Fitting in' or 'Standing Out': Working-class students in UK higher education. *British Educational Research Journal* 36:1, 107–124.

Sellar, S., & Storan, J. (2013). 'There was something about aspiration': Widening participation policy affects in England and Australia. *Journal of Adult and Continuing Education* 19:2, 45-65. doi:10.1080/01411920902878925

Shildrick T., MacDonald R., Webster C., & Garthwaite K. (2012). *Poverty and Insecurity: Life in 'low-pay, No-pay' Britain*. Bristol: Policy Press.

Taylor-Gooby, P., & Zinn, J. O. (2006). Current directions in risk research: New developments. *Risk Analysis* 26:2, 397–411. doi:10.1111/j.1539-6924.2006.00746.x

Tremlett, A. (2015) *Celebrations and Challenges: The Roma Community in the UK*. Panel Discussion. Brighton: University of Sussex. http://www.sussex.ac.uk/education/cheer/events/archive201415

Waller, R., Harrison, N., & Last, K. (2015). *Building a Culture of Participation: Interviews with the Former Directors of the National Aim Higher Programme*. Bristol: UWE. https://uwe-repository.worktribe.com/output/829528

Williams, M., & Williams, S. (2019). Higher education outreach: Examining key challenges for academics. *British Journal of Educational Studies*. doi:10.1080/00071005.2019.1572101

Chapter 6

Dispelling the myth of the 'traditional' university undergraduate student in the UK

Grace Sykes

Introduction: Problematising the myth of the traditional student

As the UK Department for Education (2019) documents, participation rates from 2017 to 2018 show 50.2% of 17- to 30-year-olds in the UK now attend university. It therefore makes much less sense to talk about 'traditional' and/ or 'non-traditional' undergraduate students. The sentiment of traditional, in its simplest definition, implies something that came before; it involves an implicit temporal comparison with a period where university attendance was completed by fewer students and less diverse cohorts. Recognising the conception of traditional as anachronistic from the outset, like all myths, the notion of the traditional student immediately implies an opposition, a newer contemporary non-traditional student. Driven by evidence that non-traditional transitions are *riskier* and more complex (Archer & Hutchings, 2000; Clayton et al., 2009), conventional distinctions between traditional and non-traditional students gained traction alongside changes to higher education landscapes (linked to consumerisation, neo-liberalisation, 1990s expansion, widening participation policies since 1997, tuition fee rise). This sparked interest in the lives of 'new' students from non-traditional backgrounds (first-in-family, parent students, mature students, international students and so on), often centred around ideas of fitting or mis-fitting (e.g. Reay et al., 2010). While this has been extremely helpful and vastly improved knowledge of the complexity and hyper/super diversity of non-traditional student experiences, it has simultaneously triggered a neglect of research focusing specifically on lived experiences of students who seemingly fit the 'traditional' category, beyond residential accounts (with the exception of Chatterton, 1999, 2010). This has enabled a problematic enduring myth that (1) there remains such thing as a traditional student demographic; (2) this is representative of the majority of students; (3) those who fall into this ostensible category of 'traditional' student move easily into, and desire, this typical transition into, and way of 'being a student', as they naturally immerse themselves in these cultures of conformity.

More recently these binaries have been problematised (Holton, 2013, 2016), as scholars recognise what it means to be a contemporary HE student is increasingly complex. Researchers have contributed, and challenged, constructions of students as consumers (Molesworth et al., 2009; Tomlinson, 2016), as hard workers (Brooks, 2018), as politically active (Morgan & Davis III, 2019), and so on, as well as criticising the lack of inclusion of the lived experience of students themselves in many popular constructions. Indeed, as an attempt to move beyond binaries and homogenising categories, I have argued elsewhere (Sykes, 2017; Sykes, forthcoming), that conceptualising university as a bubble may enhance our understanding of the ways in which multiple student identities and experiences interact – and that perhaps it is more appropriate to use the terms 'typical' and 'non-typical' as descriptors to highlight students' conflation of traditional student characteristics and expectations of student culture, in articulating their own identities and experiences.

There are some commonalities in the depictions of UK undergraduates recognised in this chapter with other conceptualisations of studenthood across the globe. Some of these ways of understanding students might be consequential to overall directions of change aligned with broader debates about neo-liberalisation in the higher education sector. For example, discussions of students as independent consumers are present, and challenged, in studies on international students studying in the UK (Lomer, 2014), in work on European student identities (Brooks, 2018), whereas ideas around drinking cultures and promiscuity are common in portrayals of American student sororities and sports teams (for instance, Tewksbury et al., 2008), in some European accounts (De Bruyn et al., 2018; Páramo et al., 2020) and beyond Europe (Nguyen et al., 2018). And indeed, more generally, there are parallels with how young people are perceived as 'emerging adults' (Arnett, 2000). This chapter contributes to these debates, focusing on the lives of UK 'traditional' undergraduate higher education students, by highlighting how homogenising, inaccurate but enduring myths impact the daily lives of students, how they understand their own identities, and how the myth serves as a measure of a legitimacy for their own experience, excluding many students who do not fit this myth. It is not only the terminology of the binary that causes hindrance here, forcing students into arbitrary categories, but the accompanying prevailing stereotype that continues to dominate discourse around representations of *being* a student.

Thus far, however, despite this widespread recognition of our increasingly hyper/super-diverse student bodies, and their varied experiences, little has been done to dispel the myth that the majority of students will adhere to expectations of a 'traditional stereotype'. In fact, commodification of student experience and increasing competition within the sector has arguably only intensified this stereotypical image. Even if this image is only an illusion, maintenance of this idealised lifestyle, some advocate, is a 'seductive' marketing tool for universities (Holdsworth, 2009a). Not only have assumptions of 'traditional' studenthood gone largely unchallenged in the mainstream media (though there are some notable exceptions), but more problematically, they persist in and through conventional divisions drawn between traditional and non-traditional students in academic accounts of traditional students. As this myth continues to dominate, the complexities and diversity of experience within these groups will be missed, as the myth overshadows new and more useful ways of imagining studenthood.

Central to the notion of the 'traditional undergraduate student' in the UK is the expectation of a smooth 'natural transition' into higher education (Patiniotis & Holdsworth, 2005), perambulating a well-trodden, normalised, superficially linear path, often assumed to be predicated upon parental history of university participation. Students in this category are presumed to enter university with a level of entitlement (Holdsworth, 2006, 2009a), armed with knowledge to utilise opportunities presented for future gain (Brooks, 2007; Holdsworth, 2010). By contrast, non-traditional students are seen to have more *complicated* transitions, with no familial background of higher education. Also entangled in this notion of 'traditional' and 'becoming' a university student are expectations of geographical mobility, through moving away from the parental home into peer shared accommodation (Chatterton, 1999, 2000, 2010; Holdsworth, 2006, 2009a, 2009b; Smith & Holt, 2007; Holton, 2013). As pockets of studentification (Smith & Hubbard, 2014) continue to engorge university towns and cities, living away from home is presented as most desirable, where students are trained into 'traditional' normalised patterns of behaviour (Holton, 2015). In contrast, non-traditional students are expected to remain in their pre-university home for the duration of their studies, less likely to indulge in rules around social behaviours, casual clothing trends, or club culture (Chatterton, 1999, 2010; Smith & Holt, 2007; Crozier et al., 2008) and painted as 'missing out' (Holdsworth, 2006; Christie et al., 2008; Reay et al., 2010).

Traditional students are historically described as young (18-21), unmarried, middle class and white (Chatterton, 1999, 2010), whereas non-traditional students may include almost any identities which fall outside these narrow categories. Notions of 'traditionality' also extend beyond demographic characteristics to behaviours and values felt to be characteristic of 'normal studenthood'. Despite cautions against stereotyping students as 'binge drinking louts' (Holloway et al., 2010), students are demonised by the media for excessive consumption (e.g. see Hubbard, 2013) and portrayed as willingly swept up in a dominant monoculture (Allinson, 2006), immersed in continuous partying (Andersson et al., 2012), with drinking positioned as a normalised component of university culture (Robertson & Tustin, 2018), alongside other risky behaviours. Such constructions are often linked to 'laddishness', problematised performances of masculinity and objectification of women (Phipps & Young, 2015; Phipps, 2017), while discussions of agency and 'ladette' culture imply women remain impelled to police their behaviour in line with notions of appropriate femininity (Hubbard, 2013).

Keeping up with the 'traditional' and idealised notion of studenthood, while subsidised by student discounts, and strengthened by geographical segregation of social activities and student nights, is not cheap, further reinforcing exclusivity, as some may be priced out of participation. However, students may find ways to maximise finances through loans, part-time work (Christie et al., 2001; Christie & Munro, 2003). The extent to which these stereotypes govern, or students indulge in, this behaviour varies depending on university destination (Chatterton, 1999; Clayton et al., 2009; Brooks et al., 2016a, 2016b). But such notions have become so well established, that to not participate in, say, drinking excessively (despite increasing numbers self-identifying as non-drinkers and many more distancing themselves from these stereotypes) is to define oneself as, de-facto, a non-traditional student.

Drawing largely on interview data from a participatory project, the findings of the research, outlined in this chapter, with self-selecting traditional students speak to these debates through articulations of students' own 'traditional' experiences. I shall go on to explain how distinctions between traditional and non-traditional students are not this clear cut, if indeed they ever were, and that students challenge these images suggesting they are an unfair, inaccurate representation of their lives. However, most interestingly, students themselves not only use aspects of this myth as a measure of authenticity and legitimacy in reference to their own experience but are also involved in the preservation of this myth. Thus, the key contribution of this chapter is to interrogate the notion of the 'traditional student' in the UK as a myth that is axiomatic to lay and policy discourse, and as a set of ideas and judgements which, somewhat paradoxically, are perpetuated by students themselves, even when their own experiences do not necessarily correspond with its main precepts.

In the remainder of this chapter, I will outline the study on which the evidence is based, before discussing three key senses in which this myth is operating. First, the term traditional is defined beyond the demographic sense, the traditional student, as this label is fused with student traditions as a set of cultures and expectations which function as a notion of what is legitimate; second, tradition as an ideal, setting judgement criteria, which students measure their own experience against, is discussed; third, the notion of idealised traditions is explored, which encourage students to preserve a myth, despite it not mirroring their own experience. While there is ample overlap between these three senses, for the purpose of this chapter they are serving heuristically to delineate how tradition operates and has different kinds of consequences.

Methods

This chapter draws on data from a 4-year participatory research project working with self-selecting traditional undergraduate students (for more information, see Sykes, 2017; Sykes, forthcoming). Rather than striving for a 'gold standard' (Kesby et al., 2005, p. 162), forcing a strict set of practices, this project ensured flexibility, adapting as necessary to maintain a participatory ethos throughout, valuing students as the expert in their own experience (Cahill, 2007).

Data were collected at a Midlands University (pseudonym used throughout), which recruited largely traditional age students, living away from home, but remaining fairly local with a large proportion moving within a 100 mile radius. The data collection for this project consisted of two qualitative phases. The first was composed of pre-defined methods including individual life history interviews and focus groups. The second phase included university life game sessions, research-led teaching/teaching-led research sessions, co-researcher diaries, informal discussions with co-researchers, and interviews with university staff. Participants were asked a wide range of questions about their lived experiences as students, including what they understood 'traditional' to mean and how, if at all, their identity and experiences related to this.

There were over 60 students involved in the study. Thirty-two students partook in all phases, from outset to completion, and nine participants from this initial sample were co-researchers, individually contributing at varying intensities from design to dissemination. Additional participants joined this original sample for Phase 2. Co-researchers and participants included students from a range of ethnic and socio-economic backgrounds, studying a range of subjects, and at different junctures in their university trajectory, but were all aged between 18 and 24. If strict mythological ideas of a traditional demographic are applied, the sample is a mix of traditional and non-traditional students, however, all students in the sample self-identified as traditional students.

For the purpose of this chapter, I focus on data from 32 life history interviews (including co-researchers), in which students reflected on, or imagined their transition into, through, and beyond university. These interviews lasted between 1 and 3 hours each.

More than traditional demographics: How student traditions function as notions of legitimacy

A key finding of this research emerged as it became evident that the characteristics of the self-selecting 'traditional' students deviated from existing definitions of this term. There were enduring aspects of historical characteristics of what constitutes a 'traditional' student in participants' accounts. However, the way in which these were interpreted and enacted was much more flexible, highlighting the subjectivity in understanding and slippage between binaries. This informs the first sense of the myth, as 'traditional' is stretched beyond demographic definitions (such as class, age and so on), but allied with student 'traditions' (e.g. around drinking, moving away from home), *typically* associated with 'traditional' students. For example, students' understandings included (1) previous knowledge and experience of higher education (though as will be explained, not always parental), (2) youth as demographic indicator of studenthood (yet being youthful in behaviour and appearance was deemed more important than being of exact 'traditional' age of 18–21), (3) living away from home (though not necessarily for the full duration, but *where* students went to university remained important). Each one of these student traditions counted towards a picture of legitimate studenthood, and when possessed together confirmed traditional student status.

I shall now highlight how this first sense of the myth operates as these student traditions include cultures and expectations such as previous knowledge of higher education and moving away from home which function as a notion of what is legitimate 'traditional' studenthood.

Previous knowledge and history of higher education as a student tradition is assumed to be built on parental experience of university participation. University is seen as a family tradition, normalising higher education as a path in the transition to adulthood (Patiniotis & Holdsworth, 2005). However, as I shall go on to explain, sibling experience played a crucial role in students' flexible interpretation of these student traditions, in identifying themselves as traditional students, and legitimatising their experience.

Unsurprisingly, those with a parental background in higher education admitted this provided a benchmark, against which students measure the legitimacy of their own life experience. To some extent, this fuelled expectations of enrolment as a family tradition. However, others in the sample stressed their parents' educational labours at best were outdated, and at worst, irrelevant; their parents had experienced university in a different era, funded by grants rather than large loans, when outcomes for, and pressures on, young people were different. Indeed, students in this research challenged the notion that this prior knowledge must come from parents, deeming generational knowledge superseded parental engagement. Rather, they favoured sibling experience as crucial in building a realistic understanding of what university was like, easing their transition, and as a measure for the legitimacy of their own experience. Duncan, a first-year student, presented a typical narrative:

> I have an older brother who was doing the process a year before...The application and the first days of going to Uni, and all that kind of thing, I learnt through him. If I need anyone to ask, I'd just ask him to find out.

For Duncan, his brother made much more sense as a reference point, as like many in my sample, sibling experience was deemed of greater significance, as a more powerful, dependable source of information. Indeed, for some students, who were first generation, but not first-in-family, their siblings had normalised university attendance. There was even further slippage between 'traditional' and 'non-traditional' backgrounds, as for some this history of university participation did not need to be a relation. Rather, having older friends, 'knowing' people that had been to university and acquiring information from people you 'know', in few cases, was deemed enough for 'traditional' entry, as Jessica, a second-year student, from a working-class background, exemplifies in her description of her previous knowledge of higher education:

> A girl that lives across the road. She's 7 years older. ... She went ... to do history. She loved it.... She's not using her degree particularly for the jobs she's doing, but that's prepared me for the fact most people don't do that. ... My parents didn't go to university.... My uncle did, but obviously long before I knew him. My mum's sister's husband, he went to Bristol to do English.

Jessica, along with few other first-generation students, self-identified as traditional students, because they believed that they had valid equivalents of 'familial' background, through older friends, etc. However, family background remained significant, as in some incidences, students, whose parents had not been to university, raised concerns around downward mobility, highlighting that to reach similar employment achievements to their parents, they would now need to gain a university degree, as entry requirements for jobs had shifted. In these cases, although there was not historically a tradition of university attendance, there was pressure to match their parents' employment status, therefore university was presented as the expected aspiration.

Moving away is another example of a student tradition deemed necessary to qualify for 'traditional' student status. Traditional students are expected to move away from the parental home to live in peer accommodation for university, and when recruited, all participants in this research had made this move. This tradition of an 'inevitable' move away from home is positioned as a binary opposite to non-traditional student experiences. A typical expectation would be that traditional students move away for the full duration of their degree. However, while all but one in the research sample agreed moving away continued to be a central component in asserting a traditional student identity, in their view, this move away could be either at the point of entry, in first year, and for the full length of their degree, or only for the duration of first year, or at a later point in their university trajectory. As long as students lived away for part, or all of their degree, with friends, rather than with a partner, they identified as traditional students. This highlights some slippage between what is deemed traditional and non-traditional. Nevertheless as I shall go onto explain, this student tradition of moving away represented an ideal, translating into a judgement criterion, employed by students to rate their own experience.

Tradition as an ideal: Measuring up to the myth

The second sense in which the myth is practised in reality is through tradition as an ideal. Tradition (including cultures and expectations for example, around drinking, moving away from home) acts as an ideal against which students measure the validity of their own 'traditional' experience. Moving away from home is presented as an ideal. Measuring their experience against this myth, one might be forgiven for assuming traditional students would feel that, having moved away, their experience was somehow more legitimate than their non-traditional peers. However, many in this sample highlighted how *where* they moved to was a significant indicator in assessing the validity of their experience. When discussing her journey to university, Helena, a first-year student, emphasised how she felt she should have gone further away:

> I was like Midlands it is, but no, I wanted to go away cos in my mind, you know, the further away I go, the more it's like I've flown the nest.

For Helena, distance served as a literal yardstick, a symbolic of legitimacy and success, as she equated moving further from the parental home for university as a more successful transition, a more substantial leap into independence and towards future 'adulthood'. Helena's views were typical of students in this sample (most of whom had moved 90 miles or less), as many hinted that the validity and legitimacy of experience could be calculated against distance from home, with those moving further claiming a more legitimate experience. Indeed, this aligns with previous work on non-traditional students which signalled a two-tier experience, in regard to university options, as non-traditional students remain restricted in choice, painted as 'missing out' as they are more likely to opt for institutions local to them (Holdsworth, 2006). Reasoning for increased legitimacy with distance from home was related to assumed increased independence and less reliance on familial support networks (although social media has dramatically changed how support is sustained and re-negotiated at a distance). Duncan, a first year, student, noted the further away you are 'you have to make it work, because it's not like you can just nip home'. The tradition of moving away for university becomes a subjective measure of validity, showing the arbitrariness in understandings of what makes an authentic/traditional experience - how far is far enough to claim traditional student status?

While Helena, like many others, initially underplayed the significance of proximity to her existing family home, it was clear it played an important role in her decision making. There was a balance between being close enough to fall back on trusted, reliable social and emotional support mechanisms, if needed, but being far enough away to grant authenticity:

> It's that nice distance away but I can go back if I want to. Or need to. Just in case. Most people I know are from quite local to Midlands. Like, most people are maybe from a hundred-mile radius.

Helena confidently defended her decision to stay relatively close to home, in asserting her experience as 'normative', by noting 'most people' were a similar distance from their parental home.

While non-traditional students are expected to manage and/or minimise the distress triggered by relocation from the familiar setting of home to an unfamiliar setting of university by simply not moving, and instead, remaining in their current home for their degree (Clayton et al., 2009), traditional students are largely absent from these discussions. The assumption is that traditional students are eager to experience university as the most 'transformative transition' (Brown et al., 2012); university is often portrayed as 'starting over', 'reinvention', 'cutting ties' and so on. This chapter tells us that there are continuities between traditional and non-traditional, presenting slippage between these binaries, as 'traditional' students in this sample shared anxieties about being somewhere new, becoming someone new. Rather than having an uncomplicated transition, some traditional students in this sample were facing similar dilemmas and negotiations, not wanting to completely cut ties with their existing network, but travelling far enough from home to engage in the possibility of self-reinvention offered by university, and to indulge in the social elements offered, without completely losing who they were, who they are. Indeed, many students mentioned maintaining connections through regular calls home, and/or the importance of continuity in routine, as Steve, a second year, student illustrated:

> Obviously, if it's the weekend I'll go home at the weekend, meet my little brother and dad and stuff.

So while fulfilling the requirement of 'normative' traditional experience, this example further highlights the complexity in 'traditional' experiences and problematises the homogenising nature of these arbitrary categories. Does 'traditional' still apply to those who live away for the full three years but return home every weekend? How frequent is too frequent, in reference to familial visits, to assert independence, associated with traditional student experience?

As well as distance from home, geographical location itself was also important. This was based on assumptions that bigger cities were overflowing with social opportunities. Therefore, these cities were presented as elevating legitimacy of experience, as students were able to engage more frequently, and more extremely, in a varied social calendar, immersed in an experience most often married with popular idealised traditions of studenthood. Steve explained his rationale in choosing which university to attend:

> I put down… three major cities, big cities. And I know (Northern City) is a big drinking city. I should say uni. (Another Northern City), heard it was a big drinking place. I'd presume I'd be out more and spending more. I can't risk that. I've come to value education and what it can do for you. I don't really want to be out all the time and I know the temptation to go out in those places would be huge.

Steve was keen to express he was satisfied that he had found a balance in his choice as he explained his Midlands choice was 'a good uni' in terms of his educational experience, but also enabled enough engagement in 'typical' social behaviours, offering 'not too much, not too little'. He compared this with other regional institutions which he felt lacked social opportunities with reputations for being 'quiet as'. He was pleased he had done enough to acquire traditional student status, weighing up adequate *typical* experience, without jeopardising his degree outcome, as he worried if he had gone to some of the bigger cities, he may have 'dropped out', or 'failed', emphasising that he believed 'everyone comes to uni to learn', and 'not to spend three years partying'.

Using moving away as an example, tradition here becomes a criterion for judging legitimate experience. Students alluded to an experience, which they felt was somewhere between the 'full' student experience, and that of those who had not moved away at all. They felt that they had done enough to claim a legitimate experience. But how much was enough? While on the surface, it appears these traditional students have followed a 'normal', 'traditional' route, their experiences are extremely diverse. Some had moved away and rarely returned home, some had only moved into accommodation with peers for a year of their study, some returned home frequently and arguably spent equal time in both locations. All had weighed up where to move, with many living within a 90 mile radius, yet all underlined the importance of moving away, measuring the legitimacy of experience against this requirement.

Idealised traditions: Students' role in reproducing the myth

The third and final illustration of the myth is how it operates as an idealised transition. These idealised traditions enable perpetuation of the myth of a traditional student, for instance, as a binge drinker, through reflexive idealisation of behaviours. As mentioned earlier in the chapter, drinking is idealised as an 'integral part' of the traditional university experience (Andersson et al., 2012). The majority of students in this sample were frustrated by popular portrayals of student drinking cultures, implying that the media had only manipulated their reporting to boost interest from the public, claiming these reports were often one-offs or extreme cases (see Sykes, 2017 and Sykes, forthcoming, for more details). Nevertheless, these students played a role in reproducing these images.

Without trying to assert themselves as non-drinkers, or denying that university culture involves drinking, students were keen to disrupt the myth that this was *all* they did. Expressing her frustration regarding the 'misconceptions about university students', Nadia, a third-year student, attempted to build a more accurate image, highlighting how university was not 'just a place of fun', where students *just* 'go out' but that they 'work ridiculously hard', emphasising how the following day she had '7 hours straight with no break'. Nadia's narrative shows she was keen to distance herself from images of students as lazy binge drinkers. Instead, Nadia's experiences, alongside many students in this sample, matched more closely to newer conceptualisations of students as 'hard workers' (Brooks, 2007). This was echoed by students in all stages of their trajectory, as Paul illustrates through his account of a typical student week for him:

> Well it depends on how much work I've got to be honest. Erm work in the library. I might go in early, in the morning... If I've got a lecture at eleven, I'll spend a couple of hours (in the library), then a couple of hours of lectures a day. In the evening, once or twice a week, we might go out somewhere – we've got the pub quiz tonight.... I'll go home at the weekend.... Most Sundays I spend going to the library and working again.

It was common in descriptions of their weeks, that students prioritised academic work, followed by extra-curricular or paid work commitments, before social endeavours. For example, Izzy, a first-year student, listed 'mountaineering', 'working at a hotel', 'volunteering for the environment team', sharing a common feeling among students of being 'busy'. Like many students, Izzy *did* go out, but less frequently than the myth would imply. In fact, as Izzy explained her week often 'lacks [...] going out', because 'I don't have the time, but I have started going out occasionally'. This suggests that Izzy felt like she should be going out more and mentioned later in her interview that she was making a conscious effort to balance work and 'doing studenthood properly'. However, although Izzy was adamant that drinking stereotypes were unfair and exaggerated, when asked about how to describe a *typical* university student, most students tended to outline behaviours that not only uphold myths of reckless anti-social behaviour but were largely dissimilar to stories of their own university experience. Nadia described how she perceives a 'typical' university student as:

> Taking cones and putting them on other people's car, people came into our kitchen and sprayed shaving foam, seen a few people here doing Harlem Shake [a dance that regained popularity in the UK as a meme a year or so prior to interview].... drinking games, ring of fire [a drinking game with playing cards], pre drinks, and sad to say but, some people getting so drunk they can't physically function.

This extract from Nadia illustrates how the fourth sense of 'traditional' operates; the tradition of heavy drinking was idealised by students themselves. The description above did not equate to this student's own experience (at least not regularly), and students were reflexive about this, but, in similar ways to how other outsider groups internalise negative stereotypes placed upon them (see Becker, 1963), students in this sample had seen enough to believe students *do* participate in this behaviour; they had seen enough to perpetuate the myth. For example, Nadia noted 'a few people doing the harlem shake' and 'some people getting so drunk', but this was enough for her to use these behaviours as an example of typical behaviour. As a consequence, drinking becomes an idealised tradition. It is a behaviour students and the public come to know as a marker of a legitimate experience, so regardless of whether or not the perceived regularity of these excessive consumption practices were true representations of reality mattered less than the pressure to demonstrate you had engaged in these idealised 'typical', 'normative' performances of studenthood. Students themselves were, therefore, as highlighted by Nadia, involved in reproducing this myth, both by occasionally indulging in the behaviour, and by portraying these experiences as a significant proportion of their time as a student.

The myth of traditional studenthood consumed by drinking, as an idealised tradition, also cascaded through students' own storytelling of university life. For example, John reported how his grandparents had been watching a university life series on television and were excited that they thought their grandson was having so much fun. The drinking was associated with being youthful, enjoying life to the full and he found his grandparents were almost vicariously living through him. Not wanting to shatter their illusion, or saddle his grandparents with the realities of the stress and worry which currently consumed his second (transitioning to third) year of university, John confessed he found himself often embellishing stories and exaggerating the frequency of partying for his grandparents' benefit.

This reproduction of the myth operating as an idealised tradition, particularly related to drinking, extended to social media. Some explained how social media played an important role in asserting idealised traditions, especially at points in time when they felt they did not have time to engage in particular pursuits in real life. For example, Holly and Lauren discussed how, during periods of intense academic labour, they would post throwback photos of night outs, where they appeared to be having fun. This included photos of them looking 'drunk' – even if in fact they were passing (which involves holding a non-alcoholic drink that would pass for an alcoholic drink) and therefore reducing interrogation. These students noted different reasons for this. For Holly, it served as proof of the idealised tradition, both to those within and outside, proof that she was making the most out of her access to increased social opportunities; Holly was highlighting her freedom from responsibility and her authentic 'fun' student experience. Displaying evidence of drinking online enabled one element of the tantalising, alluring notion of the university bubble to endure, viewed by students (in combination with other claims about university such as improved job prospects) as initially playing a role to entice prospective students and retain current students (although not necessarily helpful, nor their reason for attendance or continuation). Thus, the reputation of studenthood as a time to play was reinforced (see Sykes, forthcoming). This complements claims that this idealised tradition appeals to prospective students as they buy into student 'lifestyle' (Holdsworth, 2009a).

Relatedly, for Lauren, images of 'fun' acted as markers of safety. At times when workloads were high, some students increased contact with home, seeking support and sharing concerns about stress. However, Lauren reduced contact with home during these instances. She explained how posting old images of fun (or altering profile pictures) on social media acted to 'protect families and/or friends from the burden of worrying about her well-being', noting it 'stops mum worrying. My brother can show I'm ok, I'm just having a great time.'

Despite recognising that students themselves were involved in perpetuating this myth, some students noted the damaging impact of the presentation of this narrative to them before arrival, in giving them a false picture of what student life would include. Many students did not envisage the intensity of the academic commitments which they would experience, and the strain on their mental health. As Nadia illustrated, the prevalence of the myth left her unprepared for

> Doing too much and stress. Pressurising yourself to do well and not feeling satisfied and pushing yourself even further and staying up late. All night. And not getting sleep. And almost causing yourself to have a nervous breakdown. That's what happened to me. Tiring yourself out.

Indeed, many blamed this lack of preparedness and inability to balance differing expectations with respect to academics and social life on the overwhelming narrative centred around drinking culture. In their opinion, drinking culture dominated news headlines, stories from peers, and even open days showing off night time facilities. Nathan, a first year, explained in reference to academic pressures, he 'wasn't really prepared', 'because all you hear about is drinking'. Dispelling this myth that university life focuses only on the social life, and instead building a more realistic image of what students are likely to encounter, might better equip students to pre-empt the mental challenges a degree often presents.

Conclusion

In this chapter, I have sought to interrogate the long-standing myth of a 'traditional' undergraduate university student in the UK, and the extent to which it is relevant to the lives of students today. While a swelling volume of work has begun to unpack non-traditional student experiences of higher education, this has left traditional student lives further distanced from non-traditional experiences in academic literature. Presented as binary opposite, portrayals of 'traditional' student lives remain consumed by stereotypes which do not match up with their reality.

The need to move beyond the notion of 'traditional' student is not surprising, and not new, but understanding why we are still holding onto it, when we know that it does not correspond to student experience, offers an important insight. By interrogating four key senses in which the notion of 'traditional' operates in student experience, this chapter has attempted to dispel the myth that there remains such thing as a traditional student, yet explain, to borrow from the Thomas Theorem, whether or not it is 'real, it is real in its consequences' (Thomas & Swaine Thomas, 1928, as cited by Smith, 1995). There is widespread recognition that there is no *one* student experience – although, problematically, the term *student experience,* often used in university documents and initiatives, implies a singular experience, rather than multiple and varied experiences. Increasing complexity and diversity in university experiences is appreciated, yet 'traditional' continues to be employed in the demographic sense, positioned against non-traditional, as a marker of a 'normative' transition to university. It is not necessarily that the word 'traditional' is problematic (although, in my opinion it is unhelpful, as it tends to homogenise students identifying as traditional), but the accompanying image it conjures up, as characteristics are fused with behaviours and expectations which serve as a measure of legitimacy of experience and suggest there is a 'typical' and 'valid' way of being a student.

When received by students, 'traditional' functions as a notion of what student traditions create a legitimate experience. It becomes a stock of cultural associations and expectations. More than this, traditional dominates as an 'ideal'; it represents a measure of comparison, against which students measure their own experience. These measures are subjective and seemingly arbitrary as students discuss 'being young' and distance travelled for university. Tradition acts as an anchor in a period of uncertainty but also in a liminal life course phase. It enables a measure of what is enough. Students come to idealise this notion of tradition, aware that it does not correspond to their own experience (e.g. drinking behaviours), but having seen students engage in behaviours associated with the image, play a significant role in its perpetuation.

In questioning how this myth operates, we begin to see how it is used in problematic and damaging ways. It continues to inform services at university level, and how universities, in combination with students' unions, promote themselves, investing in flashy social facilities, and upgrading accommodation. The myth excludes students who do not measure up to this ideal, for example, by not drinking heavily, or not living away from home, positioning their experiences as non-normative, as well as overshadowing other, perhaps more helpful, ways of imagining studenthood. Yet, even within a self-identifying traditional sample, students were not 'living up' to these problematic stereotypes, but still promoted these ideals as 'typical' and 'legitimate'.

By presenting the slippage between categories, the chapter shows a need for a more holistic understanding of how student identities (and experiences) intersect and interact. In order to fully appreciate and map these complexities in experiences, and achieve greater inclusion, we must work harder to dismantle this myth, aiming to promote diverse experiences, and to present a more realistic image of university life, in university marketing, in higher education policy and through teaching practice and personal tutoring models.

References

Allinson, J. (2006). Over-educated, over-exuberant and over here? The impact of students on cities. *Planning, Practice & Research* 21(1), 79–94. doi:10.1080/02697450600901541

Andersson, J., Sadgrove, J., & Valentine, G. (2012). Consuming campus: Geographies of encounter at a British university. *Social & Cultural Geography* 13(5), 501–515. doi:10.1080/14649365.2012.700725

Arnett, J. J. (2000). Emerging adulthood: A theory of development from the late teens through the twenties. *American Psychologist*, 55(5), 469–480. https://psyc-net.apa.org/doi/10.1037/0003-066X.55.5.469

Archer, L., & Hutchings, M. (2000). 'Bettering yourself'? Discourses of risk, cost and benefit in ethnically diverse, young working-class non-participants' constructions of higher education. *British Journal of Sociology of Education*, 21(4), 555–574. doi:10.1080/713655373

Becker, H. S. (1963). *Outsiders*. New York: The Free Press.

Brooks, R. (2007). Young people's extra-curricular activities: Critical social engagement–or 'something for the CV'?. *Journal of Social Policy*, 36(3), 417–434. doi:10.1017/S0047279407001079

Brooks, R., Byford, K., & Sela, K. (2016a). Students' unions, consumerism and the neo-liberal university. *British Journal of Sociology of Education*, 37(8), 1211–1228. doi:10.1080/01425692.2015.1042150

Brooks, R., Byford, K., & Sela, K. (2016b). The spaces of UK students' unions: Extending the critical geographies of the university campus. *Social and Cultural Geography*, 17(4), 471–490. doi:10.1080/14649365.2015.1089585

Brooks, R. (2018). The construction of higher education students in English policy documents. *British Journal of Sociology of Education*, 39(6), 745–761. doi:10.1080/01425692.2017.1406339

Brown, G., Kraftl, P., Pickerill, J., & Upton, C. (2012). Holding the future together: Towards a theorisation of the spaces and times of transition. *Environment and Planning A*, 44(7), 1607–1623. doi:10.1068%2Fa44608

Cahill, C. (2007). Doing research with young people: Participatory research and the rituals of collective work. *Children's Geographies*, 5(3), 297–312. doi:10.1080/14733280701445895

Chatterton, P. (1999). University students and city centres–the formation of exclusive geographies: The case of Bristol, UK. *Geoforum*, 30(2), 117–133. doi:10.1016/S0016-7185(98)00028-1

Chatterton, P. (2000). The cultural role of universities in the community: Revisiting the university—community debate. *Environment and Planning A*, 32(1), 165–181. doi:10.1068%2Fa3243

Chatterton, P. (2010). The student city: An ongoing story of neoliberalism, gentrification, and commodification. *Environment and Planning A*, 42(3), 509–514. doi:10.1068/a42293

Christie, H., & Munro, M. (2003). The logic of loans: Students' perceptions of the costs and benefits of the student loan. *British Journal of Sociology of Education*, 24(5), 621–636. doi:10.1080/0142569032000127170

Christie, H., Munro, M., & Rettig, H. (2001). Making ends meet: Student incomes and debt. *Studies in Higher Education*, 26(3), 363–383. doi:10.1080/03075070120076318

Christie, H., Tett, L., Cree, V. E., Hounsell, J., & McCune, V. (2008). 'A real rollercoaster of confidence and emotions': Learning to be a university student. *Studies in Higher Education*, 33(5), 567–581. doi:10.1080/03075070802373040

Clayton, J., Crozier, G., & Reay, D. (2009). Home and away: Risk, familiarity and the multiple geographies of the higher education experience. *International Studies in Sociology of Education*, 19(3-4), 157–174. doi:10.1080/09620210903424469

Crozier, G., Reay, D., Clayton, J., Colliander, L., & Grinstead, J. (2008). Different strokes for different folks: Diverse students in diverse institutions–experiences of higher education. *Research Papers in Education*, 23(2), 167–177. doi:10.1080/02671520802048703

Department for Education. (2019). Participation Rates in Higher Education: Academic Years 2006/2007–2017/2018. Retrieved from https://assets.publishing.service.gov.uk/government/uploads/system/uploads/attachment_data/file/843542/Publication_HEIPR1718.pd

De Bruyn, S., Wouters, E., Ponnet, K., Van Damme, J., Maes, L., & Van Hal, G. (2018). Problem drinking among Flemish students: Beverage type, early drinking onset and negative personal & social consequences. *BMC Public Health*, 18(1), 234–242. doi:10.1186/s12889-018-5120-7

Holdsworth, C. (2006). 'Don't you think you're missing out, living at home?' Student experiences and residential transitions. *The Sociological Review*, 54(3), 495–519. doi:10.1111%2Fj.1467-954X.2006.00627.x

Holdsworth, C. (2009a). 'Going away to uni': Mobility, modernity, and independence of English higher education students. *Environment and Planning A*, 41(8), 1849–1864. doi:10.1068%2Fa41177

Holdsworth, C. (2009b). Between two worlds: Local students in higher education and 'Scouse'/student identities. *Population, Space and Place*, 15(3), 225–237. doi:10.1002/psp.511

Holdsworth, C. (2010). Why volunteer? Understanding motivations for student volunteering. *British Journal of Educational Studies*, 58(4), 421–437. doi:10.1080/00071005.2010.527666

Holloway, S. L., Hubbard, P., Jöns, H., & Pimlott-Wilson, H. (2010). Geographies of education and the significance of children, youth and families. *Progress in Human Geography*, 34(5), 583–600. doi:10.1177%2F0309132510362601

Holton, M. (2013). *Advancing Student Geographies: Habitus, Identities and (Re)sensing of Place* (Doctoral dissertation, University of Portsmouth). Retrieved from https://researchportal.port.ac.uk/portal/files/5926170/Final_submission_for_Mark_Holton.pdf

Holton, M. (2015). Learning the rules of the 'student game': Transforming the 'student habitus' through [im] mobility. *Environment and Planning A*, 47(11), 2373–2388. doi:10.1177%2F0308518X15599293

Holton, M. (2016). The geographies of UK university halls of residence: Examining students' embodiment of social capital. *Children's Geographies*, 14(1), 63–76. doi:10.1080/14733285.2014.979134

Hubbard, P. (2013). Carnage! Coming to a town near you? Nightlife, uncivilised behaviour and the carnivalesque body. *Leisure Studies*, 32(3), 265–282. doi:10.10 80/02614367.2011.633616

Kesby, M. and Kindon, S. and Pain, R. (2005). Participatory approaches and diagramming techniques. In Flowerdew, R. and Martin, D. (Eds.). *Methods in human geography: A guide for students doing a research project*. 2nd edn. Harlow, Essex: Pearson Education Limited. 144–166.

Lomer, S. (2014). Economic objects: How policy discourse in the United Kingdom represents international students. *Policy Futures in Education*, 12(4), 273–285. doi:10.2304%2Fpfie.2014.12.2.2733

Molesworth, M., & Nixon, E. & Scullion, R. (2009). Having, being and higher education: The marketisation of the university and the transformation of the student into consumer. *Teaching in Higher Education*, 14(3), 277–287. doi:10.1080/13562510902898841

Morgan, D. L., & Davis III, C. H. (2019). *Student activism, politics, and campus climate in higher education*. New York and Oxon: Routledge.

Nguyen, T. T. H., Sendall, M. C., White, K. M., & Young, R. M. (2018). Vietnamese medical students and binge drinking: A qualitative study of perceptions, attitudes, beliefs and experience. *BMJ Open*, 8(4), doi:10.1136/ bmjopen-2017-020176

Páramo, M. F., Cadaveira, F., Tinajero, C., & Rodríguez, M. S. (2020). Binge drinking, cannabis co-consumption and academic achievement in first year university students in Spain: Academic adjustment as a mediator. *International Journal of Environmental Research and Public Health*, 17(2), 542–556. doi:10.3390/ijerph17020542

Patiniotis, J., & Holdsworth, C. (2005). 'Seize that chance!' Leaving home and transitions to higher education. *Journal of Youth Studies*, 8(1), 81–95. doi:10.1080/13676260500063710

Phipps, A. (2017). (Re) theorising laddish masculinities in higher education. *Gender and Education*, 29(7), 815–830. doi:10.1080/09540253.2016.1171298

Phipps, A., & Young, I. (2015). Neoliberalisation and 'lad cultures' in higher education. *Sociology*, 49(2), 305–322. doi:10.1177%2F0038038514542120

Reay, D., Crozier, G., & Clayton, J. (2010). 'Fitting in'or 'standing out': Working-class students in UK higher education. *British Educational Research Journal*, 36(1), 107–124. doi:10.1080/01411920902878925

Robertson, K., & Tustin, K. (2018). Students who limit their drinking, as recommended by national guidelines, are stigmatized, ostracized, or the subject of peer pressure: Limiting consumption is all but prohibited in a culture of intoxication. *Substance Abuse: Research and Treatment*, 12. doi:10.1177%2F1178221818792414

Smith, D. P., & Holt, L. (2007). Studentification and 'apprentice' gentrifiers within Britain's provincial towns and cities: Extending the meaning of gentrification. *Environment and Planning A: Economy and Space*, 39(1), 142–161. doi:10.1068/a38476

Smith, D. P., & Hubbard, P. (2014). The segregation of educated youth and dynamic geographies of studentification. *Area*, 46(1), 92–100. doi:10.1111/area.12054

Smith, R. S. (1995). Giving credit where credit is due: Dorothy Swaine Thomas and the "Thomas theorem". *The American Sociologist*, 26(4), 9–28. doi:10.1007/BF02692352

Sykes, G. (2017). *The University Bubble: Undergraduate perceptions and experiences of risk/risks during their transitions to, through and beyond university*. (Doctoral dissertation, University of Leicester).

Sykes, G. (forthcoming). *The University Bubble: Conceptualising Student Experiences of Transitions to, through and beyond University (working title)*. Oxon: Routledge.

Tewksbury, R., Higgins, G. E., & Mustaine, E. E. (2008). Binge drinking among college athletes and non-athletes. *Deviant Behavior*, 29(3), 275–293. doi:10.1080/01639620701588040

Thomas W.I., & Swaine Thomas, D. (1928). *The child in America: Behavior problems and programs*. New York: Alfred A. Knopf.

Tomlinson, M. (2016). "Students' perception of themselves as 'consumers' of higher education." *British Journal of Sociology of Education* 38 (4), 450–467. doi:10.1080/01425692.2015.1113856.

Chapter 7

Imagining the constructivist student online

Actively engaged learner or vulnerable student in need?

Kate O'Connor

Introduction

The purpose of universities and what a university education should look like have been the subject of much contestation. Across the world, there is considerable debate about what university teaching should emphasise and how it can be better structured to meet the needs of a widening student body. As part of these debates, many have argued for moving university teaching away from a so-called 'instructivist', lecture-centred mode towards a more student-centred 'constructivist' approach, centred on students' own constructions of knowledge and active engagement rather than teacher developed content (e.g. Barr & Tagg, 1995; Biggs, 2014; Biggs & Tang, 2011; Lea et al., 2003; Porcaro, 2011; Wiemer, 2013). Many of these arguments also promote outcomes-based and alignment-driven education, calling for a need to focus curriculum design on the desired end-point, rather than the content to be taught (Barr & Tagg, 1995; Biggs, 2014; Biggs & Tang, 2011). There has been an emphasis on making expectations as clear and explicit as possible and ensuring content is aligned and builds towards a defined purpose.

These debates represent shifts in understandings about how knowledge is built and what good teaching looks like but are also fundamentally about how students are understood. As Brooks (2018, 2020) has argued, how students are represented, positioned and imagined in higher education institutions is not pregiven, but contested, often contradictory and changing across both time and space. Much of the recent analysis of representations of students has focused on the prominence of economic constructions of higher education, or on the positioning of students as consumers (see Brooks, 2018; Kelly et al., 2017). In this chapter, I focus on two ways students are discursively constructed in higher education debates as part of the arguments described above: as engaged constructivist learners and as vulnerable students in need of explicit teaching and additional support.

The chapter considers these two constructions in relation to the online learning context, and specifically one particular online learning initiative where constructivist ideas were a key pedagogical driver in how the initiative was structured. Online learning has become ubiquitous in higher education, and those working in the online space have been highly influenced by constructivist approaches (Selwyn, 2011), but also by the sense of the online cohort as 'non-traditional' and requiring additional supports to engage (e.g. Dyment et al., 2020). The case study initiative in question took a particular form where curriculum was developed by academics but then delivered via teaching assistants employed by an online program management provider. It is examined in this chapter as an interesting example of how the push for constructivist teaching can be taken up in practice, and the tensions which can arise in how students are imagined in relation to that.

The chapter begins with a discussion of constructivist teaching and the ways students are imagined by those calling for more constructivist forms of teaching in higher education. It then introduces the case study, and discusses how both institutional leaders and teaching staff positioned students in their policy designs and curriculum-making. This discussion highlights the importance placed on both encouraging constructivist engagement and supporting vulnerable students within this case but also shows the dominance of the latter emphasis in how teaching was actually designed and configured. The chapter argues that the focus on student vulnerabilities in arguments for constructivist teaching risks positioning students in deficit ways and, as the case study shows, can potentially work against attempts to encourage constructivist engagement in practice.

The rise of the constructivist learner

Constructivism is a term which encapsulates a collection of diverse theories, each of which has different orientations and concerns (see Sjøberg, 2010; Davis & Sumara, 2010). While individually-oriented theories focus on how individuals make sense of the world for example, social constructivist theories conceptualise learning as 'diffuse, distributed and collective', and requiring 'discussion, dialogue and interaction' (Shumar & Wright, 2016, p. 7). Yet although different in some respects, constructivist theories share common tenets which include an understanding of knowledge as actively constructed by the learner, including through their interactions with others, and a recognition that teachers have to take the learner's existing ideas seriously in order to challenge pre-existing individual views of the world (Sjøberg, 2010). There is an emphasis on ensuring teachers account for and engage with students' own pre-conceptions and understandings and an acknowledgement of a need for some openness in terms of how curriculum is preformulated and how lecturers engage with students (Sjøberg, 2010; Davis & Sumara, 2010).

Within higher education, calls for constructivist teaching have become widespread and entangled in arguments for more 'student-centred' teaching practices (e.g. Barr & Tagg, 1995; Biggs, 2014; Biggs & Tang, 2011; Lea et al., 2003; Porcaro, 2011; Wiemer, 2013). Such arguments draw a distinction between 'instructivist' teaching, understood as premised on direct instruction or didactic methods and focused on the transmission of content, and 'constructivist' pedagogies, which encourage active engagements and deep learning. Barr and Tagg's (1995) influential publication *From Teaching to Learning – a New Paradigm for Undergraduate Education* proposed a shift from an instruction paradigm, where knowledge is seen as being transferred from teachers to students and the focus is on covering content, to a learning paradigm, where the role of the teacher is to facilitate students in constructing their own knowledge and the focus is on student learning and understanding. Biggs and Tang's (2011) popular model of constructivist alignment similarly advocates for teaching focused on 'active' rather than 'passive' learning activities (see also Biggs, 2014). This work draws on a broad understanding of constructivism, whereby 'teaching is not a matter of transmitting but of engaging students in active learning, building their knowledge in terms of what they already understand' (Biggs & Tang, 2011, p. 22).

Within these arguments, calls for more constructivist teaching are typically tied to a concern with 'aligning' learning activities to build towards those predefined outcomes. Barr and Tagg (1995, p. 10) advocate for an open choice of 'means' (activities, lectures, etc.) combined with fixed 'ends' or outcomes to allow 'the means to vary in its constant search for the most effective and efficient paths to student learning'. Biggs and Tang (2011) likewise emphasise the importance of aligning (1) learning outcomes, (2) activities designed to develop those outcomes and (3) the assessment of the learning. They advocate using outcomes to encourage a 'deep' rather than 'surface' approach to learning and to 'activate' learning activities which require high cognitive level (such as reflecting, theorising and applying) rather than only those which require lower cognitive levels (such as memorising and recalling) (see also Biggs, 2014).

These arguments position students as active co-constructors in their own learning. Where constructivist teaching is enacted, students are imagined as empowered learners, actively engaged in their work and working collaboratively with both their teachers and each other. There is an emphasis on deep learning and understanding as well as a sense of increased responsibility, accountability and autonomy on the part of the student to engage in that learning (see Lea et al., 2003). Students are acknowledged as coming to university not as blank slates but with preformed ideas about the world which their education needs to build upon or challenge (Biggs & Tang, 2011).

This construct of the constructivist learner, actively taking control of their learning in dialogue with their teachers and with each other, has some resonances with but also departs from Leathwood's (2006) characterisation of the ideal independent learner. According to Leathwood, independence and the ability to be an independent learner have long been constructed as essential characteristics of a 'good' higher education student, and students have been increasingly positioned as 'active consumers of educational services, taking responsibility for their own learning as independent, autonomous and self-directed individuals' (Leathwood & O'Connell, 2003, p. 599). These characteristics of responsibility and active engagement are clearly evident within the idea of the constructivist learner. However, while the independent learner is positioned as needing little support and acting in self-directed ways, constructivist learners are understood as reliant on interactions with teachers and each other. The ideal of the independent learner has been identified as problematic for a number of reasons, including in its masculinist conceptions of both learning and student learners, and its reinforcement of a typical student as white, middle-class and able-bodied, unencumbered by caring and work responsibilities (Leathwood, 2006). In contrast, arguments for constructivist teaching (e.g. Biggs & Tang, 2011) are positioned in response to the massification of higher education and the increasing diversity of the student body, rather than on a sense of uniformity. There is an assumption of strong connections between teachers and students (Biggs & Tang, 2011), rather than a reliance on reduced student contact.

Relatedly, however, arguments for more constructivist teaching also resonate with what Brooks (2018, 2020) has identified as the discourse of the vulnerable student. As Brooks (2018) argues, higher education students are frequently discursively positioned in 'childlike' ways, as vulnerable to the 'wrong' decisions, and in terms of the academic support and teaching quality provided within universities. In a similar vein, arguments for constructivist teaching rest on assumptions that dominant 'instructivist' teaching practices leave too many students unsupported and vulnerable to failure. Biggs and Tang (2011), for example, argue that teaching that requires active engagement by students decreases the gap between students who are 'academically committed and will learn well, virtually whatever the teaching' and students who are 'not academically inclined' and 'who would not have been at university years ago' (2011, p. 3). The vast majority of students are imagined as part of this latter category, and as requiring clear direction and support to succeed at the level expected, and this is behind much of the justification for combining constructivist teaching with the explicit identification of expected outcomes. Concerns about student vulnerabilities address the student body as a whole, but also target particular groups of students identified as 'nontraditional' including those who enter university through alternative routes, students with disabilities or from working-class backgrounds (Leathwood & O'Connell, 2003). These students, as seen in Biggs and Tang's (2011) example of a typical student who would not have attended university in earlier times, tend to be constructed in deficit ways, including in relation to their abilities, backgrounds, aspirations and attitudes (Leathwood & O'Connell, 2003). This emphasis on student vulnerability and lack works against the sense of an empowered constructivist learner, actively engaged and in charge of their own learning.

These tensions are also evident in how online students are typically imagined in higher education. As Selwyn (2011) notes, constructivist ideas have been highly influential in the online learning space and constructivist theories of knowledge and learning have had a considerable impact on the framing of online programs since the 1980s. Many see digital technologies and online learning environments as aligned with constructivist pedagogies in their ability to situate learning within collaborative and supportive social contexts (e.g. Luke, 2003) and emphasise the ways peer-to-peer collaboration and interaction are supported and enabled by digital environments. This work imagines the online student as an empowered constructivist learner, actively engaging with their peers to support their learning. However, at the same time and in line with the above, online students are frequently positioned as different from 'traditional' on-campus students both as a result of age and socio-economic background and in terms of the supports required to maintain engagement and retention (see Dyment et al., 2020). And as Shumar and Wright (2016) have argued, online learning offers opportunities for enhanced interaction and co-construction but can also be used in ways which are more about control and the effective transmission of predefined content.

In this chapter, I take up two concerns arising from the construct of the constructivist student in higher education. One is the question of how the constructivist learner is being interpreted, and the extent to which students are positioned as engaged and empowered learners, or as vulnerable students in need of support. Both constructs are evident in the work discussed above, yet, as a range of work has highlighted, there is a risk of the former being undermined in a context where what, how and when students learn is highly restricted and predefined (see McFarlane, 2016; Zepke, 2018). Related to this is the question of how constructivist teaching is being interpreted in this context. Such teaching, as discussed, connects with a range of different theoretical approaches, and concerns have been raised about the forms of teaching associated with or named as constructivism (see Lea et al., 2003; Sjøberg, 2010; Van Bergen & Parsell, 2019). In what follows, the paper explores the ways in which constructivist teaching was understood in one particular online learning initiative, and how students were imagined and positioned as part of this.

Examining constructions of the student via a case study of an online 'constructivist teaching' initiative

The online learning initiative examined in this chapter was explicitly designed around a social constructivist pedagogical model. In line with the research discussed above (e.g. Biggs & Tang, 2011; Biggs, 2014), this initiative aimed to both engage students and acknowledge their own contributions and sense making practices and provide scaffolded support, alignment between activities and outcomes, and explicit identification of those outcomes.

The initiative was offered via a partnership with an online program management provider and comprised a model where subject content was developed in full prior to teaching by lecturers employed by the university, and then delivered by externally employed teaching assistants with relevant professional expertise, with the lecturer playing no role in the teaching of the subject. This model has been described as an 'unbundling' of the instructional (curriculum development) role from the delivery (teaching) activities (Neely & Tucker, 2010; Cliff et al., 2020). It works against the strong student–academic relations presumed by advocates for constructivist teaching such as Biggs and Tang (2011) (see also O'Connor, 2020), and therefore represents an interesting case through which to explore tensions in how constructivist teaching and the imagined constructivist student are being interpreted in practice.

The case study is in many ways anomalous; most online teaching in higher education is not configured in this mode. However, it is also not insignificant. Online program management of this form is a growing market and in the US was estimated to be worth an estimated $1.1 billion in 2018 (Perrotta, 2018). Moreover, the emphasis on limiting contact between academics and students is evident in other forms of online learning as well as in the rise of casual teaching globally. I therefore understand the case study as particular in context and detail, but also pointing towards challenges and contradictions that may potentially be evident in university practices more broadly.

The case study formed part of a wider research project which examined a range of different online learning reforms at two Australian universities. It was conducted across 2013 and 2014 and included interviews with staff leading each initiative, repeat interviews with selected academics and learning advisors developing new subjects over the period of development, and document analysis of policy and promotional materials and curriculum documents (including university plans, media releases, website pages, handbook entries and curriculum materials). This particular case study included a total of 17 interviews with 8 participants. These included three institutional leaders (referred to by pseudonym): Sarah, a Pro Vice-Chancellor with responsibilities for learning and teaching innovations, Lydia, the academic leader of the initiative, and Rachel, the initiative's learning design manager; three academics developing new subjects: Tara (Teacher Education), Grant (Sports Management) and Leah (Supply Chain Management); and the two learning designers assisting those academics: Zac (working on the business subjects) and Anita (working on the education subject). The academics and learning designers were interviewed at multiple points throughout the curriculum development process, while the institutional leaders were interviewed once.

The project was focused on the understandings of knowledge and students evident at the institutional level and in the curriculum development of the new subjects for the new online reforms. It was informed by traditions of curriculum inquiry (e.g. Karseth, 2006) and policy sociology (e.g. Ball, 2006), and the importance those fields place on addressing the emphases and assumptions underlying policy and curriculum-based decisions and constructions, both explicit and tacit. Drawing on understandings of policies as discursively produced, with effects that are non-linear but interpreted and contested differently across different sites of practice (Ball, 2006), the research focused on the ways in which different actors interpreted and constructed the contexts in which they work. In what follows, I discuss how these actors talked about their subject purposes and curriculum decisions and the contestations and contradictions evident in how they positioned students.

Constructions of students in the online learning initiative design and rationale

On the website for this initiative, students were advised that they will 'be engaged in an active learning environment', 'feel part of a vibrant and engaging learning community', 'find themselves members of a collaborative, supported and connected community of learners' and 'be presented with many opportunities to work collaboratively with your peers and teaching staff'. The teaching approach was defined as 'designing activities that foster collaboration among students using a social constructivist learning model', and the teaching information pack provided to new tutors defined social constructivism as 'individuals constructing knowledge through social processes (conversation, dialogue, sharing of ideas)'. It proposed that 'students in all units of study will be engaged in an active learning environment, participating regularly in communication and collaboration with staff and peers'.

In explaining the model, Lydia, the academic leader of the initiative, talked about the benefits of this in terms of developing conceptual understanding that allows students to move across and bring together different forms of information. She commented:

> it was actually about developing conceptual understanding and how you might do that. So that sort of internal conceptual structure about nodes and connections so that you kind of got information that sits in nodes but if you can't move between them then you have not got conceptual understanding. [...] So to me the social constructivist pedagogical model is all about having conversations and developing those links.
>
> (Lydia, Interview 1)

These sentiments are underpinned by a process-oriented sense of knowledge, with Lydia emphasising the importance of students understanding the wider picture and the underpinning concepts, but getting at that through discussions about the material and with other students. She saw learning and the development of broader understanding as not adequately served by transmission or telling, but as requiring work by the students to get inside or think about implications, and sees collaborative, activity-based pedagogies as necessary for effectively encouraging that within teaching. These sentiments emphasise the active work of students, positioning them as engaged learners, working collaboratively with each other, rather than absorbing predefined content in passive ways.

Alongside the emphasis on social constructivism, and in line with Biggs and Tang (2011), there was a strong concurrent emphasis on supporting vulnerable students via explicit objectives and alignment between activities and assessments. In the interviews, the institutional leaders talked about the benefits of this for students in terms of providing explicit direction and ensuring students both understood what was expected of them and developed the skills they would need to complete the assessments. Lydia, for example, noted:

> [what] the learning designers are trying to do is make sure every activity scaffolds to assessment in some way. The students can see if they do activities in week one, two and three, when they get to the assignment in week four, they've done half the work.
>
> (Lydia, Interview 1)

Institutional leaders were concerned about overloading students with content, with Rachel, for example, commenting that one of her driving emphases is the question 'Is it sort of all too much, do we need to contain that and rethink the way we do that?' (Rachel, Interview 1). Strong directions were given by staff about the number of readings they felt students could cope with (no more than two per week), and staff worked with academics to ensure content was able to be contained within a single weekly page. There was an emphasis on supporting students through explicit and detailed direction, and Lydia in particular saw this approach as critical for meeting the needs of the students likely to enrol in the initiative, many of whom are first in family:

> we absolutely believe we have the best product in the market, absolutely, because we have the support and the strategies in place to meet the needs of the students that we're recruiting [...] our students by and large are non-traditional students and therefore they're first in family or they're left school at Year Ten and are reengaging after going to TAFE [Technical and Further Education] and working for five years or you know, so I can give you journey after journey story of people who are traditionally not successful in higher education, let alone online. So they've got the double whammy of challenges for how they're going to be successful. And so we've very, very specifically designed our programs to support them in their learning.
>
> (Lydia, Interview 1).

Here the need for additional supports and explicit outcomes was framed very much in terms of the particular student cohort, and seen as necessary to ensure their success. Students are here positioned in deficit ways, as unable to cope with difficult or complex tasks, and as dependent on explicit step-by-step instruction to succeed.

Additionally, and in contrast to the sense of students as co-constructors of knowledge seen above, there was also an emphasis on subject knowledge as fixed and stable content to be learnt; something settled and predetermined prior to teaching, rather than negotiated by students with their teachers within classroom spaces. All subject materials were expected to be developed in full prior to the teaching period to allow for activities to scaffold towards the predefined outcomes and assessments, and curriculum was expected to change very little between cohorts. Lydia commented that 'one of our problems is that academics change things all the time' (Lydia, Interview 1) and talked about the issues raised for subject design where academics change assessments because it interferes with how the activities have been designed to scaffold towards their requirements. Within the thinking informing this initiative, therefore, there was an emphasis on providing space for students to actively engage with and work through concepts in ways which develop their own understandings. Yet at the same time, there was limited space for that content to reference students' own understandings, and in detailed ways that allowed for scaffolding and explicit direction. The understandings of students were here potentially contradictory, on the one hand emphasising students' own activities, interactions and concepts, and on the other framing the knowledge to be learnt as not something they were contributing to but as fixed and predefined.

Constructions of students by academics and learning advisors

Constructions of students as both engaged constructivist learners and vulnerable students in need were also evident in the thinking and practices of those developing the new subjects. When I asked the lecturers about what they were aiming to achieve with their subjects, they all talked about the complexity of their fields, and the importance of students engaging constructively with that complexity, rather than see what they are learning at university as settled or complete knowledge. The lecturers wanted to encourage students' active engagements with the content taught in ways which accord with the primary tenants of constructivist teaching discussed above and were concerned with encouraging students to think critically and to actively engage with complex problems.

Tara, one of the lecturers, explained the purpose of her Teacher Education subject as follows:

> I think what we're trying to do with this unit is to show that literacy is really, really diverse and it's not just your traditional form or traditional view of literacy. So we're trying to tackle some of the controversies with

regards to digital literacy and we're also trying to tackle how a contemporary twenty first century teacher will do that with children in the classroom.

(Tara, Interview 1).

This emphasis on the complexity and the diversity of perspectives, according to Tara, was about ensuring students appreciate the wider contexts in which they work and are able to speak back rather than passively absorb policy directions within the field of teacher education. She explained:

[Within teacher education] you are given things you're told to swallow, to basically take the policy, digest the policy, implement the policy. [...] [But] you have to be able to talk back and [...] be given the skills to actually argue back and talk to things

(Tara, Interview 2)

Here, Tara emphasised the importance of developing teacher professionalism, identity and agency in her students: student teachers active in constructing and critiquing the contexts in which they work. She wanted students taking her subject to critically engage with the contexts and purposes of their professional work, and to debate and consider controversial issues as part of that.

In relation to another subject, Supply Chain Management, Leah saw her purposes as about developing student understanding of the kinds of issues and problems likely to be encountered within professional practice. Leah explained that the subject was about getting students:

progressively to think in that multi-dimensional sort of a way and considering the complexity, the fact that these [supply chain and procurement] decisions are not black and white, there are repercussions of something that may have a great short-term benefit may actually be quite detrimental to the business in the long run. Those sorts of issues and sort of building a bit of a story about that.

(Leah, Interview 2)

Leah emphasised the importance of appreciating 'the complexity of today's business environment and the fact that there are system-like relationships, everything connects to everything else' and the importance of ensuring students understand that you cannot 'think linearly in today's world' (Leah, Interview 1). She noted that subjects within the field were predominantly taken by students with prior practical experience working within supply chain management but who had reached a ceiling in terms of their progression without further study. Because of this, she saw the subject as aiming to encourage those students:

to think critically, especially when they're so used to going 'here's a problem, here's how I solve it' and not necessarily being in a habit of rationalising or justifying 'why do I think this is a good solution for this problem [...] how do we know, is there some research that suggests that that's a good idea or have we tried it before, is there empirical evidence' or what not.

(Leah, Interview 1)

Students are here imagined as active constructivist learners, not just absorbing predefined content but engaging in the complexity of their fields, and debating key problems and dilemmas with their teachers and each other.

However, working against these aims to cultivate some openness in what was taught, the lecturers also designed their subjects based on generalised understandings of what was required to keep so called 'non-traditional' students engaged and on-task. In speaking about their students, these lecturers all tended to emphasise the importance of flexibility, reduced content and additional scaffolding and support and talked about how strongly these understandings guided their curriculum development. Tara, for example commented:

if you're a student who is working full time or have got family commitments, you need to get through the course in, human nature, the quickest way possible [...] it might be really nice for us to give them an x number of readings, and x number of videos but you want the simplest way because you just want to pass this unit.

(Tara, Interview 1)

Similarly, in relation to her subjects in Supply Chain Management, Leah commented:

we used to do a lot of concepts [...] And one of the things that I found is that it was just overwhelming, they would look at this page and there would be so much and they'd go 'oh my god I have to get through all of this in one week, I don't know where to start'. So as we went along we started to simplify it and break it down. Where now it's literally, here is the little summary [...] [Because] in reality if I give them three peer reviewed articles to read every week, they're just going to drop out by week three. [...] some people don't have enough literacy to be able to navigate through an academic article. That's really the bottom line of it and you have to account for it.

(Leah, Interview 1)

As at the policy level, these sentiments position students in deficit ways, as not capable of higher order study (cf. Leathwood & O'Connell, 2003). In contrast with the arguments of Biggs and Tang (2011), there is an emphasis on simplicity, rather than on designing activities to engage with complex thinking.

This focus was also evident in the lecturers' attention to scaffolding and alignment. In line with the policy intention, the lecturers were highly concerned with prescribing and directing student activities and with providing detailed and templated instructions regarding assessment requirements. In working with a forum which afforded them no interaction with students beyond the development of subject materials, they tended to provide comprehensive directions to the online tutors to ensure the activities and discussions proceeded as intended. Grant, an academic, for example, commented that in developing online activities he includes 'leading questions developed to try and draw out the key facts and principles from the case studies in the discussion'. He elaborated, 'My development has included quite comprehensive discussion questions that are leading the students to hopefully coming up with a particular solution or a particular answer' (Grant, Interview 1).

Each of the lecturers drafted additional notes for those tutors which directed them regarding where the discussion generated by the designed activities should go and what kinds of issues should be emphasised. For her Teacher Education subject, Tara emphasised the importance of these instructions to tutors and developed notes that were around 25 pages long. These notes provided rationales around why all the content is put together in the way it has been and included approximately five extra weekly resources for the tutors to post themselves in the discussion boards. Tara worried that if her supporting notes were not completely explicit there was a risk students might 'go into a negative deficit view of literacy or [think standardised testing] is essential and we must just do reading and writing as opposed to thinking about digital literacies and contemporary technologies' (Tara, Interview 2).

Leah who developed the Supply Chain Management subject but had also acted as an online tutor for other subjects similarly commented that her approach to online discussion tends to be more 'standardised' and more strongly directed than in on-campus delivery (Leah, Interview 1). She saw this as particularly necessary due to the asynchronous nature of the discussions, and the ways this made it harder for students to see what was relevant. Leah commented that in comparison her on-campus teaching is far more receptive to students and to the discussion in the classroom but felt there was less openness to achieve this kind of work without confusing the students within the online discussion space.

Across the subjects, the approach taken to the discussion boards and activities tended to be more template-driven and directed towards the predetermined outcomes and the assessments, rather than oriented to students developing their own constructions of knowledge. In developing curriculum for students with whom they would not interact, the lecturers worried about students misinterpreting activities which were too open and focused more on prescribing defined tasks for students that linked explicitly with their assessment tasks than on opening up broader discussion spaces.

Similar emphases were also evident in relation to the assessment design, where the lecturers were concerned with providing students with clear rubrics and templated instructions. For Tara's subject for example, the primary assessment comprised a portfolio task which required students to complete a template about a collection of resources. This template asked students to provide a brief description of each resource, evidence of it (such as a link or screenshot), a description of how it could be used and why it is relevant to the weekly topic and a critical analysis of its merits and limitations. In relation to this task, Anita, the learning advisor responsible for the course commented:

> They've got quite a lot of guidance. So, for instance, in the week on writing and primary, they need to find two creative and contemporary strategies to develop children's writing skills in primary classes. So there's guidance on the number of things they have to find on the broad sort of category, so here it's strategies for developing writing skills. They're told that it needs to be creative and contemporary but then within that they can go as far afield as they like as long as they're still doing that analysis of explaining what it is, how it's used, the advantages, limitations and finding the academic resources to support its usage.
>
> (Anita, Interview 2)

Here, what students were expected to do in respect of the assessment was highly prescribed. Within this assessment, what was left up to students – where they can go 'as far afield as they like' – was the selection of the resource, but what they were asked to do with that conformed to rigid template expectations, with set lengths allocated to defining use, advantages, limitations and the like. Students were provided with a detailed rubric with marks allocated for each element and the expected content was clearly defined. The assessment task was very self-contained and there was little that asked students to go beyond the resources they were provided when formulating their thinking. Students were required to source their own resources but their engagement with theoretical and conceptual concepts was very much defined to the content provided.

Across all three subjects, the use of the discussion boards and the design of the assessments was far less open than the policy rhetoric about student discussion and social constructivism might suggest. The approaches taken by the lecturers tended to restrict activities and assessments to what could be most easily directed, rather than what might be the most important substantive issues to discuss or engage with. Although the lecturers I spoke with wanted students to engage in open and constructive ways and to understand the evolving and complex nature of knowledge within their fields, their subject development tended to focus predominantly on issues of clarity and control. Students were primarily directed in ways that were more about fulfilling pre-set requirements than making connections with or building from their own concepts and understandings, potentially limiting their opportunities to engage in potentially more meaningful ways.

In summary, these academics' curriculum development was informed by the two dominant understandings of students evident at the policy level and in debates about constructivist teaching – of engaged constructivist learners, and vulnerable students in need. However, although both orientations were evident in the ways the lecturers talked about their purposes, their actual subject design tended to be oriented more towards concerns about student vulnerabilities and the need for additional support. While those leading the initiative hoped it would encourage more constructivist teaching with more emphasis on student activities, the lecturers saw the move online as encouraging and necessitating a greater degree of explicitness and standardisation and focused on these issues in their subject development.

Conclusion

As Brooks (2018, 2020) has highlighted, students are discursively constructed in multiple and at times contradictory ways. This chapter has explored the dominant ways students are imagined in arguments for constructivist teaching as well as within a particular case study of an online learning initiative, arguing that students are typically positioned as actively engaged constructivist learners, but also as vulnerable and in need of support.

These conceptions are at odds with each other, and as the case study shows, attention to student vulnerabilities can risk undermining aims to encourage constructivist forms of engagement and learning. In talking about their subject purposes, the case study lecturers imagined students as engaged constructivist learners, expressing desires to engage with students' own interpretations and thinking about the concepts they were trying to teach, rather than require them to passively absorb predefined content. However, in developing their curriculum, they worried more about what their students were capable of and became more concerned with rigid assessment expectations and parameters, and with prescribing and directing student activities. Students were here not positioned as active co-constructors working with lecturers and each other in collaborative ways, but as passively fulfilling preset requirements, and as needing explicit direction to succeed. This potentially restricted the ways in which students were invited to engage within their subjects, tying them to rigid predefined requirements, rather than encouraging them to take their learning in new directions. At the institutional level, the leaders responsible for the online initiative likewise imagined students as engaging in constructivist forms of learning, but also emphasised the importance of clarity and simplified content to ensure the success of 'non-traditional students' and positioned subject knowledge as something fixed and predetermined prior to teaching, undermining the sense of students as active co-constructors of knowledge within the classroom. Students were here framed in deficit ways, with the focus on what leaders and lecturers imagined they were not capable of, rather than on what they might bring to the educational situation (cf. Leathwood & O'Connell, 2003).

The case study considered in this chapter was configured in a particular mode, where academics designing new subjects had no contact with the students taking them.

In this case, limited opportunities for interacting with students meant that lecturers were not able to develop their curriculum content in ways which referenced where students were coming from, and they were not able to teach that content in a way which allowed them to engage with students' own understandings and concepts in meaningful ways, exacerbating the problems identified above. This highlights the difficulty of practicing constructivist teaching in contexts where contact between those designing subjects, and those taking them is limited. As Sjøberg (2010) and Davis and Sumara (2010) have argued, constructivist teaching typically requires some openness in terms of how curriculum is preformulated, and this is challenged in contexts where subjects are not taught by those designing them.

Constructivist teaching potentially brings many benefits to students, encouraging attention to student engagement and interactions. However, these benefits risk being undermined if constructivist teaching is introduced in contexts where students are also positioned in deficit ways. Although specific in some ways to the case in question, the issues highlighted in this chapter underline the importance of considering in more detail how constructivist teaching is being interpreted within higher education, and the extent to which students are recognised as agentic and empowered learners as part of this.

References

Ball, S. J. (2006). *Education policy and social class: The selected works of Stephen Ball.* Abingdon, Oxon: Routledge.

Barr, R. B., & Tagg, J. (1995). From teaching to learning – a new paradigm for undergraduate education. *Change*, November/December, 13–24. https://www.tandfonline.com/doi/abs/10.1080/00091383.1995.10544672

Biggs, J. (2014). Constructive alignment in university teaching. *HERDSA Review of Higher Education*, 1, 5–22.

Biggs, J. B., & Tang, C. (2011). *Teaching for quality learning at university* (4th Ed.). Maidenhead, Berkshire: Society for Research into Higher Education & Open University Press.

Brooks, R. (2018). The construction of higher education students in English policy documents. *British Journal of Sociology of Education* 39:6, 745–761. https://www.tandfonline.com/doi/full/10.1080/01425692.2017.1406339

Brooks, R. (2020). Diversity and the European higher education student: Policy influencers' narratives of difference. *Studies in Higher Education*. Advance online publication. https://www.tandfonline.com/doi/full/10.1080/03075079.2018.1564263

Cliff, A., Walji, S., Mogliacci, R.J., Morris, N., & Ivancheva, M. (2020). Unbundling and higher education curriculum: a Cultural-Historical Activity Theory view of process. *Teaching in Higher Education*. Advance online publication. https://www.tandfonline.com/doi/abs/10.1080/13562517.2019.1711050

Davis, B., & Sumara, D. (2010). Curriculum and constructivism. In P. Peterson, E. Baker, & B. McGaw (Eds.), *International encyclopedia of education* (3rd Ed., pp. 488–489). Oxford: Elsevier Ltd.

Dyment, J., Stone, C. & Milthorpe, N. (2020). Beyond busy work: rethinking the measurement of online student engagement. *Higher Education Research & Development*. Advance online publication. https://www.tandfonline.com/eprint/MSFMIB8EEG4PNBRPTHBK/full?target=10.1080/07294360.2020.1732879

Karseth, B. (2006). Curriculum restructuring in higher education after the Bologna Process: A new pedagogic regime? *Revista Española de Educación Comparada* 12, 255–284.

Kelly, P., et al. (2017). The engaged student ideal in UK higher education policy. *Higher Education Policy* 30:1, 105–122.

Lea, S. J., Stephenson, D. & Troy, J. (2003). Higher education students' attitudes to student centred learning: Beyond 'educational bulimia'. *Studies in Higher Education* 28:3, 321–334. https://www.tandfonline.com/doi/abs/10.1080/03075070309293

Leathwood, C. (2006). Gender, equity and the discourse of the independent learner in higher education. *Higher Education* 52:4, 611–633.

Leathwood, C., & O'Connell, P. (2003). 'It's a struggle': The construction of the 'New Student' in higher education. *Journal of Education Policy* 18:6, 597–615. https://www.tandfonline.com/doi/pdf/10.1080/0268093032000145863.

McFarlane, B. (2016). *Freedom to learn: The threat to student academic freedom and why it needs to be reclaimed.* London: Routledge

Neely, P., & Tucker, J. (2010). Unbundling faculty roles in online distance education programs. *The International Review of Research in Open and Distance Learning* 11:2, 20–32.

O'Connor, K. (2020). Constructivism, curriculum and the knowledge question: tensions and challenges for higher education. *Studies in Higher Education*. Advance online publication. https://www-tandfonline-com.ezp.lib.unimelb.edu.au/doi/full/10.1080/03075079.2020.1750585

O'Neill, G., & McMahon, T. (2005) Student-centred learning: What does it mean for students and lecturers? In O'Neill, G., Moore, S., McMullin, B. (Eds). *Emerging issues in the practice of university learning and teaching.* Dublin: AISHE. http://www.aishe.org/readings/2005-1/oneill-mcmahon-Tues_19th_Oct_SCL.html

Perrotta, C. (2018). Digital learning in the UK: Sociological reflections on an unequal marketplace. *Social Sciences* 7:10, 170. doi:10.3390/socsci7100170

Porcaro, D. (2011). Applying constructivism in instructivist learning cultures. *Multicultural Education & Technology Journal* 5:1, 39–54.

Selwyn, N. (2011). *Education and technology: key issues and debates.* London; New York: Continuum International Publishing Group.

Shumar, W., & Wright, S. (2016). Digital media and contested visions of education. *Learning and Teaching: The International Journal of Higher Education in the Social Sciences* 9:2, 1–11. doi:10.3167/latiss.2016.090201

Sjøberg, S. (2010). Constructivism and learning. In P. Peterson, E. Baker, & B. McGaw (Eds.), *International encyclopedia of education* (3rd Ed., pp. 485–490). Oxford: Elsevier Ltd.

Van Bergen, P. and M. Parsell. (2019). Comparing radical, social and psychological constructivism in Australian higher education: A psycho-philosophical perspective. *The Australian Educational Researcher* 46:1, 41–58.

Wiemer, M. (2013). *Learner-centered teaching: Five key changes to practice.* 2ndEd. San Francisco, CA: Jossey-Bass.

Zepke, N. (2018). Student engagement in neo-liberal times: What is missing? *Higher Education Research & Development* 37:2, 433–446. https://www.tandfonline.com/doi/abs/10.1080/07294360.2017.1370440

Chapter 8

Dominant higher education imaginaries

Forced perspectives, ontological limits and recognising the imaginer's frame

Matt Lumb and Matthew Bunn

Introduction

With a focus on the Australian and UK higher education (HE) contexts, this chapter considers how dominant social imaginaries construct the HE student as a fully agentic individual and the way this narrows the possibilities of how to *be* a student. We implement a sociological perspective on the notion of *frame* to analyse policy texts from Australia for empirical evidence regarding the ways in which the prevalent notion of *employability* increasingly patterns the purpose of study. While recognising that 'understandings of "the student" differ in significant ways both across countries and, to some extent, within them' (Brooks, 2019, p. 1), we explore in this work how a reified 'individual' student in HE is commonly imagined as a decontextualised container through a dominant construction or frame that enables certain horizons of student being while limiting others. Notably, this imagined individual is one that 'possesses' ability, aspiration, even education, for rational use orientated towards the maximisation of self-interest and the instrumental pursuit of HE for gaining well-paid careers. These epistemological constructions directly shape the possibilities of student *being* – across the field of policy, research, evaluation and practice – into an ontology that forecloses the promise of valuing education in any way contrary to the dominant framing. This forced perspective also works to hold in place a 'naturalness' of the purpose of HE, one that allows for 'employable' modes of self, practice and affect to appear as the benchmark of success. Simultaneously, this provides the conditions for stigmatising those who are unsuccessful in leveraging 'their' participation in HE towards industry interests, with worrying implications for projects of equity.

This chapter first sets out a theoretical explanation of a dominant epistemological construction of the student in HE as part of a set of contemporary *social imaginaries* (Taylor, 2003) that sustains a deeply inequitable status quo. We begin by drawing together sociological conceptualisations of *misrecognition* in relation to HE. We then relate this to how forced (privileged) perspectives of 'imaginers' construct educational spaces and the limits of ontological possibilities within these, including building on previous work that unsettles taken-for-granted assumptions regarding conceptualisations of *agency* in educational policy and practice.

The chapter then builds on critiques of employability as it is variously conceived in HE; not to rehearse these or to accept and reinforce them, but to further trouble the underpinnings that facilitate the imagined student in contemporary contexts. To do so, we undertake a deconstruction of policy and programming texts in the Australian context, guided by Ball's (2010) account of a shift from *government* to *governance* that has increasingly involved a blurring across different tiers of government and between private and public sectors. It is evident that these new ways of governing need new knowledge (and new knowledge brokers) to facilitate them. Our analysis aims to apprehend this constitution of 'ongoing transformation of the values, meanings and possibilities within our day-to-day activities in HE' (Ball, 2010, p. 124). Our concern here is to question persistent notions of employability by paying attention to how the way that HE students are imagined within governmental and institutional discourse coerces students into adopting these conditions as the limiting 'common-sense' that underpins the possible formations of the future. This question leads to our final move in this chapter, in which we draw on Barad's agential realism in an effort to identify conceptual material for an ongoing project of *reimagining our responsibility* to students.

A contribution we seek to make throughout this chapter is to question the foundations from which processes of reimagining the HE student might be made and to articulate how this relates to projects of equity. 'Widening Participation' in HE is an accelerating concern in many western contexts yet it is power relations that effectively shape the horizon of possibilities. We therefore hold concern for the ways in which the discourses of employability within the current dominant social imaginaries forge realities for students in HE.

Forced perspectives in higher education

The notion of dominant social imaginaries is useful for illustrating how hegemonic constructions of the student in HE limit possible forms of becoming and reinforce problematic conceptualisations of agency. Rizvi and Lingard (2011) define a social imaginary as:

A way of thinking shared in a society by ordinary people, the common understandings that make everyday practices possible, giving them sense and legitimacy. It is largely implicit, embedded in ideas and practices, carrying within it deeper normative notions and images, constitutive of a society

(Rizvi & Lingard, 2011, p. 34).

We adopt this concept of dominant social imaginaries to foreground the presence of 'the imaginer' as part of any project to reimagine the HE student. Whether it be a HE professional, or policymaker or scholar, 'the imaginer' brings a lens or gaze to bear on this process. These forced perspectives are contextually produced and are commonly the product of dominant social positions. In a similar manner to the Bourdieusian conceptualisation of *doxa*, dominant imaginaries operate in the symbolic and arbitrary social systems as 'common-sense', natural, and thus 'go without saying', *misrecognising*[1] the deep historical struggles that have formed them. Doxa hence reflects a 'particular point of view, the point of view of the dominant, which presents and imposes itself as a universal point of view' (Bourdieu, 1998, p. 57). In the Australian HE landscape, we have seen a particular doxa of aspiration (Sellar, 2013) within policy agendas to 'raise aspirations' for university study among students from low socio-economic status (SES) backgrounds.

A recently developed Ames Room analogy (Lumb & Burke, 2019) helps here to consider the assumptions we make as 'imaginers' regarding the arrangements in our social realities that might be more ambiguous or pre-constituted (rather than natural) than might appear to be the case. The Ames Room illusion is a heavily distorted physical construction commonly used in filmmaking and set construction that misleads the subject into accepting a particular 'reality' through a forced perspective or lens. The illusion can lead to unsettling experiences as underlying assumptions support the subject to deal with ambiguity and 'make sense' of improbable arrangements. Stepping away from the compulsory physical viewpoint reveals the concealed dimensions of the experience, yet, as the subject steps back to the forced perspective, the assumptions return effortlessly and the illusion holds again, even with this new 'knowledge' of the deceit.

Lumb and Burke (2019) argue that we 'know' students in HE in ways that are analogous to an Ames Room, as socially dominant imaginaries *force perspectives* that are construed as legitimate ways of being, doing and knowing in HE. As highlighted earlier, policy and programme language in the UK and Australian HE sectors consistently deploys the term aspiration with the discursive framing of particular aspirations as legitimate, adhering to the hegemonic neoliberal ideal of the entrepreneurial and socially mobile competitor-individual, de-meaning and de-valuing 'Other' personhoods (Sellar, 2013). Social policy operates to frame as desirable and legitimate only certain ways of being, knowing and doing (Ahmed & Swan, 2006) and we would argue that this framing is conducted through a largely male, white, middle class background forming an 'implicit collusion among all the agents who are products of similar conditions and conditionings' (Bourdieu, 2000, p. 145). While playing out differently in different contexts, these framings create the conditions for multiple misrecognition(s) that are themselves difficult to recognise, raising again the importance of acknowledging the frame 'the imaginer' brings to projects of reimagining.

It is important to consider the assumptions dominant social imaginaries bring to projects of equity or widening participation in HE. Forced perspectives within dominant social imaginaries shape ontological possibilities including what it is possible for students to legitimately be and become. An example of which are the predominant conceptualisations of *agency* and *employability* in education. In previous work (Bunn & Lumb, 2019a), we have problematised conceptualisations of agency in education by considering how the rampant construction of an individual student determined by his or her own internal capacities has become the norm within educational policy. This, we have argued, yields undemocratic educational spaces that ignore the contextually bound ways production and reproduction of disadvantage and advantage occurs within the educational system. In this sense, it too is a forced perspective, a construction and subsequent *reification* of the HE student as a 'hyper-individual'. We want to further this interrogation to consider how the hyper-individual interacts with the increased focus on *employability* as both the doxic purpose and product of HE. *Reification* (a concept with a diverse history in Marxist theoretical traditions and popularised by Lukacs in connection with processes of alienation) is the 'error of regarding an abstraction as a material thing, and attributing causal powers to it' (Scott, 2015, p. 638). This arguable danger of misplaced 'concreteness' is an important consideration here in terms of the ways in which dominant constructions or frames enable certain horizons of student being in HE while limiting others or closing them entirely.

It needs to be stressed how powerful these imaginaries are, and how much energy is required to make a break with them, if only briefly and partially. Indeed, as Barad (2014) points out, one of the important contributions of the physicist Niels Bohr's work was to provide a break with a dominant Cartesian imaginary. She points towards how, in order to understand emerging problems in physics were to fundamentally rethink epistemology and ontology, and in doing so, required a break from the subject–object dualism that had become taken-for-granted to produce a 'new quantum epistemology' (Barad, 2014, p. 173). While this chapter is not *about* quantum or particle physics, we are however interested in the implications for scientific approaches and attendant methods when it has been demonstrated that the apparatus used to measure/know is co-implicated and entangled with that being measured/known. We are attentive here to the deceit of the masculinised rational sciences that we can escape perspective and attain God's eye view (Bennett, 2010) of the world. In this we want to recognise the history of feminist work in education interrogating historical formations reproducing inequalities and facilitating understandings of power relations within and across both micro and macro level politics (e.g. Lather, 1991; Epstein, 1998; Butler, 1999; Kenway & Epstein, 1996; Burke, 2012; Mirza, 2014). We also want to acknowledge how traditional universalisms of science feel all too familiar and neat:

> Matter is discrete, time is continuous. Place knows its place. Time too has its place. Nature and culture are split by this continuity, and objectivity is secured as externality. We know this story well, it's written into our bones, in many ways we inhabit it and it inhabits us.
>
> (Barad, 2010, p. 249).

These universalisms form part of a 'common sense', a doxa seemingly beyond the need for interrogation, and unfortunately helpful for a continual complicity within the reproduction of domination.

In contemporary times, these universalisms are being taken up enthusiastically in fields of education (including HE) as increasingly our systems, practices and experiences are 'datafied' around quantum notions; that is, how much. It seems irresponsible in these contexts not to question the apparatus by which we know students in HE, particularly given that increasingly our relations seem grounded in an economic rationality via a generalisation of neo-liberal epistemology (Shamir, 2008). This *Tyranny of Metrics* (Muller, 2018) privileges a now longstanding 'regime of numbers' in which 'research is equated with particular forms of data collection and comparison and its quality is judged in relation to its usefulness in assessing comparative performance' (Ozga, 2008, p. 264). McGowan (2016) contends that a conceptual lack exists regarding 'understandings of what the university is and is for, and of how systems interact with and impact the rest of society' (McGowan, 2016, p. 506). In a context of rampant commodification of HE, and also 'unbundling' (whereby there is a separating into constituent elements for consumption that which was previously held/sold together), we tend to agree with McGowan that political claims to quality on which the broad project of HE rests are deeply connected to the project of reimagining the HE student. Harwood (2010) explains how the imagination is connected to politics, in that 'The imagination not only enables us to appreciate the plurality of the world, it is invaluable in supporting the ongoing task of identifying exclusion: in the world, in our own assumptions...' (Harwood, 2010, p. 366). It is with this in mind that we move to the next section, seeking to trouble assumptions that arguably hold in place a mainstream discourse of employability within the Australian HE context, a discourse that simultaneously colludes and *excolludes* (Goffman, 1974). For Goffman, this term is used to consider fabrications that occur when primary frames are reworked to induce a 'false belief' about activities. These can be more benign (playful deceit or practical joking) or more exploitative (demonstrably against the interests of the deceived). Goffman argues that when groups are involved in these processes of deception, there is collusive interaction required involving 'those in on it constitute a collusive net and those the net operates against, the excolluded' (Goffman, 1974, p. 84).

The cunning of 'employability'

A formidable presence in the dominant social imaginaries is the notion that HE serves the broader interests of economy and industry. While there are longstanding debates and contestations surrounding the purposes of education, in recent relevant policy and program language employability forms part of a new *governing* of the education landscape, shaping HE institutions and practices (e.g. Moreau & Leathwood, 2006; Clegg, 2010).

Debates regarding education systems and practices contain readily visible recitations such as *globalisation, marketisation* and *commodification*. These cultural products circulate across different scales of policy and practice, carrying relatively openly their meaning and allowing for debate *about* them and their consequences. More sinister, we would argue, are the coded policy slogans underpinning current HE policy such as *employability:*

> isolated and apparently technical terms such as 'flexibilité' (or its British equivalent, 'employability') which, because they encapsulate and communicate a whole philosophy of the individual and of social organisation, are well-suited to functioning as veritable political codewords and mottoes (in this case: the downsizing and denigration of the state, the reduction of social protection and the acceptance of the generalisation of casual and precarious labour as a fate, nay a boon)
>
> (Bourdieu & Wacquant, 1999, p. 42).

As sites of cultural reproduction, universities (and the policies that shape their practices) are important locations for considering the ways in which social inequalities circulate. Our interest here is the ways in which concepts such as employability operate as tools in the reproduction of social inequality.

Neo-liberal perspectives and outcomes underpin the contemporary HE imaginaries 'with a focus on the types of employability, human capital, development of skills and competencies that promote an efficient and competitive workforce in global knowledge economies and markets' (Burke, 2016, p. 2). Since the 1980s, there has been growing pressure on HE in many nation state contexts to contribute to national economic regeneration and growth. Influential governmental reports, such as the Dearing Review in the UK, are driven by an implicit declaration that the primary purpose of HE is the preparation of students for the world of work (Harvey, 2000). Worryingly for projects of access and equity, the HE employability discourses continue the historical process of 'laundering' privilege (Crossley, 2003, p. 43) into 'clean' cultural and economic currency that legitimates students from more privileged backgrounds gaining greater access to higher paid careers. The skills, qualifications and pacing of an individual student relies on a focus on *what an individual contains* and not the uneven contexts and circumstances that produce particular modes of being.

In this way, discussions relating to employment have been reformulated (Brown & Hesketh, 2004), commonly around a focus on skills, in a 'shift from a systematic view of the labour market to a focus on the individuals and their qualities' (Garsten & Jacobsson, 2003, p. 2). Notions of job or career 'readiness' continue to abound in HE (Universities Australia, 2019) in ways that arguably respond to employers having cut their investment in training and support of workers and with the responsibility for employment shifting from society to individuals. Unemployment is also seen as the individual's problem, with no recognition of context. As Crisp and Powell (2017) show, the contemporary UK policy focus on promoting employability to address youth unemployment in the UK has been underpinned by a static and simplistic notion of employability rooted in supply-side orthodoxy, which presents worklessness as a behavioural and cultural shortcoming among individuals. The effectiveness of employability thus relies on a broader performativity that 'invites and incites us to make ourselves more effective, to work on ourselves and to feel inadequate if we do not' (Ball, 2010, p. 125).

Nation states have simultaneously accelerated investment in, and pressure on, individuals to become equipped for the 'knowledge-driven' economies with a responsibility for their own employment and employability. In Australia, HE policy has been part of this process. The Bradley Review of HE proposed open-ended public funding of all eligible students via a demand-driven system.

> It was expected that the demand-driven system would establish a virtuous circle between student demand (which was assumed to partly reflect labour market demand for skills), institutional program offerings, and teaching quality, generating continuous improvement over time. This was wishful thinking. Over-subscribed elite universities are not compelled by student preferences. The education/work relation is too distanced and fragmented to drive nuanced student demand according to the needs of each individual sector of the labour markets. The primary university competition turns on not teaching quality or graduate employability, but research. Only in lower status institutions does competition turn more on graduate employability than on research.
>
> (Marginson, 2013, p. 65)

This increasing emphasis in HE on the economic realm drives rationalities underpinning policy, with universities' increasing focus on employability and framing equity policy and practice via logics of the market. In addition, there is arguably a gendered dimension to *employability* with a strong rational, technical and utilitarian construction of HE study (Burke, forthcoming). A recent Australian Government report (DET, 2019a) has prepared the groundwork for a performance-based funding model for HE, supported by claims from the then Australian Government Education Minister Dan Tehan that 'Graduate employment outcomes will be the most important factor under the performance-based funding model for universities' (Tehan, 2019, para.2). Yet, as Jackson and Bridgstock (2019) point out in the title of their article: 'Universities don't control the labour market: we shouldn't fund them like they do'. At the same time, Australian research is telling us that:

> Graduates newly entering the workforce and with less work experience generally experience greater difficulty finding work. This is consistent with the broader long run trend since the Global Financial Crisis (GFC)

where new graduates have found it more difficult to make a successful transition to the labour market upon completion of their studies.

(QILT Graduate Outcomes Survey, 2019, p. 2)

We see here the misplaced 'concreteness' of reification in operation again as the abstract notion of some imagined *employability,* supposedly developed in the context of HE and against which Australian universities are proposed to be measured and funded, is rendered immediately meaningless in a labour market in which employment is not possible.

Fabricating 'economic fatalism'

Standing (2011) argues that there is an emerging class in many contexts across the globe: a 'precariat' characterised by *distinctive relations of production* (i.e. people habituated into accepting and internalising a life of unstable labour and unstable living in the form of zero hour contracts and internships), *a lack of an occupational narrative for their lives,* and *distinctive relations of distribution* (i.e. reliance on money wages that are falling in real terms and becoming more volatile). Standing's work has been critiqued in terms of his use of class as an explanatory framework. Yet there are certainly examples in the Australian context that demonstrate efforts to coerce young people in particular to develop something of an economic fatalism around the unpredictability of the labour market and their potential participation within it. By engaging the entrenched logics of employability, and the way that they frame the limits of what is possible to 'make real' and to 'real-ise', we want to offer here a problematisation of the imaginer in HE and to explore the limits and possibilities of recognising our location in HE social imaginaries.

Ball (2010) describes contemporary times having seen a shift from *government* to *governance* that involves a blurring of the connections and disconnections across different tiers of government and between private and public sectors. This shift requires new forms of knowledge to make this governance 'work' and has meant that 'public sector HE institutions are being displaced as knowledge brokers and at the same time "enterprised" and "hybridised", in a new education policy knowledge market.' (Ball, 2010, p. 124). A recent report commissioned by the previous Australian Government Education Minister, Dan Tehan, and delivered by consulting firm Ernst and Young (2019), found an urgent need to boost the number of 'job ready' graduates to meet workforce needs, with a central claim that this would boost economic productivity by $3.1 billion (AUS) dollars annually. This report positions *employability* as primarily of value to industry, not the student. This is part of the emergence of an *evaluative state* in which the state now oversees HE for the market rather than as a guardian of learning (Neave, 2012). This is exemplified by the ways in which processes of educational evaluation reflect a spirit of capitalism rather than any lateral understanding of the value of educational process and in which for example 'gender, race and social class are often seen as background variables, rather than constructs embedded within evaluation processes and politics themselves' (Borrelli, Gavrila, Spanò, & Stazio, 2019, p. 26).

The Foundation for Young Australians (FYA) *The New Work Mindset In Action: South West Victoria* (FYA, 2019) is an example of a contemporary brand of 'research reports' produced by not-for-profit organisations, backed by industry (and commonly governments also), that are helping to cement the dominant social imaginaries in the Australian context: 'The new reality of work is here to stay. We can't press pause on change, or halt the increasing demands on our workers' (Foundation for Young Australians, 2019, p. 3). Under the guise of being *for* young Australians, this work is a kind of 'moralisation of the market' (Shamir, 2008). Signed by five CEOs and produced with the support of Victorian Department of Education and Training's Workforce Training Innovation Fund, the 'New Work Mindset In Action' promises to deliver '…data driven insights [that] can help learning systems in the region deliver training more responsive to employer demands and enable industries to provide future focussed workforce planning' (FYA, 2019, p. 7). These recitations are of the type that Hogan and Thompson (2019) argued in schooling contexts have become the 'languages and practices that are shaping public schooling, particularly in regards to increasing commercialisation caused by (and contributing to) the quasi-marketisation of schooling' (Hogan & Thompson, 2019, p. 391). These dynamics play out across the Australian education system and increasingly there is an increasing focus at transitional moments between secondary and tertiary levels. For example, the Australian Government *National Career Education Strategy* cites further FYA reports – *The New Work Order* (FYA, 2015) and *The New Work Smarts* (FYA, 2017) – in a call for 'educating students for a world yet to be imagined' (Hogan & Thompson, 2019, p. 16). Moreover, in Victoria, Australia, an Employability Skills Framework presents the following declaration:

> All young people need a set of skills and attributes that will prepare them for both employment and further learning. The Employability Skills Framework includes what employers think makes a good employee.
>
> (VIC DET, 2006, p. 1)

Across the country, *Work Education* syllabi operate in high school contexts to establish the vanguard of the employability agenda in the tertiary sector. The current syllabus was established in 2003 (with a new syllabus to be launched in 2020) and it explains how:

> Understanding and development of employability skills will assist students to achieve the flexibility required for the workplaces of today and of the future. … The development of enterprising capabilities will empower students with the skills necessary to succeed in a labour market

that is increasingly characterised by self-employment and part-time or casual work.

(NSW BOS, 2003, p. 8)

We see here a clear precursor or antecedent to the sort of *flexibilité* (Bourdieu & Wacquant, 1999) that is part of the contemporary HE apparatus. The hidden challenges of hegemonic neoliberal framings of 'flexibility' produce students that are made individually responsible for the management of their time, many of whom consequently experience guilt and self-blame (Bunn, Bennett, & Burke, 2018).

A theme of the book in which this chapter resides is the ways in which conceptualisations 'jostle uncomfortably' in relation to each other, with students portrayed often in contradictory or divergent terms. In the Australian context, *Driving Innovation, Fairness and Excellence in Australian HE* (Commonwealth of Australia, 2016) promotes the Federal Government as an advocate for 'choice', 'support', and the 'removal of barriers for under-represented groups' (Commonwealth of Australia, 2016, p. 2). This commercialised language of 'return on investment for both the student and the nation' performs an exemplary neo-liberal version of fairness that individualises and responsibilises the student. We see how the Ames Room forced perspective operates here as the imaginer is disciplined into accepting how 'HE is more important to the future of Australia's industry, businesses and families than ever before' (Commonwealth of Australia, 2016, p. 2) with the ordering here of to whom HE participation is of value, and why, establishing a human capital position on nation-state competition as the driving economic policy imperative. This sits in tension with a fairness discourse where 'all Australians with the ability and the motivation to succeed in tertiary education are supported to do so' (Commonwealth of Australia, 2016, p. 6). This tension helps to forge the ethically fraught (Burke, 2012) territory of equity and widening participation in HE, whereby programs of research, evaluation and practice (e.g. outreach, access, transition, success, graduation) are positioned between goals that are often at odds.

In Australia, career education interventions within universities are now common. Careers services in particular now 'build employability' as part of their core business. There is also an accompanying and growing body of uncritical research and evaluation work which takes up the constructed challenge. An example below quotes the Foundation for Young Australians to state that:

A clear change in graduate employment outcomes over the past 30 years, coupled with a renewed focus on employability rankings as a key factor in why students choose a university (Bridgestock, 2016; Kinash, n.d.) has required a paradigm shift in the way employability is approached by HE institutions (Foundation for Young Australians, 2018).

(Warr Pederson & Gibbons, 2018, p. 2).

We would argue that this type of evaluative research helps to embed the cunning of employability within an overly-individualised frame as part of a forced perspective, as it simultaneously suggests that:

> While previous studies have indicated the value of complimentary career education interventions on increasing graduate employability (Bridgstock, 2009, Kalfa & Taksa, 2015, Jackson, 2016), the measurable impact, and most effective format of these interventions remain under researched.
>
> (Warr Pederson & Gibbons, 2018, p. 3)

It appears that in the race to measure *everything*, nothing is safe from construction, reification and quantification. In the UK, employment destinations of university graduates have become an important proxy measure of the value of a university education. There have certainly been various efforts to define and measure employability (Harvey, 2001) and institutions use their 'destinations' data to highlight their success in this area, increasing their attractiveness to prospective students. There is however little opportunity to open up debate as to why this framing of education and the labour market holds such sway.

In the Australian context, there are efforts to *do* employability *to* those positioned as disadvantaged 'equity students'. Recommendations made in a report by Harvey, Andrewartha, Edwards, Clarke, and Reyes (2017) were as follows: increased strategic collaboration between different university areas; increased data collection in relation to employability and equity; increased integration of employability into mainstream curricula and increased promotion and support for the extra-curricular participation of equity groups. This report also raises the likelihood of unwittingly exacerbating inequalities via intervention, for example, via a focus on particular forms of cultural capital 'through employer-driven activities that emphasise 'cultural fit' and networking, and the exclusive recognition of particular types of 'volunteering' and other contributions' (Harvey et al., 2017, p. 50). We want to extend this problematisation to suggest that a capitals approach (however carefully implemented) carries with it a concept of the student in HE that frames them via an epistemology that forecloses particular ways of being. And it is to these questions that we turn in the next section, looking for paths forward in reimagining that can help to trouble and perhaps even begin to break with the dominant epistemologies that shape HE ontologies for students.

Agency, ontological limits and responsibility

In this final section, we offer to the project of reimagining the HE student something of a provocation, an appreciation of and attention to the 'tissue of ethicality that runs through the world' (Hickey-Moody, 2015, p. 809). Elsewhere we (Bunn & Lumb, 2019a) have problematised how overly individualised conceptualisations of agency have become the norm within educational policy. In the framing of the individual as rational agent maximising self-interest, the contextually bound conditions of 'choice' and the resultant inequalities become invisible, seen merely as 'backgrounds' (Bunn, Threadgold, & Burke, 2019). This produces and reproduces disadvantage and advantage within the educational system. We thus experimented with how the ontological assumption of the individual might be unsettled, with a focus shifting to relations rather than interiorised individuals. We drew on Karen Barad's (2003, 2007, 2010, 2014) agential realism, to suggest that educative spaces are the enactments and realisation of knowledge and, thus, an enactment of education is not reducible to separate or separable individuals. This theorisation is a tool to reimagine the student in HE. However, we need to further consider the ethical implications in the theorisation of agency as a contextually bound enactment within HE.

The HE landscape, with a significant focus on equity and Widening Participation, is an ethically fraught (Stevenson & Leconte, 2009) field of policy and program making. Carstens (2016) following Barad asks how we might foster a type of transversal thinking of a post-human cyborg that takes 'issue with human exceptionalism while being accountable for the role we play in the differential constitution and differential positioning of the human among other creatures' (Barad, 2007, p. 136). This approach does require a type of *uncanny* reflexivity, a 'patient praxis' (Bunn & Lumb, 2019b) that demands counterintuitive waiting while in the midst of urgency. Indeed, in projects of reimagining we would promote here methodologies of practice (and research) in HE that require prolonged engagement without the expectation that a path of action simply ameliorates enduring inequalities built through a deep historical inertia. We want to encourage a patience in reimagining the HE student in ways that disrupts the dominant social imaginaries and their accompanying temporalities of urgency. This reimagining is complimented by the need to carefully rethink how we conceive of agency within education. We need to consider that 'a whole host of other relata – including human actors, the character of place, and the material and symbolic attributes of these relations – make this agentic enactment possible' (Bunn & Lumb, 2019a, p. 14). These relata host the conditions for the enactment of agency. Yet, it should not be mistakenly conveyed here that agency is a simplistic causal event, one that, given a certain series of objective conditions, a certain mode of action is likely. These conditions that limit and delimit what is possible or even likely are shaped by the narrowed ontological boundaries set within dominant imaginaries and prevent the possibility of lateral possibilities, imaginations, anticipations and futures to arrive. The way that the student is imagined within governmental and institutional discourse bends HE students into adopting these conditions as the limiting "common-sense" that underpins the possible formations of the future. Employability for example is constructed as 'navigable trajectories for individual students to produce, pursue and negotiate' (Bunn & Lumb, 2019a, p. 14). There is growing advocacy for applying alternative theoretical perspectives that might allow a movement away from individualised graduate employability discourses (Burke, Scurry, Blenkinsopp, & Graley, 2017).

If we are however to ethically reimagine the HE student, we need to acknowledge the difficult contemporary politics of Widening Participation (Harwood, Hickey-Moody, McMahon, & O'Shea, 2017) that ignores the ways in which community members imagine the university, often from precarious circumstances. Largely, HE language and practices 'have tended to avoid discussing the structural inequalities that inform employment practices and opportunities for work (such as unequal pay, access to networks, or graduate mobility)' (Coffield, Markham, Crosby, Athanasiou, & Stenbom, 2019, p. 8). To more adequately consider a way forward, we must recognise how the ab/use of employability challenges us not only to reimagine 'the student' in HE but also to reimagine our responsibility to students.

> Responsibility is not an obligation that the subject chooses but rather an incarnate relation that precedes the intentionality of consciousness. Responsibility is not a calculation to be performed. It is a relation always already integral to the world's ongoing intra-active becoming and not-becoming. It is an iterative (re)opening up to, an enabling of responsiveness. Not through the realization of some existing possibility, but through the iterative reworking of im/possibility, an ongoing rupturing, a crosscutting of topological reconfiguring of the space of response-ability.
>
> (Barad, 2014, p. 183)

The notion of the 'always already' Barad uses here is important to consider for one further moment in relation to the project this chapter and book engages. Certainly, in the reimagining of the student, we would argue for a need to recognise the way that imaginaries *produce* the limits of student possibility. We need to examine and carefully analyse the way that dominant social imaginaries pervade the 'always already'. As scholars, we must also recognise how our own positions as imaginers are 'always already' informed and produced in order to wrestle free (as much as possible) from these doxic positions, and to offer lateral and alternative imaginaries of the HE student.

Concluding thoughts

Discourses of employability have been effective in producing the precarious labour a contemporary economy needs to grow. The concept of employability in higher education needs further and ongoing analysis (Holmes, 2013). As noted above, this is of concern for projects of equity in HE as it risks more deeply embedding processes of 'laundering' privilege (Crossley, 2003) into 'clean' cultural and economic currency. The Australian HE context sees fragmented rules of the game deploy systemic metrics to govern the value of the student in relation to the labour market, producing new, agile and pernicious forms of inequality. Privilege will undoubtedly remain yet, for those swept up in the wider net of participation, receiving an education that tacitly educates students into an acceptance of precarity is deeply unethical. Indeed, it can be so boldly organised as to blame the subjects who can be demonstrated quantifiably to lack employability (or aspiration, resilience, skills, etc.) and, that 'if they had only tried harder', they would have succeeded in avoiding their casualised, insecure and precarious fate.

In this chapter, we have considered how dominant social imaginaries construct the HE student as a fully agentic individual and then looked to articulate how this narrows the possibilities of how to *be* a student. Having set out a theoretical explanation of a dominant epistemological construction of the student in HE as part of a set of contemporary social imaginaries that sustain an inequitable status quo we then moved to build on critiques of employability as it is conceived in HE, to further trouble the underpinnings that facilitate the imagined student in contemporary contexts. Building on previous work, we have drawn on Barad's agential realism to identify conceptual material for the project of *reimagining our responsibility* to students. In an unprecedented time of intersecting global crises (e.g. COVID-19, ecological collapse, gendered violence), the contribution this work has sought to make is to question the foundations from which processes of reimagining the HE student might be made, and to articulate how this relates to projects of equity.

Note

1 Misrecognition is a notion with differing uses within sociology, predominantly between Axel Honneth, Nancy Fraser, and Pierre Bourdieu – with Lois McNay (2008a, 2008b) offering a powerful juxtaposition of the merits of these accounts. Burke (2012, p. 182) has taken the politics of recognition into the context of EWP, drawing on McNay to highlight the strengths and limitations of Fraser's (Fraser & Honneth, 2003) use of the concept. The concept is also deployed meaningfully from a Bourdieusian conceptualisation of HE, see: Bunn et al., 2019; James, 2015.

References

Ahmed, S., & Swan, E. (2006). Doing diversity. *Policy Futures in Education* 2. http://www.doi.org/10.2304/pfie.2006.4.2.96

Ball, S. (2010). New voices, new knowledges and the new politics of education research: The gathering of a perfect storm? *European Educational Research Journal* 9:2 doi:10.2304/eerj.2010.9.2.124

Barad, K. (2003). Posthumanist performativity: Toward an understanding of how matter comes to matter. *Signs: Journal of Women in Culture and Society* 28:3, 801–831.

Barad, K. (2007). *Meeting the universe halfway: Quantum physics and the entanglement of matter and meaning.* Durham: Duke University Press.

Barad, K. (2010). Quantum entanglements and hauntological relations of inheritance: Dis/continuities, spacetime enfoldings, and justice-to-come. *Derrida Today* 3:2, 240–268. doi:10.3366/E1754850010000813

Barad, K. (2014). Diffracting diffractions: Cutting together-apart. *Parallax* 20:3, 168–187. doi:10.1080/13534645.2014.927623

Bennett, J. (2010). *Vibrant matter: A political ecology of things.* Duke University Press: Durham and London.

Bourdieu P (1998). *Practical reason: On the theory of action.* Stanford: Stanford University Press.

Bourdieu, P. (2000). *Pascalian meditations.* California: Stanford University Press.

Bourdieu, P., & Wacquant, L. (1999). On the cunning of imperialist reason. *Theory, Culture and Society* 16:1, 41–58.

Borrelli, D., Gavrila, M., Spanò, E., & Stazio, M. (2019). Another university is possible: Towards an idea of meridian university. *Italian Journal of Sociology of Education* 11:3, 16–39. doi:10.14658/pupj-ijse-2019-3-2

Brooks, R. (2019). The construction of HE students within national policy: A cross-European comparison. *Compare: A Journal of Comparative and International Education.* doi:10.1080/03057925.2019.1604118

Brown, P., & A. Hesketh. (2004). *The mismanagement of talent: Employability and jobs in the knowledge economy.* Oxford: Oxford University Press.

Bunn, M., Bennett, A., & Burke, P.J. (2018). In the anytime: Flexible time structures, student experience and temporal equity in HE. *Time & Society* 28:4, 1409–1428.

Bunn, M., & Lumb, M. (2019a). Education as agency: Challenging educational individualization through alternative accounts of the agentic. *The International Education Journal: Comparative Perspectives* 18:1, 7–19. https://openjournals.library.sydney.edu.au/index.php/IEJ

Bunn, M., & Lumb, M. (2019b). Patient praxis: A dialogue between equity practice and research, *International Studies in Widening Participation* 6:1, 1–9. https://novaojs.newcastle.edu.au/ceehe/index.php/iswp/article/view/117/141

Bunn, M., Threadgold, S., & Burke, P. J. (2019). Class in Australian higher education: The university as a site of social reproduction. *Journal of Sociology.* doi:10.1177/1440783319851188

Burke, C., Scurry, T., Blenkinsopp, J., & Graley, K. (2017). Critical perspectives on graduate employability. In Tomlinson, M. & Holmes, L. (Eds) *Graduate employability in context: Theory, research and debate.* Palgrave Macmillan, London, doi:10.1057/978-1-137-57168-7

Burke, P.J. (2012). *The right to HE: Beyond widening participation.* London and New York: Routledge.

Burke P.J. (2016). Access to and widening participation in HE. In: Shin J., Teixeira P. (eds) *Encyclopedia of international HE systems and institutions.* Springer, Dordrecht.

Burke, P.J. (forthcoming). Gender, neoliberalism and corporatized HE. In: Niemi, S., Weaver-Hightower, M. *The Wiley handbook of gender equity in HE*, Wiley-Blackwell Publishers.

Butler, J. (1999). *Gender trouble: Feminism and the subversion of identity.* Routledge.

Carstens, D. (2016). The Anthropocene crisis and HE. *South African Journal of HE* 30:3, 255–273. doi:10.20853/30-3-650

Clegg, S. (2010). Time future – the dominant discourse of HE. *Time and Society* 19: 3, 345–364.

Coffield, E., Markham, K., Crosby, J., Athanasiou, M., & Stenbom, C. (2019). *Beyond employability*. Newcastle University. https://eprints.ncl.ac.uk/file_store/production/260239/6438E3A9-950D-4535-829F-819E1135124C.pdf

Commonwealth of Australia (2016). *Driving innovation, fairness and excellence in Australian HE*. https://docs.education.gov.au/documents/driving-innovation-fairness-and-excellence-australian-education

Crisp, R., & Powell, R. (2017). Young people and UK labour market policy: A critique of 'employability' as a tool for understanding youth unemployment. *Urban Studies* 54:8, 1784–1807.

Crossley, N. (2003) From reproduction to transformation: Social movement fields and the radical habitus. *Theory, Culture and Society* 20:6, 43–68.

Department of Education and Training (2019a). *Performance-based funding for the Commonwealth grant scheme*. Commonwealth of Australia. https://docs.education.gov.au/system/files/doc/other/ed19-0134_-_he-_performance-based_funding_review_acc.pdf

Department of Education and Training (2019b). *National career education strategy*. Commonwealth of Australia. https://docs.education.gov.au/system/files/doc/other/future_ready_a_student_focused_national_career_education_strategy.pdf

Epstein, D. (1998). *Failing boys*. McGraw-Hill Education UK.

Ernst & Young (2019). *The productivity uplift from better outcomes for our university students*. Ernst and Young Australia. https://asia-pac.ey-vx.com/44/13606/landing-pages/ey-productivity-uplift-higher-education-finaldraft-updated.pdf

Foundation for Young Australians (2015). *New work order report*. https://www.fya.org.au/report/new-work-order/

Foundation for Young Australians (2017) *The new work smarts*. https://www.fya.org.au/report/the-new-work-smarts/

Foundation for Young Australians (2018) *The new work reality*. https://www.fya.org.au/wp-content/uploads/2018/06/FYA_TheNewWorkReality_sml.pdf

Foundation for Young Australians (2019). *The new work mindset in action: South West Victoria* https://www.fya.org.au/wp-content/uploads/2019/02/TheNewWorkMindsetAction_SWVic.pdf

Fraser, N., & Honneth, A. (2003). *Redistribution or recognition?: A political-philosophical exchange*. London and New York: Verso.

Garsten, C., & Jacobsson, K. (2003) Learning to be employable: An introduction. In Garsten, C. & Jacobsson, K. (eds) *Learning to be employable: New agendas on work, responsibility and learning in a globalizing world*, Palgrave Macmillan: London.

Goffman, E. (1974) *Frame Analysis: An essay on the organisation of experience*. Harper & Row, New York.

Harvey, A., Andrewartha, L., Edwards, D., Clarke, J., & Reyes, K. (2017). *Student equity and employability in HE*. Report for the Australian Government Department of Education and Training. Melbourne: Centre for HE Equity and Diversity Research, La Trobe University

Harvey, L. (2000). New realities: The relationship between HE and employment. *Tertiary Education and Management* 6: 3–17.

Harvey, L. (2001). Defining and measuring employability. *Quality in HE* 7: 2. doi:10.1080/13538320120059990

Harwood, V. (2010). The place of imagination in inclusive pedagogy: Thinking with Maxine Greene and Hannah Arendt. *International Journal of Inclusive Education* 14: 4, 357–369, doi:10.1080/13603110802504572

Harwood, V., Hickey-Moody, A., McMahon, S., & O'Shea, S. (2017). *The politics of widening participation and university access for young people*. Oxfordshire and NY: Routledge.

Hickey-Moody, A. C. (2015). Beside ourselves: Worlds beyond people. *British Journal of Sociology of Education* 36:5, 802–813, doi:10.1080/01425692.2015.1043187

Hogan, A., & Thompson, G. (2019). The quasi-marketization of Australian public schooling: Affordances and contradictions of the new work order. *Asia Pacific Journal of Education* 39:3, 391–403, doi:10.1080/02188791.2019.1598849

Holmes, L. (2013). Competing perspectives on graduate employability: Possession, position or process? *Studies in HE* 38:4, 538–554, doi:10.1080/03075079.2011.587140

James, D. (2015). How Bourdieu bites back: Recognising misrecognition in education and educational research. *Cambridge Journal of Education* 45:1, 97–112.

Jackson, D., & Bridgstock, R. (2019). Universities don't control the labour market: We shouldn't fund them like they do. *The Conversation*, https://theconversation.com/universities-dont-control-the-labour-market-we-shouldnt-fund-them-like-they-do-124780 (Accessed 13/11/2019)

Kenway, J. & Epstein, D. (1996) Introduction: The marketisation of school education: Feminist studies and perspectives. *Discourse: Studies in the Cultural Politics of Education* 17:3, 301–314, http://www.doi.org.au/10.1080/0159630960170301

Lather, P. (1991) *Getting smart: Feminist research and pedagogy with/in the postmodern*. New York: Routledge.

Lumb, M., & Burke, P.J. (2019). Re/cognising the frame: Discursive framing, 'legitimate' aspirations and misrecognition in the sociological Ames room. *International Studies in Sociology of Education* 28:3–4, 215–236, doi:10.1080/09620214.2019.1619470

Marginson, S. (2013.) Labor's failure to ground public funding, In *Tertiary education policy in Australia*, (Ed. Marginson S.) Centre for the Study of HE, University of Melbourne.

McGowan, T. (2016). Universities and the post-2015 development agenda: An analytical framework. *Higher Education* 72: 505-523. doi:10.1007/s10734-016-0035-7.

Moreau, M-P., & Leathwood, C. (2006). Graduates' employment and the discourse of employability: A critical analysis. *Journal of Education and Work* 19:4, 305–324, https://www.doi.org/10.1080/13639080600867083

McNay, L. (2008a). The trouble with recognition: Subjectivity, suffering and agency. *Sociological Theory* 26: 3, 271–296.

McNay, L. (2008b). *Against recognition*. Cambridge: Polity Press.

Mirza, H. (2014). Decolonizing higher education: Black feminism and the intersectionality of race and gender. *Journal of Feminist Scholarship* 7:8, 1–12.

Muller, J. (2018). *The tyranny of metrics*. New Jersey: Princeton University Press. www.jstor.org/stable/j.ctvc77h85.4

Neave, G. (2012). The Evaluative State: A Formative Concept and an Overview. In: *The evaluative state, institutional autonomy and re-engineering HE in Western Europe*. Issues in HE. Palgrave Macmillan, London. doi:10.1057/9780230370227_3

NSW Board of Studies (2003). *Work education years 7–10 syllabus*. NSW Government. ISBN 1 7409 9270 9

Ozga, J. (2008). Governing knowledge: Research steering and research quality. *European Educational Research Journal* 7:3, 261–272. doi:10.2304/eerj.2008.7.3.261

QILT (2019) *Graduate Outcomes Survey*. https://www.qilt.edu.au/docs/default-source/gos-reports/2019-gos/2019-gos-national-report.pdf?sfvrsn=cdceec3c_4

Rizvi, F., & Lingard, B. (2011). Social equity and the assemblage of values in Australian HE. *Cambridge Journal of Education* 41:1, 5–22. doi:10.1080/0305764X.2010.549459

Scott, J. (2015). *Oxford dictionary of sociology* (4th Edition). Oxford, UK: Oxford University Press.

Sellar, S. (2013). Equity, markets and the politics of aspiration in Australian HE. *Discourse: Studies in the Cultural Politics of Education* 34:2, 245–258.

Shamir, R. (2008). The age of responsibilization: On market-embedded morality. *Economy and Society* 37:1, 1–19. doi:10.1080/03085140701760833

Standing, G. (2011). The precariat – The new dangerous class. *Policy Network*, https://core.ac.uk/download/pdf/9831737.pdf

Stevenson, J., & Leconte, M.-O. (2009). 'Whose ethical university is it anyway?': Widening participation, student diversity and the 'ethical' HE institution. *International Journal of Diversity in Organisations, Communities and Nations* 9:3, 103–114.

Taylor, C. (2003). *Modern social imaginaries*. Durham, NC: Duke University Press.

Tehan, D. (2019). *The future of Australian universities focuses on achievement*. https://ministers.dese.gov.au/tehan/future-australian-universities-focuses-achievement

Universities Australia (2019). *Career ready graduate*. https://www.universitiesaustralia.edu.au/wp-content/uploads/2019/06/Career-Ready-Graduates-FINAL.pdf

Victorian Department of Education (2006). *Employability skills framework*. https://www.education.vic.gov.au/Documents/school/teachers/teachingresources/careers/employabilityskills1.pdf

Warr Pederson, K., & Gibbons, T. (2018). *Assessing impact: Exploring the assessment of careers education interventions in HE: A UTAS pilot*.

Chapter 9

Reframing the 'traditional learner' into the 'partner' in higher education

Conflicting subjectivities and behavioural expectations of the undergraduate 'student' in UK universities

*Eloise Symonds**

Introduction

'What it means to be a student in the UK appears to have changed radically' (Williams, 2013, p. 1); the subjectivity of the undergraduate student is being reconstituted. McMillan and Cheney note that, 'in the past [...] we were content simply to call students "students"' (McMillan & Cheney, 1996, pp. 12–13); however, the positioning of undergraduates is not as simple in the modern climate. The concept of partnership, which is often framed as a response to the pedagogical damage caused by the legal imperatives of positioning undergraduates as consumers (Neary & Winn, 2009; Symonds, 2020), has become increasingly popular in UK universities. This concept encourages undergraduates to adhere to a partner subjectivity, which changes the behaviour expectations within the learning process (Little, 2010; Tong et al., 2018b). Daniels and Brooker acknowledge that subjectivity is a 'fluid and flexible process' (Daniels & Brooker, 2014, p. 69) dependent upon an individual's 'ability to shape, adapt and apply the self to the needs of a particular role' (Daniels & Brooker, 2014, p. 69). The literature about subjectivities is vast and polyvocal. The concept of subjectivity is fluid and there is often an interchange between discursive terms representing a similar idea; as such, this chapter will utilise the terms subjectivity, subject position, identity and social role interchangeably when drawing on literature that employs differing discursive terms to explore similar concepts.

This chapter presents a conceptualisation of subjectivities based on Weber's concept of ideal types, which are constituted through 'the one-sided *accentuation* of one or more points of view' and 'the synthesis of a great many

---

* This chapter is based on doctoral research that has been published as part of a PhD thesis entitled 'Reframing power relationships in higher education: An integrated understanding of conflicting power relationships and undergraduate subjectivities in the current university climate' at Lancaster University.

diffuse, discrete, more or less present and occasionally absent *concrete individual* phenomena' (Weber, 1949, p. 90). The two subjectivities explored in this chapter are presented as heuristic constructs, or ideal types, which allows the tractability of 'limiting concepts against which reality is to be measured' (Weinert, 1996, p. 75). Despite recognition that ideal types are only limited representations of empirical reality, they provide a valuable tool in emphasising specific elements that are common within the given phenomena; ideal types allow a structured and coherent examination of the dynamic nature of subjectivities.

During their university experience, undergraduates are encouraged to adopt the partner subjectivity, through both institutional structures and interaction with academics. This positioning entails different behavioural expectations from that of the traditional learner subjectivity; these two social roles are the central concern of this chapter. Despite the popularity of partnership models in UK universities, there is a lack of consensus in terms of what partnership models, and thus the partner subjectivity, specifically entail. Nevertheless, they share similar characteristics; partnership is underpinned by authenticity, inclusivity, reciprocity, empowerment, trust, challenge, community and responsibility (Healey et al., 2014). The majority of the UK and international literature that deals with partnership, or the partner subjectivity, references either all or some of the above characteristics. The traditional learner subjectivity, on the other hand, emphasises passive deference to pre-determined authoritative knowledge through transmission teaching. The traditional learner subjectivity is an established social role in the sense that it is internalised throughout UK compulsory schooling as the appropriate position to take up during face-to-face contact with teachers in educational contexts (Hargreaves, 1972). Other forms of learning, such as online learning, may incite undergraduates to take up different social roles, such as a silent or private learner role, that require less performative behaviour (Macfarlane, 2015); the purpose of this chapter, though, is to explore the behaviour of undergraduates in face-to-face learning environments. This chapter focusses on these two subjectivities because, although it is acknowledged that social roles are dynamic and individuals occupy multiple subjectivities simultaneously, these two roles, and the conflict between them, are pertinent in the framing of the current undergraduate experience in UK universities. The ideal types of the traditional learner and the partner subjectivity have specific characteristics that are familiar to each through their social construction: the partner subjectivity is constituted through the expectations of taking responsibility for learning, actively participating in the learning process and sharing authority within reciprocal relationships with academics (Little, 2010), while the traditional learner subjectivity is constituted through the behavioural expectations of deference and passive acceptance of authoritative knowledge (Shor, 1996).

Ball and Olmedo argue that 'the subject is the result of endless processes of construction of identities' (Ball & Olmedo, 2013, p. 87); subjectivities are the product of social rules determining appropriate ways of being and refer to 'a set of guidelines which direct the behaviour of the role' (Hargreaves, 1972, p. 71). As a social construct, subjectivities are contingent upon pre-determined characteristics that define that particular role. Atkins notes that taking up a socially constructed role 'provides the individual with knowledge and rationale for actions with which the individual unwittingly identifies' (Atkins, 2005, p. 208). Behaving within specific social subjectivities is based not on agents' 'unique characteristics as individuals, but their social identities as participants in enduring, socially structured relationships' (Isaac, 1987, p. 21). This chapter argues that the undergraduates in this study adopt the subject position of the traditional learner while simultaneously being encouraged by their institutions to take up the social role of the partner; it explores the conflict in behaviour that arises from these two subjectivities.

The extent to which undergraduates adhere to the ideal type of the traditional learner and the partner differs; the literature on undergraduate subjectivity can sometimes focus on one particular subjectivity, be it the partner or the traditional learner role (Isaac, 1987; Shor, 1996; Little, 2010). However, this provides a limited perspective and fails to relate to the conflict that arises in the attempted reconciliation of opposing subjectivities. It is essential to understand the different characteristics of each subjectivity in order to appreciate how and why conflict arises in undergraduates' attempts to reconcile the behavioural expectations of each.

Conceptualising the 'traditional learner' and the 'partner'

The 'traditional learner' subjectivity

Freire, from a critical pedagogical perspective, argues that in the traditional learner subjectivity and within the socially structured relationship in which it participates, 'educators are the possessors of knowledge, whereas learners are "empty vessels" to be filled by the educators' deposits' (Freire, 1985, p. 100). He surmises that education is where 'the educator as "the one who knows" transfers existing knowledge to the learner as "the one who does not know"' (Freire, 1985, p. 114). Although dated, Freire's conceptualisation of the 'banking method' of education is a pervasive concept in many Western educational contexts; it details the traditional mode of education in which the learner demonstrates understanding through recitation of predisposed knowledge. As a traditional learner, then, individuals are expected to be dependent upon the authority of the individual occupying the teacher role, with little need to discover knowledge for themselves. Shor, an American educator, argues that this characteristic is naturalised to such an extent that 'what has been socially and historically constructed by a specific culture becomes presented to students as undebatable and unchangeable' (Shor, 1996, pp. 10–11). The traditional learner is a socially constructed subjectivity but, because of its pervasiveness as an 'enduring relation' (Isaac, 1987, p. 22) over a number of decades, it still appears as natural.

The natural adoption of the traditional learner subjectivity is framed as a negative barrier to the implementation of collaborative learning in HE. McMillan and Cheney argue for the need to move away from 'the old-fashioned model of passive information transmission, in which the student is viewed merely as a receptor and mirror' (McMillan & Cheney, 1996, p. 13). However, implementing collaborative partnerships is far more complex than stating a necessity for departing from the transmission model of teaching which is closely aligned with the traditional learner subjectivity; two decades on from McMillan and Cheney's consideration, MacFarlane notes the continued difficulty in attempts to move away from the pervasive transmission model because of the 'wealth of evidence that students prefer to learn in ways that are often labelled negatively as "traditional" or "passive"' (Macfarlane, 2015, p. 342). The passivity encouraged by particular teaching methods is closely aligned to the characteristic of deference which constitutes the traditional learner subjectivity.

Moreover, as an established social role, the traditional learner has little authority over class content, the assessment process or the creation and distribution of knowledge because 'the power resides with the authority of the lecturer and is often reinforced through our social practices of teaching' (Allin, 2014, p. 97). UK universities are still 'dominated by traditional teaching methods: lectures, seminars and tutorials' (Morris, 2009, p. 104); these face-to-face interactions with academics, that often mimic classroom environments used in Western compulsory schooling, frame the traditional learner subjectivity as the most appropriate position to adopt. While many authors acknowledge that 'in any act of learning, prior experiences, perceptions, approaches and outcomes are simultaneously present in a student's awareness' (Trigwell & Ashwin, 2006, p. 244), the majority fail to recognise how these particular pre-existing notions play out in HE and what impact they have on the ability to reconstitute appropriate behaviour within universities. Equally, while the literature recognises that undergraduates have pre-existing notions of how they should behave within educational institutions, it fails to illuminate how these notions reconcile with the behavioural norms of the partner subjectivity, a social role which undergraduates within UK universities are also expected to take up.

The 'partner' subjectivity

Levy et al. define partnership in terms of 'shared responsibility and cooperative or collaborative action, in relation to shared purposes' (Levy et al., 2010, p. 1); many authors emphasise the encouragement of taking responsibility for learning in partnership models, in direct contrast to the traditional learner subjectivity. Jensen and Bennett argue that 'partnership goes beyond listening to students and offers them a central role in developing teaching and learning' (Jensen & Bennett, 2016, p. 51) and Levy et al. surmise that the goal of partnership is to 'share authority in the process of jointly constructing meaning' (Levy et al., 2010, p. 4).

In order for partnership models to be successful, there needs to be an emphasis on shared responsibility within the learning process, and so taking responsibility for learning is an important characteristic of the partner subjectivity. Telfer argues that partnership increases undergraduates' ability to retain and create knowledge 'through the double-loop learning model and the act of designing one's own approach to learning' (Telfer, 2018, pp. 249–250). The partner subjectivity emphasises responsibility in the learning process and the creation of knowledge. However, as Australian critics Bovill and Felten note, this presents 'unfamiliar territory for students, staff and institutions' (Bovill & Felten, 2016, p. 2). The partner subjectivity:

> Requires active engagement with the entire learning process [...] and sees the student as an active participant in the development of knowledge.
> (McCulloch, 2009, p. 178)

Adhering to the partner subjectivity requires that undergraduates, alongside academics, partake 'in the production of knowledge through active participation, rather than act as, respectively, providers and passive recipients of its transmission' (Naseem, 2018, p. 228). In addition to taking responsibility for learning and actively participating in the learning process, adhering to a partner subjectivity entails forming a reciprocal relationship with academics 'whereby students and staff work together to achieve common goals' (Matthews et al., 2018, p. 31). In order for reciprocal partnerships to work, they 'require a structure that is formed by the exchange of ideas and agreed by all participants' (Sotiriou, 2018, p. 57); however, reciprocity must be negotiated differently within a partnership model because the 'balance of power should not shift to the students [...] partners should be equally valued by their different areas of expertise' (Matthews et al., 2018, p. 38). Adhering to a partner subjectivity, then, not only requires undergraduates to take responsibility for learning and actively participate but also requires them to continuously negotiate the distribution of contextually dependent power; these characteristics are difficult to reconcile with the traditional learner subjectivity.

There is a wide consensus across the literature that introducing partnership models into universities poses considerable challenges, not only in the UK, but also internationally as Bovill and Felten conclude: 'partnership does not always fit easily within existing cultures in higher education' (Bovill & Felten, 2016, p. 1). This is because the partnership subjectivity and subsequent relationship:

> Poses a threat to the 'taken-for-granted' way of approaching education, which sees the teacher as expert and the student as inexperienced listener.
> (Tong, Clark, Standen, & Sotiriou, 2018, p. 315)

This is the traditional dynamic, whereby 'teachers hold all the power and knowledge and only they can bestow it on the learners, who remain passive recipients' (Pilsworth, 2018, p. 127). The literature that deals with the subjectivity of partners in universities frequently recognises the tension that stems from the conflicting behavioural expectations of positioning individuals within the dual roles of the partner and the traditional learner because there are 'accepted teaching and learning norms which may be difficult to deviate from' (Bovill, 2014, p. 22). There is significant recognition in the literature that the subjectivity of the partner conflicts with the expectations of the traditional learner subjectivity:

> When students are treated as students, it appears that they are kept in a subordinate place [...] However, when students are thought of as junior colleagues, the dynamic of their relationship to their teachers and to the university changes.
>
> (Brew, 2006, p. 96)

The social role of partner is less established than that of the traditional learner and as such, it is more ambivalent. However, the literature does emphasise a consistent expectation for undergraduates to behave as equal contributors and participate with 'reciprocity, mutual respect, shared responsibility and complementary contributions' (Bovill, 2017, p. 720). This chapter explores how these dual roles are conceptualised by undergraduates and academics and how their co-existence is creating conflict when behaving within sites of learning and teaching in two UK universities.

Research design

This chapter draws from a research project conducted in two post-1992 universities in England, hereafter referred to as University A and University B (A or B in the data). Both universities in this study have institutional policies which outline methods for engaging undergraduates as partners. For University A, the policy is based on 'mutual expectation and aspirations' (2018a), and for University B, the policy defines undergraduates and staff as 'co-producers of knowledge' (2018a). Although the institutional discourse from both universities is similar in terms of defining a partnership model, the way in which it is embedded differs. University A has a specific strategy to configure a collaborative learning process at the structural level and was chosen to explore how the positioning of undergraduates within a partner subjectivity plays out within interpersonal relationships with academics. University B was chosen to provide a comparative model within the same categorisation of institution, to explore the variation in perspectives and practices; although University B has a partnership strategy in place, it is presented, and perceived, as guidance for engaging students in learning, rather than an institutionally embedded policy as it is in University A. This project included 32 semi-structured interviews with undergraduates and academics (6 academics and 10 undergraduates from each institution); the interviews explored interpersonal relationships, the methods of engagement for undergraduates, the impact of policy documents and the relationships between undergraduates and academics, conceptualised in visual drawings produced by participants. The chapter draws on observational data of three seminars and three lectures (Sem or Lec in the data) from each university as well as six institutional documents from each. Participants were all volunteers and included academics within the humanities and undergraduates within the humanities, in different years of study (Year1, Year2 or Year3 in the data). All participants have been given pseudonyms to ensure confidentiality.

The study uses Faircloughian critical discourse analysis to interpret the spoken discourse of the interviews, the written discourse of institutional policy and images drawn by interviewees to conceptualise undergraduate–academic relationships. All data were analysed as a text (vocabulary and grammar), a discursive practice (situational context and intertextuality) and a social practice (social determinants influencing the text) (Fairclough, 2015). This model allows for a richer understanding of the relationship between structure and agency and the resulting formation and perpetuation of subject positionings. Participants were asked explicitly about the partner role and their conceptualisation of it, as well as their perception of its implementation within their institution. The majority of undergraduates were unfamiliar with the concept of partnership and thus, once the premise was explained, the majority attempted to understand the model in relation to what they perceived to be the more familiar dynamic between them and academics.

Findings

Managing dual roles

The traditional learner subjectivity is a role that was conceptualised by participants as '*unavoidable*' (B, Academic, Michelle) within a UK HE context because it appears 'so similar to [...] school' (B, Year3, Bethany). The subjectivity of the traditional learner has solidified over years of socialisation within UK compulsory schooling, to form part of the 'enduring relations' (Isaac, 1987, p. 22) of the learner–teacher dynamic. As a result, 'the socially competent actor becomes constrained internally [...] because he or she knows what to expect (Haugaard, 2012, p. 39). Undergraduates are used to passively receiving knowledge from teachers: 'the natural tendency of a student [...] is to expect eternal knowledge, finite verities' (Ribéreau-Gayon, 2018, p. 140); it is a characteristic that forms the internal constraint of the 'socially competent actor' (Haugaard, 2012, p. 39) in UK educational contexts. Undergraduates in this study identified strongly with the traditional learner subjectivity and considered the role and its characteristics to be necessary within an educational context, perceiving it to be 'naturally' (B, Year2, Vera) present because, despite the difference in the level of education, it remains 'very much student and teacher and there's that separation' (A, Year2, Ben).

The characteristics of the traditional learner subjectivity, though, conflict with those behavioural expectations that constitute the partner subjectivity. While the traditional learner is granted little to no power in the classroom, the partner is expected to share power equally. One academic argued: 'partnership can be a bit misleading because we're not *equals*' (B, Academic, Michelle). Equality was often cited as a concern when considering a partnership approach. The traditional learner–teacher relationship is constituted through unequal dispositional power on the premise of a teacher's expertise; as Isaac notes, 'powers to act are part of the nature of the relationship' and constitute 'routinely performed and purposeful activities' (Isaac, 1987, p. 22). The findings of this study highlight the ambiguity and conflict that surrounds the attempted reconciliation of the behaviours associated with the partner subjectivity and the traditional learner subjectivity and the impact this conflict has for fostering effective partnerships.

Taking responsibility for learning

As mentioned previously, the discourses of the institutional documentation from both universities share similarities in their definition of the partnership model, but differ in the way in which the model is perceived, and thus embedded, throughout the university; discourse from both institutions reflected the positioning of undergraduates as partners through the emphasis on the characteristic of taking responsibility for learning. University A's Student Charter, which is an official set of expectations from the university, the student and the Student's Union as part of the undergraduate's contract to undertake study, expects undergraduates to 'take responsibility for [their] own learning and research' (2018a). Similarly, University B's Student Charter expects undergraduates to 'take responsibility for managing their own learning' (2018b), which is fostered through an emphasis on 'challenging accepted thinking' (2018a).

The majority of academics emphasised the behavioural expectation of taking responsibility for learning, arguing that 'it's about *their* learning experience' (A, Academic, Mary). One recognised the importance of undergraduates doing 'as much of the talking as possible' (B, Academic, Janice) because academics are 'trying to steer *them* to do something not do it *for* them' (B, Academic, Janice). Undergraduates recognised that the responsibility for learning went beyond the behavioural expectations of the traditional learner because 'nobody's holding your hand' (A, Year3, Jane). One said: 'I like the independence of it, but then, also I initially found it quite difficult' (A, Year2, Lisa) and another said:

> It's very different because they give you A and they want you to get to C, they're not going to give you the B in the middle, whereas High School, you're used to, "Right, A, B, C, got it".
>
> (A, Year1, Claire)

This perception emphasises undergraduates' natural expectation of adhering to the traditional learner subjectivity, whereby learners rely on teachers and a passive approach to learning encourages them to 'think it's the tutor's responsibility to do the work for [them]' (A, Academic, Bernard).

As one academic noted, the familiar space of the seminar, which are small group classes similar to tutorials, can perpetuate the behavioural expectations of the traditional learner subjectivity:

> They're all sat round and they're looking at you and there's that expectation that you are going to give them and they will just consume.
>
> (A, Academic, Louise)

The expectation that undergraduates are the passive recipients of knowledge was felt by another academic who argued:

> They perceive that I know a lot more about the topic than they do and they want me to *tell* them about it.
>
> (B, Academic, Michelle)

Another felt that some undergraduates enjoy being lectured because 'it makes them feel safe because they're being *told* what it is they need to know' (B, Academic, Alistair). Part of the traditional learner subjectivity is an expectation that teachers will transmit knowledge to learners because socialisation has 'led us to internalise the unilateral authority of the teacher as the normal, "common sense" way to do education' (Shor, 1996, p. 27). There was a predominant perception from participants that undergraduates are less knowledgeable and, therefore, teachers should transmit knowledge to the learner; it constitutes 'the "taken-for-granted" way of approaching education' (Tong et al., 2018a, p. 315). One undergraduate participant conceptualised this in her drawing of a 'good' relationship with an academic (Figure 9.1).

The figure representing the academic is larger and positioned as a central point of transition; the undergraduate appears miserable until the academic has validated her work, after which she appears happy. The observations also supported the view that undergraduates are socialised into solely trusting the authority of the teacher role; some undergraduates only wrote down their peers' contributions once the academic had verified the validity of the idea (A, Year1, Sem; B, Year2, Lec). One even said:

> You're often apprehensive to note down what other students have said in seminars *until* the lecturer's gone, "That's a good idea".
>
> (B, Year2, Henry)

Figure 9.1 Drawing of a 'good' relationship with an academic (B, Year 2, Vera)

The naturalised authority of the teacher makes transmission teaching more appealing to undergraduates because of its familiarity, which makes them less likely to take responsibility for their own learning. The conflict between the partner subjectivity and the traditional learner subjectivity was furthered by participants' recognition of the irreconcilability between the characteristic of deference and the characteristic of active participation.

Actively participating in the learning process

The importance of undergraduates actively discussing and sharing ideas collaboratively was emphasised by academics. One thought it was 'invaluable for students to have the chance to discuss' (B, Academic, Michelle) and another said: 'the most important point about a seminar is that […] they do need to participate' (A, Academic, Mary). The discursive nature of seminars meant that the majority of participants considered them more engaging than lectures where 'the tendency is for students to sit there passively for 50 minutes' (A, Academic, Mary). One academic reflected that the lecture can be '*problematic* because it's so passive' (B, Academic, Alistair) and another noted that 'lecture theatres are *hopeless* for engaging anybody' (A, Academic, Andrew). Some undergraduates, though, felt that the encouragement of active participation was a forced means of learning:

> I think sometimes seminars try and *force* an opinion out of you […] *force* you to think, and sometimes that's not necessarily useful […] I don't think it helps you *understand* the topic more, it just makes you […] feel as though you've said something.
>
> (A, Year 2, Ben)

The observations also demonstrated academics pushing for active participation and being met with resistance or silence from undergraduates (A, Year 2,

Lec; A, Year2, Sem; A, Year1, Sem; B, Year3, Lec; B, Year3, Sem; B, Year2, Sem). It was evident that academics were keen to get undergraduates to actively participate, but as reflected in the discourses of the undergraduate interviews and the behaviour during observations, attempts to force active participation were often met with resistance.

Some undergraduates in this study demonstrated their reluctance to actively participate because of the internalised notion that teacher roles have greater knowledge:

> Because some of them are, like, so intelligent, that I just feel like anything I'm going to say they're going to be, like, "*Really?* Really?"
>
> (A, Year2, Ben)

Another said:

> You always feel *stupid*, like literally, you could have the *best* point ever and [...] it's almost, like, they've already thought of it when they're brushing their teeth.
>
> (A, Year1, Claire)

The intelligence associated with the academic role in the above perceptions posits that they will naturally hold authority over knowledge. Traditional learners are used to accepting 'what the teacher says goes' (Hargreaves, 1972, p. 139); as a social practice, deferring to the academics' authority of knowledge is in virtue of their social role as a teacher and the expectation that 'they know what they're doing' (A, Year1, Claire). This notion of authoritative knowledge was reflected by one undergraduate:

> I said before that they don't spoon-feed us but they, kind of, *do* in a way [...] they basically give us everything that we *need* for essays.
>
> (A, Year2, Daisy)

Despite the level of learning being elevated compared to compulsory schooling, there was still a noticeable reliance on academics to provide authoritative knowledge and this was conceptualised as 'naturally' (B, Year2, Vera) appropriate; this reliance makes it less likely that undergraduates will actively participate in the learning process.

Sharing authority within reciprocal relationships

A number of academics reflected on the behavioural expectation of sharing authority in their drawings of positive relationships:

The academic responsible for the drawing in Figure 9.2 described the conceptualisation as 'something that's reciprocal, so it's equal and the conversation is two-way' (B, Academic, Lizzie). Mutuality or equal contribution was

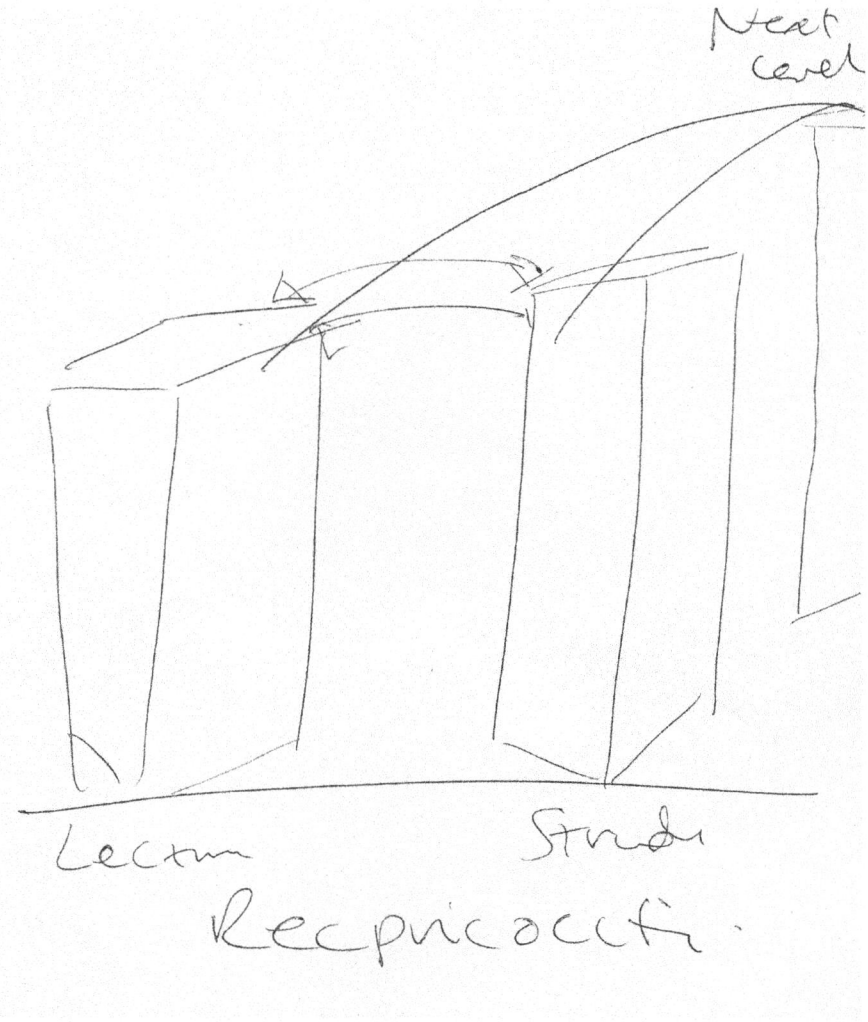

Figure 9.2 Drawing of a 'good' relationship between undergraduates and academics (B, Academic, Lizzie)

cited frequently as being a necessary characteristic and this notion is pervasive throughout the literature on student-staff partnership (Little, 2010; Tong et al., 2018b). Another academic drew the figure below (Figure 9.3).

By way of explanation, this academic said: 'we've *both* got things to say, equally' (A, Academic, Mary). A large proportion of undergraduates also maintained a sense of mutuality, arguing for '*interaction* between two people [...] open both ways' (A, Year3, Daniel). One called it a 'two-way process' (A, Year2, Susan) and another referred to it as a 'two-way street' (B, Year3, Bethany). Yet another said 'it's more of a two-way, rather than lecturers just

A good relationship w/ a student

Figure 9.3 Drawing of a 'good' relationship between undergraduates and academics (A, Academic, Mary)

standing there talking at you' (B, Year3, Phoebe) and another argued for reciprocity 'rather than it being just a one-way street' (B, Year2, Edith). The repetition of the phrase 'two-way', or similar, emphasises the importance of reciprocity, which is reiterated in the institutional discourse of both universities, encouraging undergraduates to be 'co-creators' (University A, 2018b; University B, 2018a).

Although undergraduates and academics perceived reciprocity to be a positive behaviour of the partner subjectivity, there was still ambivalence towards embedding shared authority because of the internalised expectation of the teacher's authority. One undergraduate said: 'I don't feel that we are at a high enough level to, kind of, *add* to what they already know' (A, Year2, Daisy). This perception illuminates the strength of the traditional learner subjectivity in assuming the impracticality of a partner subjectivity because undergraduates are 'not on the same level' (A, Year2, Ben). Generally, undergraduates felt as though academics held the authority of knowledge; as a social practice, the teacher role possesses a 'discrete body of knowledge that's, kind of, in a box' (B, Academic, Alistair). This idea is subsumed into HE, despite the fact that 'at university, there's no box' (B, Academic, Alistair). There was consistent acknowledgement of an academics' authority, perpetuating the assumption that '"*they're* right. *I'm* wrong"' (A, Academic, Louise). Although most academics felt that the characteristics of the partner subjectivity were positive behaviours, there was still a reliance on the behavioural expectations of the traditional learner subjectivity: 'I am willing to *listen* but ultimately, I am the specialist' (B, Academic, Vicky). The strength, and seeming naturalness of the traditional learner subjectivity, creates stark challenges for the implementation of the partner subjectivity and the willingness of undergraduates to adhere to its behavioural norms.

Conclusion

The universities in this study position their undergraduates as partners through institutional discourse and policies with little attention paid to the pervasiveness of the pre-existing subjectivity of the traditional learner and the way in which it negates the adherence to the partner role. The findings of the study demonstrate that undergraduates are reliant on the behavioural characteristics of the traditional learner subjectivity. Moreover, the findings relay a natural inclination for academics to position undergraduates as traditional learners in sites of learning and teaching, despite their consistent recognition that the partner subjectivity, and its behaviours, are more appropriate for HE contexts. Telfer writes:

> Innovation does not happen by following the rules [...] It happens when we rewrite the rulebook, and to do that we need to know how the rulebook has been written.
>
> (Telfer, 2018, p. 251)

In order to effect successful partnership models, an understanding of the conflict between the partner subjectivity and the traditional learner subjectivity is crucial. As Morrissey argues, 'the first challenge in reworking conditioned agency is recognising it' (Morrissey, 2015, p. 628); acknowledging the structural barrier of the traditional learner subjectivity is essential, without which reconfiguring undergraduate behaviour to reflect the expectations of the partner subjectivity becomes incredibly difficult. It is widely accepted in the UK HE literature that 'we need to depart from the old-fashioned model of passive information transmission' (McMillan & Cheney, 1996, p. 13) and move towards a partnership model based on 'shared responsibility and cooperative or collaborative action' (Levy et al., 2010, p. 1). In order to implement new approaches to learning through new subjectivities, there must be an understanding of the conflicting behaviours encouraged by the pertinent subjectivities of the partner and the traditional learner.

Those who perform as traditional learners are used to passively receiving and consuming relevant knowledge from those performing as teachers, who represent 'the unilateral authority who tells them what things mean, what to do' (Shor, 1996, pp. 11–12). Moreover, the traditional learner has little responsibility, instead relying on the teacher to impart necessary and required knowledge. This dynamic 'cultivates passivity, conformity, obedience, acquiescence and unquestioning acceptance of authority' (Kreisberg, 1992, p. 8). The passive acceptance of knowledge that characterises the traditional learner poses a challenge for adherence to the partner subjectivity. The findings of this study demonstrate that undergraduates are having to negotiate two opposing behaviours: one which they are familiar with, in which they are expected to passively listen and absorb knowledge, and another which is unfamiliar to them, in which they are expected to actively collaborate to produce knowledge.

Moreover, the behaviour of deferring to the teacher's authority was highly apparent in this study and other research has recognised it as a barrier when attempting to implement partnerships (Allin, 2014). Danaher argues that 'we make sense of ourselves by referring back to various bodies of knowledge' (Danaher, 2000, p. 50); as the findings suggest, undergraduates refer back to the knowledge that constitutes appropriate behaviour and they draw on what they have internalised from other educational contexts. They draw on their internalisation of the 'enduring relations' (Isaac, 1987, p. 22) of the learner–teacher relationship within Western compulsory education: they consider the teacher's knowledge to be 'authoritative [because] many have learned to manipulate the teacher for a good grade by mimicking the teacher's opinions' (Shor, 1996, p. 51). Despite recognition that undergraduates prefer passive and traditional methods of learning (Macfarlane, 2015), the reasons behind the preference have never been fully explored. Evidence from this study suggests it stems from their reliance on the familiarity of the traditional learner subjectivity and its behavioural expectations. The strength of this subjectivity, the characteristics of which undergraduates naturally adhere to in educational contexts, creates conflict when attempts are made to behave in accordance with competing subjectivities. Foucault argues that 'in our culture, human being are made subjects' (Foucault, 2002, p. 326); throughout UK compulsory schooling, individuals are positioned as traditional learners and the social role is constituted through behavioural expectations, which have become internalised as 'naturally' (B, Year2, Vera) appropriate within educational contexts. In addition, although institutional discourse is similar in defining partnership models, there is a lack of consistency in academics' positioning of undergraduates as partners in the learning process; this naturalisation and ambiguity causes conflict when undergraduates are encouraged to adhere to a partner subjectivity by their institutions.

As the literature explains, the partner subjectivity necessitates an emphasis on collaboration and shared responsibility in the learning process, both of which negate the passive deference to finite knowledge. The hierarchy implicit in UK universities is structured upon the subjectivities of the traditional learner and the traditional teacher; partnership subjectivities threaten to erode what is perceived of 'as undebatable and unchangeable' (Shor, 1996, pp. 10–11). Behaving as a partner was frequently met with resistance by participants in this study owing to the conflict it presents for the more naturalised learner subjectivity. According to Haugaard,

> If an actor can be socialised into taking certain structural practices for granted, as part of the natural order of things, any practice that contravenes these structures are perceived as unreasonable, which constitutes a powerful structural constraint.
>
> (Haugaard, 2015, p. 153)

Reframing undergraduate students as partners constitutes traversing the natural adherence to the traditional learner subjectivity and poses a challenge for practical implementation. Marquis et al. note: 'partnerships involve the formation of reciprocal relationships between students and academic staff, with the capacity to mitigate traditional hierarchies' (Marquis et al., 2016, p. 4). However, the findings of this study suggest that while undergraduates and academics consider the partner subjectivity and its associated behaviours to be positive for HE contexts, this does not correlate to its 'capacity to mitigate traditional hierarchies' (Marquis et al., 2016, p. 4). Both institutions in this study deliberately position their undergraduates as partners, as shown in the institutional discourse, but the data have demonstrated that the traditional learner subjectivity, and the hierarchy it invokes, is difficult to overcome simply by discursively positioning undergraduates as partners.

Because the traditional learner and the partner subjectivity are constituted through adherence to incompatible behavioural expectations, undergraduates have little option but to prioritise one subjectivity over the other. The prioritised role differs for individuals, with external factors influencing their choice, and this leads to ambiguity and variation across undergraduate behaviour. The adherence to different subjectivities, and thus behaviours, has the potential to cause discord, with undergraduates adopting different approaches and seeking different outcomes. While this research is situated within the UK HE context, it relates to international contexts in which the traditional learner and the partner subjectivity are present; it highlights the need to recognise and understand the conflicting behavioural expectations of undergraduate subjectivities in universities more broadly. The partner subjectivity is becoming more popular both nationally and internationally

(Bovill, 2017; Brew, 2006; Cook-Sather, 2014; Tong et al., 2018b; Symonds, 2020); to continue the development of HE requires that we look more closely at the ways in which undergraduates are framed within institutions and what this framing entails for the ways in which they choose to behave during their studies.

References

Allin, L. (2014). Collaboration between staff and students in the scholarship of teaching and learning: The potential and the problems. *Teaching and Learning Inquiry: The ISSOTL Journal* 2:1, 95–102.

Atkins, K. (Ed.). (2005). *Self and subjectivity*. Malden, MA: Blackwell Publishing.

Ball, S. J., & Olmedo, A. (2013). Care of the self, resistance and subjectivity under neoliberal governmentalities. *Critical Studies in Education* 54:1, 85–96. doi:10.1 080/17508487.2013.740678

Bovill, C. (2014). An investigation of co-created curricula within higher education in the UK, Ireland and the USA, *Innovations in Education and Teaching International* 51:1, 15–25. doi:10.1080/14703297.2013.770264

Bovill, C. (2017). A framework to explore roles within student-staff partnerships in higher education: Which students are partners, when, and in what ways? *International Journal for Students as Partners* 1:1, 1–5.

Bovill, C., & Felten, P. (2016). Cultivating student–staff partnerships through research and practice. *International Journal for Academic Development* 21:1, 1–3. doi:10.1080/1360144X.2016.1124965

Brew, A. (2006). *Research and teaching: Beyond the divide*. Basingstoke, Hampshire; New York: Palgrave Macmillan.

Cook-Sather, A. (2014). Multiplying perspectives and improving practice: What can happen when undergraduate students collaborate with college faculty to explore teaching and learning. *Instructional Science* 42:1, 31–46. doi:10.1007/s11251-013-9292-3

Danaher, Geoff. (2000). *Understanding Foucault*. London; Thousand Oaks, CA: Sage Publications.

Daniels, J., & Brooker, J. (2014). Student identity development in higher education: Implications for graduate attributes and work-readiness. *Educational Research* 56:1, 65–76. doi:10.1080/00131881.2013.874157

Fairclough, N. (2015). *Language and power* (3rd ed.). Abingdon: Routledge.

Foucault, M. (2002). *Power* (J. D. Faubion, Trans.). London: Penguin.

Freire, P. (1985). *The politics of education: Culture, power, and liberation* (D. Macedo, Trans.). Basingstoke, Hampshire: Macmillan.

Hargreaves, D. H. (1972). *Interpersonal relations and education*. London, Boston: Routledge and K. Paul.

Haugaard, M. (2012). Rethinking the four dimensions of power: Domination and empowerment. *Journal of Political Power* 5:1, 33–54. doi:10.1080/21583 79X.2012.660810

Haugaard, M. (2015). Concerted power over: Concerted power over: Mark Haugaard. *Constellations* 22:1, 147–158.

Healey, M., Flint, A., & Harrington, K. (2014). *Framework for partnership in teaching and learning in higher education*. York: Higher Education Academy.

Isaac, J. C. (1987). Beyond the three faces of power: A realist critique. *Polity* 20:1, 4–31.

Jensen, K., & Bennett, L. (2016). Enhancing teaching and learning through dialogue: A student and staff partnership model. *International Journal for Academic Development* 21:1, 41–53. doi:10.1080/1360144X.2015.1113537

Kreisberg, S. (1992). *Transforming power: Domination, empowerment, and education*. Albany: State University of New York Press.

Levy, P., Little, S., & Whelan, N. (2010). Perspectives on staff-student partnership in learning, research and educational enhancement. In S. Little (Ed.), *Staff-student partnerships in higher education* (pp. 1–15). Retrieved from http://ebookcentral. proquest.com/lib/lancaster/detail.action?docID=742925

Little, S. (Ed.). (2010). *Staff-student partnerships in higher education*. Retrieved from http://ebookcentral.proquest.com/lib/lancaster/detail.action?docID=742925

Macfarlane, B. (2015). Student performativity in higher education: Converting learning as a private space into a public performance. *Higher Education Research and Development* 34:2, 338–350. doi:10.1080/07294360.2014.956697

Marquis, E., Puri, V., Wan, S., Ahmad, A., Goff, L., Knorr, K., ... Woo, J. (2016). Navigating the threshold of student–staff partnerships: A case study from an Ontario teaching and learning institute. *International Journal for Academic Development* 21:1, 4–15.

Matthews, K. E., Cook-Sather, A., & Healey, M. (2018). Connecting learning, teaching and research through student-staff partnerships: Toward universities as egalitarian learning communities. In V. C. H. Tong A. Standen, & M. Sotiriou (Eds.), *Shaping higher education with students: Ways to connect research and teaching* (pp. 23–29). London: UCL Press.

McCulloch, A. (2009). The student as co-producer: Learning from public administration about the student–university relationship. *Studies in Higher Education* 34:2, 171–183. doi:10.1080/03075070802562857

McMillan, J. J., & Cheney, G. (1996). The student as consumer: The implications and limitations of a metaphor. *Communication Education* 45:1, 1–15.

Morris, A. (2009). The stretched academy: The learning experience of mature students from under-represented groups. In L. Bell, M. Neary, & H. Stevenson (Eds.), *The future of higher education: Policy, pedagogy and the student experience* (p. ch. 10). London: Continuum International PubGroup.

Morrissey, J. (2015). Regimes of performance: Practices of the normalised self in the neoliberal university. *British Journal of Sociology of Education* 36:4, 614–634. doi: 10.1080/01425692.2013.838515

Naseem, J. (2018). Connecting graduates with the real world: Transferring research-based skills to the workplace. In V. C. H. Tong, A. Standen, & M. Sotiriou (Eds.), *Shaping higher education with students: Ways to connect research and teaching* (pp. 224–241). London: UCL Press.

Neary, M., & Winn, J. (2009). The student as producer: Reinventing the student experience in higher education. In L. Bell, M. Neary, & H. Stevenson (Eds.), *The future of higher education: Policy, pedagogy and the student experience* (pp. 126–138). London: Continuum International PubGroup.

Pilsworth, E. (2018). Research = Teaching = Dialogue? Dialogue as a model for research-based learning at university. In V. C. H. Tong, A. Standen, & M. Sotiriou (Eds.), *Shaping higher education with students: Ways to connect research and teaching* (pp. 126–138). London: UCL Press.

Ribéreau-Gayon, A. (2018). Interdisciplinary research-based teaching: Advocacy for a change in the higher education paradigm. In V. C. H. Tong, A. Standen, & M. Sotiriou (Eds.), *Shaping higher education with students: Ways to connect research and teaching* (pp. 139–149). London: UCL Press.

Shor, I. (1996). *When students have power: Negotiating authority in a critical pedagogy.* Chicago: University of Chicago Press.

Sotiriou, M. (2018). Investigating student perceptions of student-staff partnership. In V. C. H. Tong, A. Standen, & M. Sotiriou (Eds.), *Shaping higher education with students: Ways to connect research and teaching* (pp. 53–63). London: UCL Press.

Symonds, E. (2020). The depersonalised consumer subjectivity and its effect on fostering meaningful relationships between undergraduates and academics in higher education. *Critical Studies in Education.* 1–17. doi:10.1080/17508487.2020.17 55330

Telfer, J. (2018). Can research-based education be a tool to help students prepare for the world of work? In V. C. H. Tong, A. Standen, & M. Sotiriou (Eds.), *Shaping higher education with students: Ways to connect research and teaching* (pp. 244–255). London: UCL Press.

Tong, V. C. H. Clark, L., Standen, A., & Sotiriou, M. (2018a). Inspiring change: Advancing student-staff partnership and research-based education together. In V. C. H. Tong, A. Standen, & M. Sotiriou (Eds.), *Shaping higher education with students: Ways to connect research and teaching* (pp. 313–320). London: UCL Press.

Tong, V. C. H., Standen, A., & Sotiriou, M. (Eds.). (2018b). *Shaping higher education with students: Ways to connect research and teaching.* London: UCL Press.

Trigwell, K., & Ashwin, P. (2006). An exploratory study of situated conceptions of learning and learning environments. *Higher Education* 51, 243–258.

University A. (2018a). Student charter. Retrieved November 16 2018, from Website redacted for ethical reasons

University A. (2018b). Student engagement – university a learning & teaching. Retrieved March 19 2019, from Website redacted for ethical reasons

University B. (2018a). Policy document on 'Learning and Teaching Strategy 2015–20'. Retrieved November 16 2018, from Website redacted for ethical reasons

University B. (2018b). Policy document on 'Student Charter'. Retrieved May 12 2017, from Website and accurate name redacted for ethical reasons

Weber, M. (1949). 'Objectivity' in social science and social policy (1904). In E. A. Shils & H. A. Finch (Eds. & Trans.), *Max Weber on the methodology of the social sciences.* Glencoe: The Free Press.

Weinert, F. (1996). Weber's ideal types as models in the social sciences. *Royal Institute of Philosophy Supplement* 41, 73–93. http://dx.doi.org.ezproxy.lancs.ac.uk/10.1017/S1358246100006056

Williams, J. (2013). *Consuming higher education: Why learning can't be bought.* London; New York: Bloomsbury Academic.

Chapter 10

Constructing the university student in British documentary television

Kay Calver and Bethan Michael-Fox

Introduction

In this chapter, we argue that an increase in documentary television detailing the lives of university students was coincident with the increase in tuition fees in 2012 and the removal of student number controls for England in 2013. These documentaries reflect and negotiate a range of prominent socio-cultural concerns about students. According to the Department for Business, Innovation and Skills (2016, p. 7), there has been a shift from a university sector 'that serves only a narrow band of people, to a broader, more diverse and more open system'. The documentaries examined here are indicative of greater interest in this 'broader' and 'more diverse' population of students and their experiences, though the extent to which they actually reflect and represent them is questionable. We argue that these documentaries can be seen to reflect a broader shift in thinking about 'the university student' in contemporary Britain. The consequences of the high cost of university to both the student and the taxpayer are consistently at the fore and students are often conceptualised in terms of risk. The earliest documentaries examined tend to construct students in terms of perhaps more 'traditional' risks associated with the university student: binge drinking, a lack of independent living skills and promiscuity. More recent examples focus on mental health, sexual assault and the pressures of higher education. The chapter begins with a consideration of the approach taken and discussion of the complexity of the terms 'British', 'documentary' and 'television' in categorising the texts examined here. It then explores the documentaries in terms of their figuration of the higher education student as 'at risk' and 'a risk' in a range of different ways.

Approach

Television forms a space in which people engage with complex social understandings (Livingstone, 1998). Williams (2010, p. 170) has emphasised that:

> media representations of students are worthy of analysis as they reflect back to society some of the dominant ways in which what it means to be a student is understood.

Williams (2010, p. 70) also suggests that representations of students in the media might play a part in constructing 'ways of being' for new generations of students. As Tyler (2008, p. 18–19) has pointed out, mediation should be recognised 'as a constitutive and generative process'. The documentaries examined here offer a valuable space for the negotiation and consideration of the university student but are also active in the construction of the student in the popular imagination in particular ways. In outlining a figurative methodology for the analysis of media representations, Tyler (2008, p. 18) writes that 'representational struggles are often played out within highly condensed figurative forms'. Tyler (2008, p. 18) utilises the term 'figure' as a way to describe how at particular historical and cultural junctures 'specific "social types" become over determined and are publicly imagined (are figured) in excessive, distorted, and caricatured ways'. It is argued such figures are always 'expressive of an underlying social crisis or anxiety' (Tyler, 2008, p. 18). It is perhaps inevitable that these documentaries' condensed representations coupled with the requirement to be 'entertaining' has meant that at times they reinforce the notion of there being particular 'types' of students. Roberts (2014) suggests that:

> every fly-on-the-wall documentary or dramatic representation of British students casts the same collection of characters; 'the lad', 'the slut', 'the introvert' and 'the geek'.

Tyler (2008, p. 19) states that it is through a figure's repetition in and across media that it acquires both 'accreted form' and 'affective value in ways that have significant social and political impact'. It is for this reason that we have examined a range of examples of British documentary television focused on the university student. We seek to identify the dominant 'figure' that emerges of the student while considering the shifts, complexities, contradictions and social anxieties evident.

The phrase British documentary television is far from straightforward. Though the channels these documentaries are featured on can be defined as British, their audiences might not be. The students they document are not representative of British students as a whole, nor of students studying at British universities, as this chapter will show. *Students on the Edge*, the longest 'episode' of which is 9 minutes, seems designed less for consumption on a television than on a device, problematising the use of the term television. The term documentary is also complex, with a range of competing meanings. The rise in television documentaries focused on students is reflective of a broader rise in hybridised documentary television. According to Dovey (2000, p. 232), in recent years, there have been 'anxieties about "popular factual television" displacing or marginalising profound (or "serious") documentary output'. Though Dovey (2000, p. 4) cautions against 'stultifying binaries', he suggests that 'traditional' documentary might be associated with words like 'authoritative', 'boring', 'elitist', 'argument' and 'investigation', while 'popular' documentary might be understood in terms of words like 'fun', 'reality TV', 'entertainment', 'video' and 'reflexive'. Most of the shows under consideration here can be seen to adhere more closely to the terms associated with 'popular' documentary. Many include video diaries, seeking to present the 'truth' of the student experience through this technique. *The Secret Life of Students* takes this effort to new levels by 'employing a brand new technological innovation which enables students to share their digital lives' (Channel 4, 2014). This is achieved by collecting the participants' text messages and social media posts and incorporating this with documentary footage. This series imagines and constructs a particular notion of the student: a 'digital native' (Prensky, 2001) who is connected, on social media, and sharing their intimate thoughts via digital technology. Though not all of the documentaries examined here take this approach, the majority reflect a shift towards, as Dovey (2000, p. 55) writes, more 'subjective, local and confessional rather than objective, generalising and rational' formats.

When selecting the texts, a series of searches were completed via online search engines and the academic broadcast database Box of Broadcasts (BoB) for programming including the terms 'student' and 'university'. We selected only shows that were included in the category 'documentary' by BoB or by the channel broadcasting them. Programming focused on a particular profession was excluded – for example, those focused on young vets, nurses or junior doctors as the emphasis was on the professional and placement dimensions of students' study. We chose instead to focus on programming which feature students from across a range of different courses with an emphasis on a generic notion of 'the student experience' (a term we will critique at the end of this chapter). The documentaries discussed are outlined in Table 10.1 below.

We first became interested in the construction of university students in documentary television when we worked as lecturers at the University of Bedfordshire, which was the setting of the first iteration of *Freshers*. We experienced having camera crews on campuses and worked directly with a number of the students involved in the production. At open days, we began to hear that prospective students had been attracted to the university via this series, adding support to Williams' (2010, p. 170) assertion that the representation of students in the media might play a part in constructing 'ways of being' for new generations of students. The anecdotal conversations we had with students and prospective students about *Freshers* suggested that they experienced the construction of the student within the series in a range of ways: as relatable, as contrastable with their own experience, as something they wanted to challenge, and as aspirational. As such, we became interested in the ways that different media can open up productive spaces for the negotiation of what, and who, a student is.

Table 10.1 Summary table of television programmes analysed

Title	Place of Broadcast	Content	Date
Dispatches: Cashing in on Degrees	Channel 4	Journalist Laurie Penny explores fee rises at British universities and focuses on the pay of top earning bosses and 'predatory' university recruitment practices, rather than on students themselves.	2011
Freshers	ITV2	Freshers begins a trend in 'reality tv' style documentaries focused on students, with series one filmed at the University of Bedfordshire and series two at Swansea University. Freshers follows a group of students during 'freshers', the term given to both the early weeks of the first year of university in Britain and a term used to describe those students who are participating in 'freshers', often with connotations of those students being young, drinking alcohol and engaging in sexual activity. It is related to the US term 'freshman'.	2013; 2014
The Secret Life of Students	Channel 4	Observational documentary series focuses on 12 students over three months of their first year at university. The documentary utilises students' social media posts, internet search histories, calls and text messages to provide insight into their 'secret' lives.	2014
Freshers, Sex and Suspicious Parents	BBC Three	Follows two 'freshers' embarking on their first days at university. Includes footage of the parents of students Cleo and Joe secretly watching their children on video from a local hotel, often shocked by their behaviour.	2015
Death on Campus: Our Stories	BBC Three	Thirty-minute documentary using interviews to piece together the last days of three students who died by suicide at three different British universities.	2017
Panorama: Student Loan Scandal	BBC One	Richard Watson investigates agents who recruit what are referred to in the programme as 'bogus' students seeking student loans to private colleges whose degrees are awarded by British universities.	2018

Table 10.1 (Continued)

Title	Place of Broadcast	Content	Date
Students on the Edge	BBC Three	Series of short documentaries taking a 'confessional' format as students, often anonymously, discuss their experiences of sexual assault, drug dealing, sex work, poor mental health, cheating and drug use at university.	2018
Freshers 2018: In Our Own Words	BBC Three	Shot entirely on students' own phones, this documentary follows seven brand new students as they experience freshers' week at different universities.	2018
Student Sex Workers	Channel 5	Devoted to students who fund their way through university with sex work, consisting of two episodes titled Stripping to Study and Porn Star Graduate.	2019
The Warwick Uni Rape Chat Scandal	BBC One and BBC Three	Thirty-minute documentary on the handling of a case at the University of Warwick where female students were targeted with rape threats.	2019
Dying for a Degree	BBC One	Features interviews with the family and friends of Natasha Abrahart, one of 11 students who died by suicide at the University of Bristol over a period of 18 months.	2019

'At risk' or 'a risk'

The theme of risk emerges time and again in the documentaries. This is, in part, a consequence of the ways in which they focus without exception on students aged between 18 and 21. Kemshall (2009) argues youth and risk are increasingly intertwined in contemporary social policy, yet the relationship between young people and risk seems pervasive beyond this. Constructions of young people as 'at risk' or 'a risk' can be seen to reflect deep seated anxieties about the behaviour of young people and a desire to control them (Kelly, 2000). This persistent dichotomy emerges across policy, media representations and in research. We argue here that the 'at risk'/'a risk' dichotomy is also evident in British documentary television focused on university students. In reading the documentaries in terms of the categories of 'at risk' or 'a risk', we might be guilty of reiterating reductive understandings and constructions of students and young people. Yet we contend that, as Badmington (2003, p. 16) points out, repetition 'can be a form of questioning: to restate is not always to reinstate'. By analysing the breadth of these televisual texts and offering one way in which they might be interpreted, we seek to understand and critique the figuration of the university student in British documentary television and to explore how constructions of the student as both 'at risk' and 'risky' function across these examples.

'Cash cows' and 'bogus students'

Dispatches: Cashing in on Degrees can be seen as beginning a trend in documentaries focused on students, in particular in terms of risk and the high cost of education. Laurie Penny, who left university with a total of £9,000 in debt, investigates the rise in tuition fees and emphasises that going forward this would be a 'drop in the ocean'. Current figures estimate that the average UK student graduates with £36,000 of debt (Bolton, 2019). However, a student featured in the 2019 documentary *Student Sex Workers* explains that they will be leaving university with just under £60,000 in debt, and this second figure appears frequently in news reporting (Fazackerley, 2017; Binns, 2019). The emphasis of *Dispatches: Cashing in on Degrees* is not on students but on the significant pay received by university bosses and the ways in which universities might be understood to be 'selling' education and exploiting students with both home and international fee statuses. International students are explicitly discussed in terms of being viewed by universities as 'cash cows'. A significant focus on the cost of education is evident in all of the documentaries examined here, but the figure of the international student shifts from one of being 'at risk' of exploitation ('cash cows') in *Dispatches: Cashing in on Degrees* to one of posing 'a risk' as they become 'bogus students' exploiting the loans system for cash in *Panorama: Student Loan Scandal*.

This shift is reflective of the ways in which, in recent years, 'students have become the latest object of fear and panic within the debate about immigration and global population mobility' (Back, 2016, p. 33). Back highlights:

> new phrases like 'bogus students' (accused of using higher learning illegitimately to gain visas) and 'backstreet colleges' (who are selling immigration and not education) are gaining currency. (Back, 2016, p. 33)

Both of these phrases feature heavily in *Panorama: Student Loan Scandal*. At the beginning of the documentary, the audience is told 'at a time when student debt has topped 100 billion pounds, we reveal how student loan scams are costing us all millions'. The narrator positions an 'us', the taxpaying non-student, as 'at risk' from 'them', the 'fraudsters' and 'bogus students'. International students are not featured in any of the other documentaries discussed here and as such their construction is limited to that of 'cash cows' and 'bogus students'. This resonates with Brooks' (2018a) findings in relation to the construction of university students in policy, where international students were mostly absent. When they did appear, a juxtaposition between the 'brightest and best' and those deemed a 'sham' emerged. In the documentaries examined here, however, there is no notion of international students as the 'brightest and best'. Their construction is almost entirely focused on financial risk. Initially, the risk posed to international students and latterly, the risk posed by them.

Dumbing down

In the majority of these documentaries, the students featured do not align with stereotypical notions of the 'ideal' university student. In Wong and Chiu's (2018, p. 8) study of lecturers' expectations of the ideal student staff expected students to be 'prepared, engaged and committed, as well as being critical, reflective and making progress'. Tomlinson (2017, p. 453) problematises this 'notion of the student as academic disciple, liberally immersed in intellectual pursuits' and suggests such a construction has always been a myth. In the first episode of *Freshers*, Anita does not know what course she has signed up for. As Cleo in *Freshers, Sex and Suspicious Parents* states, freshers' week is not about getting prepared, it 'is all about going out, that's why they created it'. Jane in *Students on the Edge* says that:

> first year was really, really fun and there were parties going on all the time [...] I basically had vodka and MDMA [drug] for breakfast

suggesting that students continue to party well beyond freshers' week. Partying is positioned as what students do, with the narrator in *Freshers* describing drinking as 'what students do best'. One student featured in *The Secret Life of Students* tells audiences there are:

> three things on everyone's mind when you come to uni, fun, action and friends, and that is all bolted together with alcohol.

Though students who are positioned as academically focused are featured, they are situated as an exception and associated with degrees such as medicine (*The Secret Life of Students*) and physics (*Freshers; Death on Campus: Our Stories; Dying for a Degree*).

Students are frequently constructed as at university to 'have a good time' and to delay their entry to adulthood, with academic studies being an unfortunate consequence of this wider 'student experience'. In *Freshers*, the narrator tells audiences that '73% admit to missing lectures because of a hangover'. The tension between academic study and partying is often emphasised. For example, Hassan in *The Secret Life of Students* misses lectures because he is too tired after a night out. He jokes 'they shouldn't have had freshers and lectures at the same time, it's not my fault they're fuckin' stupid... the university'. Abbie in *Freshers* asserts that 'you've gotta study but it's all about the partying isn't it'. In the same programme, Bailegh explains how far she is from the 'ideal student'. Visiting the bookshop she explains:

> actually, I read one book once. On holiday I read the Madeline McCann book. Maybe I can do this, maybe I can read a whole book.

The value and importance of reading is seen to be integral to students' success at university (Wong and Chiu, 2018). The notion that someone at university has only ever read a whole book once jostles uncomfortably with:

> a common-sense understanding of the student as a learner, an individual who is, above all else, dedicated to his or her studies.
>
> (Brooks 2018b, p. 501)

Media representations of students lacking intellectual merit can be linked to concerns about the lowering of academic standards within UK higher education. Certainly, a number of these documentaries imply that some of those studying are not 'academically talented'. Since the initiation of the removal of student number controls in 2013, Bekhradnia and Beech (2018, p. 28) highlight:

> there had been speculation that cash-hungry institutions might recruit more students than they had previously been allowed, in order to bolster their finances, and specifically that institutions might lower their entry demands.

The supposed growing ease of entry to higher education has led to concerns about illegitimate students who are unprepared or unfit for study. While there are significant costs to the student, each student is also entitled to a loan which is heavily subsidised by the taxpayer. In *Freshers*, Abbie says:

> coming to university wasn't just about getting a degree it was about growing up and it kind of gives you life experience doesn't it and I think that's something I needed more than a degree.

Yet in a context where it is estimated that 70% of current full-time undergraduates who take out loans will not repay them in full (Bolton, 2019), university represents a financial risk to society at large. Audiences might justifiably question whether some of the students figured in these documentaries should be at university, and whether they are there for the 'right reasons'.

In Tomlinson's (2017, p. 463) study of students' own perceptions of the student as consumer, some expressed the view that other students were 'unclear on their motivation' for study and were going to university 'by default'. This resonates with Aiden's experience in *The Secret Life of Students*. Aiden is arguably a student who is at university 'by default' and not to pursue a passion for academic study. We learn that his knowledge of his course is inaccurate, suggesting he has done little prior research. He is disappointed with the infrequency with which other students go out, stating:

> first year is about going out... just drinking so much... just enjoying yourself. But everyone takes their work so seriously here and it's kinda

shit. I thought there'd be at least like four or five who wanna go out every night. It's just such a weird situation it's just me. It's just not a uni…it just doesn't feel like a uni.

Aiden considers dropping out and his peers ask him what his options are if he does. He says 'go on the dole, grow a beard, drink frosty jacks [a high strength cider]'. Though Aiden is joking, this highlights a very real anxiety about what young people's options are should they not graduate with a degree, as well as about what a 'positive' outcome for a young person entering adulthood is. As Tanya, a single mum who appears briefly in the same series, states 'any job that's got any standing in society these days you need a degree'. Aiden and Tanya are not positioned as being at university for intellectual pursuit but because they need to be, because it is the only way to gain economic security and 'good standing' in society. The risk (of the cost to taxpayers; of the 'dumbing down' of academic content) posed by students studying for the 'wrong reasons' is here contrasted with the risk to young people of *not* going to university, the consequences of which are positioned as significant.

In light of the consumerist culture within higher education, it has been suggested that today's students seek to have a degree rather than to be learners (Molesworth et al., 2009). Brenda in *The Secret Life of Students* is one of the few black students featured in these documentaries. The absence of black students on some UK campuses is emphasised by Cleo and her friend in *Freshers, Sex and Suspicious Parents* when they approach a group of young men and say:

> we saw you guys and thought we should come and talk to you cos you're the first black people we've seen, no offence!

Unlike the students around her who have financial support from their parents, Brenda is a first-generation university student whose family does not have the economic means to subsidise her time at university. Brenda worries about dropping out and explains that:

> if I don't have a degree then I don't know what else I can do […] I don't want it to be a thing where I end up still in the same circle, still being working class, still living in a deprived area and everything. I don't want that for myself. So having a degree is really important for me because then I can get out of that, but at the moment I can't see that happening because of money.

Failure at university poses a significant risk for Brenda's future but her lack of financial resources also puts her 'at risk' of dropping out. Again, the potential impact of not having a degree is central.

Skint or flush?

Brenda, discussed in the section above, is also concerned about the significant cost of university. She is called to meetings about her attendance and does not perform as well in assessments as she would like. She finds lectures boring, posting a video on social media saying:

> what exactly am I paying for? I have seen a lot on Twitter about people and their lectures and how their lectures are so boring [...] lecturers should have a course in public speaking if you're asking me to pay 9 grand.

Here the significant financial cost of study is emphasised, as is what Brenda perceives as a disappointing return on her investment. In her failure to attend lectures, Brenda is positioned as in deficit of the skills and traits required to succeed within higher education (a commitment to study translated as the ability to endure what she deems lengthy and unstimulating lectures). Later, Brenda is unable to attend lectures due to taking on a 30 hour a week job at a retail store to pay for her accommodation. In one sense, Brenda shows significant commitment to her studies because without the job, she would have to leave university. However, with it, her ability to engage with her studies is significantly limited. Complicating her construction in the documentary further, Brenda is positioned as 'skint' (a colloquial term for having little or no money) when she needs to get a job to pay for accommodation. However, the series also emphasises one occasion when she spends £300 on beauty products and shoes, positioning her as 'flush' with money and irresponsible.

In *Freshers*, a member of staff regales the time a student complained of being in financial difficulty after having spent their loan on an expensive car, emphasising how irresponsible some students can be with their money. Yet students are not always positioned as financially irresponsible. For example, Amelia in the same series explains that she needs a job because 'my loan only just covers my accommodation', showing she has budgeted and is prepared to work. Michael, a first-generation student, has saved up for university, stating 'I see it as my responsibility, my burden'. According to Kelly et al. (2017, p. 106):

> higher education policy in the UK increasingly conceives undergraduate students as individual entrepreneurs, transacting their way through higher education, preparing themselves for high-earning success in the global field of market competition.

Student Sex Workers and *Students on the Edge* are the documentaries that most closely adhere to a construction of the student as financially savvy, though not quite in the way that higher educational policy documents do.

In *Student Sex Workers*, one student explains that they undertake sex work because they want to 'be able to earn enough money to be able to pay for [university] instead of getting a loan'. In *Students on the Edge*, a drug dealer explains his approach to finances:

> I'm a student, I'm a drug dealer. When you're a student everyone is on drugs around you and it's easy to sort of capitalise off that market.

These students are constructed as financially aware, making considered choices about their income to debt ratios.

Sugar Baby on Campus, an episode of *Students on the Edge*, begins by foregrounding that Penny has been trying to get a job but finds:

> so many jobs it's like, you need experience, but then, you need a job to get experience so it's just like, such a vicious cycle so obviously I just turned to other stuff.

Penny is shown in her accommodation which has not been well maintained and is a significant distance from campus, as she cannot afford anything closer. However, empty alcohol bottles and branded beauty products are scattered around. She complains of the house being freezing, showing the audience her goose bumps, but wears very little clothing, implying she might be lacking in 'common sense' or spending her money 'irresponsibly'. When choosing 'dates' with 'sugar daddies', she explains:

> I'd rather have a date and get food out of it rather than just go to a hotel room and have sex with them. I don't really want that because that's quite prostitution-y.

Penny is unaware of how much she will be paid by a man she is going to meet but does not mind as last time he gave her £80 worth of cocaine. Unlike many of those in *Student Sex Workers*, she is not a savvy entrepreneur:

> I don't know what I'm doing with my life [...] but I know that my student loan isn't gonna get any bigger. I doubt I'm gonna get a good job where they pay really well...so I'm just gonna carry on doing it.

Her behaviour is positioned as risky, but she sees no alternative to undertaking sex work.

There are tensions in the documentaries that reflect broader notions about whether students are 'skint' or 'flush'. In *Student Sex Workers*, one student says 'you do live very close to the breadline when you're at uni' and this documentary repeatedly emphasises the high cost of university, stating that many of those featured undertake sex work in order to pay for essentials. Yet in *Students on the Edge* a drug dealer suggests:

> there is sort of a myth surrounding students and skintness, I think people have a lot of money they just spend it on nights out and not really what they should be spending it for. I know people who say they can't afford to eat, or they have to steal food, but they're still buying drugs every week.

Max in *Freshers* exemplifies this point when he is given a budget of £50 a week by his parents on top of his loans, but jokes that this will not be enough and that he knows they will provide more, explaining that his parents:

> won't be annoyed at me as long as I don't spend it on stupid stuff and just spend it on necessities like going out at night and eating.

This arguably reflects a broader juxtaposition in the popular imagination between those who perceive students as well off and spending money irresponsibly and those who see them as 'broke' and 'on the breadline'.

Stress and vulnerability

Hayes (2009, p. 127) has argued that:

> the changed conception of a student is not as an autonomous person embarking on the pursuit of knowledge, but as a vulnerable learner.

This construction of students plays out across the documentaries examined here. The title *Students on the Edge* implies the students featured are in an extreme situation, perhaps at the fringes of 'the student experience', or more broadly 'on the edge' due to high stress levels caused by academic pressure and financial cost. In one episode about drugs taken to enhance study skills, a student tells the audience:

> some people are just naturally smart, I wasn't. I was smart but through studying rather than it being a natural ability.

The student is highly organised, is committed and seems to be performing well academically. He explicitly links his drug taking to the financial and academic pressure of attaining a degree, stating:

> there's increased pressure on education. There's increased pressure in paying £9,000 a year for university students. People want more for their money. Whether they're pushing themselves to the limit by taking smart drugs, that's one way of looking at it, but is that not because of the pressures of university?

Williams (2010, p. 178) has pointed out that in news reporting:

> the experience of attending university is presented to students as 'stressful' and it is the consumption model that is blamed by some for causing this stress.

The earlier documentaries examined here all have sections of varying lengths focusing on homesickness, students wanting to 'drop out' or being worried that they are not sufficiently academically talented to succeed. Yet these themes become much more prominent in recent documentaries where the focus shifts from a construction of students as 'party goers' to one more in line with the notion of a 'vulnerable learner', stressed and under pressure.

The confessional video diary format of *Freshers 2018: In Our Own Words* means that audiences get insight into the students' anxieties, which focus both on the social and academic side of university. One student explains 'I'm really nervous, I don't think I'm very good at making friends' and another states:

> to be honest I'm actually shitting myself because I'm scared that I'm gonna sit down and they're gonna start saying shit that I know literally nothing about.

Rue in *Student Sex Workers* has dropped out of university. She was attaining first class grades but felt the pressure to do so was overwhelming. In an episode of *Students on the Edge* focused on essay mills, from which students buy tailor made essays, a graduate who writes these essays to sell asks:

> what makes [students] feel so much pressure to succeed that they have to go and literally purchase parts of their degree? It's the system itself that is flawed. Having students that rack up 5 maybe even 6 figures of debt...essentially it requires them to succeed. They can't fail so that is why they turn to services like this.

Here, the financial and academic pressures of university coalesce. In a *Students on the Edge* episode titled Breakdown on Campus, Amy, who has a diagnosed mental health condition, reflects on her university experience, saying:

> people always say like oh it's the best years of your life blah blah you have so much fun party, party, party but they don't mention like the social pressure, there's a pressure to join teams and be part of things, you've got like you're work pressure, then your living arrangements, then your student loan and balancing money and finding a job and it's just like so difficult [...] Sometimes you just need someone else to care for you.

Amy balances paid work with study, party-going and other social activities and achieves first class grades. Yet she feels like 'no one listens, no one tries' when it comes to her mental health. We are informed mid-episode that Amy attempted suicide. In *Students on the Edge*, a construction of the student as a 'party goer' extending their period of youth shifts towards a more complicated construction of the student as 'under pressure', expected to achieve, to earn, to enjoy themselves and to be an independent adult caring for themselves all at once.

Institutional failures

Concerns about universities are evident in most of the documentaries examined here. These concerns focus on universities' recruitment practices (aggressively recruiting students, failing to detect 'bogus students', being more concerned with 'bums on seats' than standards), the broader structural issue of the cost of university to students and society at large and, finally, the issue of universities failing to safeguard their students. Institutional and structural failure comes to the fore in the 2019 documentary *The Warwick Uni Rape Chat Scandal*, which examines a high-profile case relating to rape threats sent in a Whatsapp group in 2018. The documentary's focus is on the university's mishandling of the case and failure to support the students at whom the rape threats were directed. However, it is notable that in this documentary the male students involved are referred to consistently as men, emphasising their adult status, and not as 'lads' or 'boys' as they often are in the earlier documentaries. This represents a shift from positioning sex and sexuality in terms of 'fun', 'experimentation' and students placing themselves 'at risk' (of sexually transmitted infections, of regret after a 'one night stand' or what one student in *The Secret Life of Students* eloquently calls a 'smash and dash') to an emphasis on sexual assault and misconduct which form the focus of later documentaries including *Students on the Edge* and *The Warwick Uni Rape Chat Scandal*.

The underlying argument made in *The Warwick Uni Rape Chat Scandal* is that the university was more concerned with its reputation than safeguarding students. Student Anna explains:

> honestly at the start of this I really did have a lot of trust in my university that they'd be able to deal with it properly and that was broken down at every single point.

The university is positioned as failing to adequately manage risk towards its students. The theme of the university as posing a risk to students is also evident in *Freshers 2018: In Our Own Words*, though in quite a different way, when Beckett, a transgender student, becomes extremely distressed at having their birthname printed on their student ID card rather than their chosen name. At the end of this documentary, there is a note stating that the university apologises and made an error, and that students could have any name they chose on their ID card. Ella in *Student Sex Workers* explains how she was bullied by peers at her university. She felt the university failed to support her or provide a safe environment, going on to complete her degree via a distance learning institution. In all of these examples, the university is positioned as failing to meet the individual needs of students.

The risk that university can pose to students is especially evident in documentaries focused on student suicide. *Death on Campus: Our Stories* focuses on three students and emphasises the academic, financial and personal pressures they faced. It features friends and families of the deceased as well as social media footage of those who died. *Death on Campus: Our Stories* and *Students on the Edge* both place an emphasis on the importance of students who are having suicidal thoughts 'reaching out' and speaking to others. We are told via writing on the screen in *Death on Campus: Our Stories* that 'nearly half of students with a mental health condition do not disclose it to their university', perhaps implying that in failing to disclose, students have failed to adequately protect themselves, or that students are reluctant to disclose this information for fear of negative consequences. Yet as student suicide has become a significant concern in recent years, universities have come under scrutiny for a lack of support for students (Morris, 2019; Shackle, 2019).

Death on Campus: Our Stories is careful not to criticise the universities involved, but the underlying argument seems to be that the high cost, high pressure environments of UK universities are at least partially responsible for these young people's deaths. *Dying for a Degree* is much more explicit in its critique. It focuses on 'one family's fight for answers after their daughter took her own life' at the University of Bristol, where there have been a high number of suicides in recent years. The parents of Natasha, who died by suicide at the university, are shocked to discover they have been sent a Certificate of Higher Education for her year one credits and insulted by the university's offer of a plaque in the walled garden, questioning 'have they got a plaque for every dead student? They'd need a big wall'. Her parents state 'the people who were meant to look after her, whatever they did, tended to make matters worse not better'. They engage a legal team to try to prevent other deaths, seeking systemic 'change on the national stage'. Natasha's flatmate Luke says that 'everyone's petrified coming to university' and talks about the 'the stress of first year', where you have this 'ridiculous pressure put upon you immediately'. In contrast to earlier representations, students are constructed as highly academic. Stress, a 'toxic' environment and pressure 'to perform academically' when surrounded by people who were the 'smartest' in their schools are all emphasised. The student is also constructed as vulnerable, stressed, under pressure and uncared for by an institution that has failed to support them. However, this construction jostles with the construction, in both *Dying for a Degree* and *The Warwick Uni Rape Chat Scandal*, of students as capable of protest. In both of these documentaries, students can be seen as engaging in active protest about their universities, with *Dying for a Degree* featuring students chanting 'people not profit'. Natasha's parents worry that at the inquest into their daughter's death, their evidence will be 'glossed over by some sort of PR machine', emphasising again the construction of the university as concerned predominantly with financial gain. Though the construction of the student seems to shift in these documentaries, that of the university as mainly concerned with income remains consistent throughout them all.

Conclusion

In a context of shifting understandings about university students in Britain and when the expansion, cost, 'worth' and 'value' of higher education are all under scrutiny, this chapter has analysed how documentary television makes prominent a range of socio-cultural concerns about both students and universities. The documentaries examined here are active in constituting and perpetuating particular constructions of the student, but the experience of the university student is represented as fairly homogeneous. Initially, as one where party-going is the norm and study is an unfortunate consequence of being a student. Later, one where students are under pressure to do it all: expected to achieve academically, to work for an income, to take part in activities and, of course, to party – footage or images of 'nights out' are featured in almost all of the documentaries.

The trend in documentaries focused on university students identified here begins in 2011 and is coincident with the announcement of an increase in tuition fees from 2012. All of the documentaries feature discussion of the cost of higher education in some form. This ranges from the financial risk students pose in terms of being a 'burden on the taxpayer' to the risks students can experience, with a focus on the concomitant pressures of a high cost education becoming ever more apparent in the later documentaries. Though we argue that all of these documentaries are notable for their figuration of the higher education student as 'at risk' or 'a risk', the ways in which students are constructed as 'risky' shifts and is, at times, complex and contradictory. The earlier documentaries tend to construct students in terms of more 'traditional' risks associated with the university student including binge drinking, promiscuity and a lack of life skills. The later documentaries focus on standards and the academic integrity of institutions and students themselves as well as the figuration of the student as vulnerable, under pressure, at 'at risk' of breakdown, suicide and assault. As such, we have argued here that documentary television can be understood to reflect, inform, contribute to and make sense of broader shifting constructions of the British university student in recent years.

Some things remain consistent, with all students featured in these documentaries aged between 18 and 21. As such, a range of students suffer erasure and are notable only by their absence, with no representation of part-time, distance or mature students in any of these documentaries. There is some, but scarce, representation of students with caring responsibilities, international students or those declaring disabilities. Arguably, the representation and construction of the university student in these documentaries is based on a narrow understanding of what 'the student experience' is. Sabri (2011, p. 658) examines the normative notion of 'the student experience' and concludes that its 'sacralisation' in the higher education sector has led to the obscuration of the experiences of an 'ethnically and socio-economically highly diverse body of students' and, furthermore, obscured differences between institutions. Most of the documentaries examined here can be seen to do the same. As such, the analysis of the construction of the university student in British documentary television offered here has emphasised the ways in which media representations can both serve to highlight and to evade the complex lived realities of university students.

References

Back, L. (2016). *Academic diary: Or why higher education still matters.* London: Goldsmiths Press.

Badmington, N. (2003). Theorizing posthumanism. *Cultural Critique* 52:1, 10–27. doi:10.1353/cul.2003.0017

Bekhradnia, B. and Beech, D. (2018). *Demand for higher education to 2030.* Retrieved from https://www.hepi.ac.uk/2018/03/15/demand-higher-education-2030/

Binns, K. (2019). University fees: My daughter's student debt will be triple my son's. *The Times.* Retrieved from https://www.thetimes.co.uk/article/university-fees-my-daughters-student-debt-will-be-triple-my-sons-xbmn35wp7#

Bolton, P. (2019). *Student loan statistics.* Retrieved from https://researchbriefings.parliament.uk/ResearchBriefing/Summary/SN01079

Brooks, R. (2018a). The construction of higher education students in English policy documents. *British Journal of Sociology of Education* 39:6, 745–761. doi:10.1080/01425692.2017.1406339

Brooks, R. (2018b). Understanding the higher education student in Europe: A comparative analysis. *Compare: A Journal of Comparative and International Education* 48:4, 500–517. doi:10.1080/03057925.2017.1318047

Department for Business, Innovation and Skills (2016). *Success as a knowledge economy: Teaching excellence, social mobility and student choice.* Retrieved from https://www.gov.uk/government/uploads/system/uploads/attachment_data/file/523396/bis-16-265-success-as-a-knowledge-economy.pdf

Dovey, J. (2000). *Freak show: First-person media and factual television.* London: Pluto Press.

Fazackerley, A. (2017). Grace is 25. Her student debt: £69,000. *The Guardian.* Retrieved from https://www.theguardian.com/education/2017/jul/11/student-debt-raduates-tuition-fees

Hayes, D. (2009). Academic freedom and the diminished subject. *British Journal of Educational Studies* 57:2, 127–145. doi:10.1111/j.1467-8527.2009.00432.x

Kelly, P. (2000). Youth as an artefact of expertise: Problematizing the practice of youth studies in an age of uncertainty. *Journal of Youth Studies* 3:3, 301–315. doi:10.1080/713684381

Kelly, P., Fair. N. and Evans, C. (2017). The engaged student ideal in UK higher education policy. *Higher Education Policy* 30:1, 105–122. doi:10.1057/s41307-016-0033-5

Kemshall, H. (2009). Risk, social policy and young people. In: J. Wood, and J. Hine (Eds.) *Work with young people* (pp.154–162). London: Sage.

Livingstone, S. (1998). *Making sense of television: The psychology of audience interpretation* (2nd ed.) London: Routledge.

Molesworth, M., Nixon, E. and Scullion, R. (2009). Having, being and higher education: The marketization of the university and the transformation of the student into consumer. *Teaching in Higher Education* 14:3, 277–287. doi:10.1080/13562510902898841

Morris, S. (2019). She went through torment: Parents criticise Bristol over student suicide. *The Guardian*. Retrieved from https://www.theguardian.com/education/2019/may/16/she-went-through-torment-parents-criticise-bristol-university-over-student-suicide

Prensky, M. (2001). Digital natives, digital immigrants: Part 1. *On the Horizon* 9:5, 1–6. doi:10.1108/10748120110424816

Roberts, L. (2014). The secret life of students isn't an accurate portrayal of student life. *The Guardian*. Retrieved from https://www.theguardian.com/education/2014/jul/18/tv-shows-secret-life-students-use-same-stereotypes

Sabri, D. (2011). What's wrong with 'the student experience'? *Discourse: Studies in the Cultural Politics of Education* 32:5, 657–667. doi:10.1080/01596306.2011.620750

Shackle, S. (2019). The way universities are run is making us ill: Inside the student mental health crisis. *The Guardian*. Retrieved from https://www.theguardian.com/society/2019/sep/27/anxiety-mental-breakdowns-depression-uk-students

Tomlinson, M. (2017). Student perceptions of themselves as 'consumers' of higher education. *British Journal of Sociology of Education* 38:4, 450–467. doi:10.1080/01425692.2015.1113856

Tyler, I. (2008). Chav mum chav scum: Class disgust in contemporary Britain. *Feminist Media Studies* 8:1, 17–34. doi:10.1080/14680770701824779

Williams, J. (2010). Constructing consumption: What media representations reveal about today's students. In M. Molesworth., R. Scullion, and E. Nixon (eds.), *The marketisation of higher education and the student as consumer* (pp. 170–182). Abingdon: Routledge.

Wong, B. and Chiu, Y. (2018). University lecturers' construction of the 'ideal' undergraduate student. *Journal of Further and Higher Education* 44:1, 54–68. doi:10.1080/0309877X.2018.1504010

Chapter 11

Constructing students as family members

Contestations in media and policy representations across Europe

Anu Lainio and Rachel Brooks

Introduction

Many scholars have observed that, within countries of the Global North, parents have become increasingly involved in the decisions their children take about higher education, and their subsequent lives while at university (e.g. Lamprianou et al., 2019; Symeou et al., 2018; West & Lewis, 2017). However, such studies have tended to be carried out in single (and often Anglophone) nations. We thus know relatively little about how such involvement is patterned cross-nationally. An important exception to this is Antonucci's (2016) research, which focused on three countries (England, Italy and Sweden). On the basis of her data, she argues that, across Europe, there has been a shift in welfare provision from the state to the family, which has had the consequence of placing students in a position of 'semi-dependence' (at least economically) in relation to their families. However, her analysis focuses largely on structural factors, such as the mechanisms put in place by the state to fund higher education; cultural differences between countries, and how these might impact family relationships during higher education are largely omitted from her discussion.

In this chapter, we explore the ways in which students are constructed as family members within newspaper articles and the narratives of a range of policy actors. These two sources have been chosen because of their often-important contributions to establishing the parameters of public debate and the substantive content of dominant discourses. To broaden the focus from single-nation, Anglophone studies, we draw on data from five European nations (Denmark, England, Germany, Ireland and Spain), teasing out important similarities and differences. In explaining the patterns, we identify cultural and structural influences and contend that a complex combination of both underpins the constructions of student–family relationships in Europe.

Background

Two bodies of work provide an important background to the discussion that follows. The first comprises various comparative studies that explore family ties across Europe. At the core of these is the debate over whether structural or cultural factors are more important in shaping family relationships. The second body of literature focuses on different types of family support and involvement, and the consequences of these for students' experiences. With these two bodies of literature, we aim to establish a framework to explore and compare student–family relationships in our cross-national study. Another significant branch of research addressing student–family relationships highlights the influence of socio-economic status (e.g. Bathmaker et al., 2016). While we acknowledge the importance of such analyses, we have excluded them from our analysis, as we would not be able to justice to them within the available space.

Comparative studies of the family

There is a great deal of comparative research that seeks to categorise European countries into clusters based on perceived similarities and differences in regard to family relations. Reher (1998) argued, on the basis of measuring two key variables (age at which children left the parental home, and how care for the elderly was organised), that there were two main types of family tie – weak and strong. According to his categorisation, weak family ties were dominant in the centre and north of Europe (Scandinavia, UK, the Low Countries, much of Germany and Austria), whereas strong family ties were characteristic of the Mediterranean region. Even though he acknowledges that this divide is not exhaustive and regional differences occur, he contends that such exceptions do 'not negate the existence of more general regularities affecting large areas of Europe' (Reher, 1998, p. 204) – which he explains in terms of cultural and historical factors. Moreover, while he recognises that family structures are not static and change over time, he does not believe that a process of overall convergence is taking place in which economic and social changes will come to override cultural and historical traditions. Instead, he argues that convergence might happen with respect to various 'external indicators of family life' (p. 221) (such as demographics, improvement of social welfare and women entering working life) but, due to the nature of 'path-dependency' in the development of societies, weak and strong family systems will remain. Even though Reher's work initially faced much criticism, it has become an influential text upon which many other scholars have built. Mönkediek and Bras (2014), for example, have revisited Reher's model, arguing that the divide between weak and strong family ties becomes more complex when different parameters are introduced to measure such ties. They show that family regimes can be 'regarded as a construct of multiple dimensions of which one dimension may be classified as weak while the other can be strong at the same time', thus highlighting the complexity of geographical categorisation (Mönkediek & Bras, 2014, p. 235).

Focusing on youth policies within Europe, Chevalier (2016, 2018) argues that much comparative research in this area tends to focus on specific welfare measures – and thus commonly overlooks the influence of cultural and historical factors in the formation of social policy and, particularly, assumptions about the appropriate role for the family. Our aim here is not to engage with debates regarding the origins of social policies or explain Chevalier's theoretical model in detail, but rather to highlight the usefulness of his work in examining student–family relationships across European countries. Of particular relevance is his distinction between familialised and individualised citizenship. The former is, he maintains, characteristic of continental European countries and has its roots in the Bismarckian (corporatist) welfare state, and in the 'principle of subsidiarity'[1], that is the assumption that responsibility for less independent individuals, for example children and elders, must reside primarily with the family, and not the state, whenever possible (Chevalier, 2018). This 'familialisation of social rights' means, for example, that parents are legally responsible for supporting their children financially while they are in education (Chevalier, 2018, p. 307). Indeed, student support is seen as part of family policy; student grants and loans are dependent on parental income as it is viewed as the parents' duty to take care of their children (Chevalier, 2018, p. 307). In contrast, 'individualised citizenship' is prevalent in Nordic and English-speaking countries and, Chevalier (2016) asserts, can be traced back to their Protestant social traditions. Instead of viewing young people as dependent children, this understanding of citizenship positions them as social citizens with their own rights, and parents have no legal obligation to support them after compulsory schooling or upper-secondary education (ibid.). Moreover, in countries with individualised citizenship regimes, young people are able to claim their rights directly – not through their families – and student support systems tend to be universal, and based on grants and/or loans that are not dependent on parental income (ibid.).

Other scholars have placed emphasis more on material and structural factors in explaining student–family relationships than the cultural and religious traditions that are foregrounded in Chevalier's analysis. For example, Moreno (2012) and Antonucci (2016) are both critical of the 'individualisation thesis' (Beck, 1992), propounded by many youth scholars, for over-emphasising the choices available to young people in contemporary society, and neglecting structural and material conditions. Antonucci (2016) argues that the role of family in providing welfare to students has gained more importance across Europe as a result of austerity policies and the associated decline in the role of the state and labour market. As discussed previously, this kind of reliance on family sources is traditionally seen as a characteristic of southern European countries. Thus, although Antonucci recognises some enduring differences in the welfare mixes that underpin student support systems, she suggests that we are witnessing a process of 'southern Europeanisation' of policies for young people. We return to these debates below.

Different types of family support and involvement

The second body of literature focuses more specifically on different types of parental involvement and their impact on students' experiences. One group of studies explores which types of involvement are seen as beneficial and which more harmful for students. For example, Williams (2011) has argued that in English newspapers students are represented as emotionally and financially dependent on their parents due to high tuition fees which may result in the infantilisation of students. Similarly, in the context of the US, Zaloom (2019) maintains that the large debt students and families are forced to take on creates intergenerational dependencies, rather than enabling students to establish independent lives of their own. Symeou et al. (2018) suggest that when families are required to make substantial financial contributions, parents do not view their children's university experience as a time for self-discovery and growth, but rather as an investment in their future. Other researchers have focused on the psychological effects of family involvement, and its influence on students' independence from or dependence on their families. For example, Bradley-Geist and Olson-Buchanan (2014) found in their study of college students that parental involvement was generally associated with a range of positive outcomes. However, some forms of involvement were related to more negative consequences, such as lower levels of self-efficacy. This type of involvement is often referred to as 'over-parenting' or 'helicopter parenting', where parents 'apply overly involved and developmentally inappropriate tactics to their children' (Segrin et al., 2012, p. 237). In the context of higher education, this type of behaviour could include visiting university, interacting with academic staff and helping with assignments (Lamprianou et al., 2019). Other studies have also shown the negative impact of helicopter parenting on students' academic performance, social relations and adjustment to university life (Schiffrin et al., 2014). Interestingly, however, Lamprianou et al. (2019) suggest that students' reactions to parental involvement are mainly positive, and that emotional and financial supports are particularly welcome.

Research methods

The data we draw on in this chapter were collected as part of a European Research Council-funded project, which explores conceptualisations of students across and within various European countries. In each country, we examined the perspectives of the media, policy actors, higher education staff (and their institutions) and undergraduate students. In this chapter, we focus specifically on the ways in which students are understood in the media and by those involved in making, or seeking to influence, higher education policy, drawing on data from Denmark, England, Germany, Ireland and Spain[2]. The countries in the study were chosen to provide diversity in terms of welfare regime and mechanisms for funding higher education (see Table 11.1 for details).

Table 11.1 Characteristics of the countries involved in the research

Country	Welfare regime[3]	Tuition fees for full-time undergraduates in public universities (2018/2019)	Student support for full-time undergraduates (2018/2019) – € per annum[4]
Denmark	Social democratic	No tuition fees	c.89 per cent receive needs-based grants (average of €9810); loans available to those entitled to state grant
England	Liberal	Fees typically €9998 per year, paid by all students	No grants; income-contingent loans available to all for tuition[5]; needs-based loan for maintenance costs
Germany	Corporatist	No tuition fees; in 10 Länder, small administrative fee of up to €70 paid	c.22 per cent of students receive need-based grants (average of €5568 – includes integrated loan)
Ireland	Catholic corporatist	'Student contribution' of €3000 per year paid by c.57 per cent of students	c.43 per cent of students receive need-based grants (average of €4600); no loans available
Spain	Mediterranean/ sub-protective	Tuition fees paid by c.70 per cent of students; average amount of €1081 per year	c.28 per cent of students receive need-based grants (average of €2166); no loans available

Table 11.2 Newspapers included in the media sample

Country	Newspapers
Denmark	Politiken, BT
England	The Guardian, The Daily Mail
Germany	Süddeutche Zeitung, Die Welt
Ireland	The Irish Times, The Irish Independent
Spain	El País, ABC

The media data comprise newspaper articles from two national newspapers (see Table 11.2), and selected through purposive sampling (Berg & Lune, 2012). Sampling was based on the following criteria and steps: (1) only national (not regional) newspapers were included; (2) the newspaper was available through an online database or archive; (3) two different newspapers from each country were sampled: either 'a tabloid' and 'a quality'[6] newspaper or two 'quality' papers that differ in terms of political alignment. The data consist of 1159 articles that were gathered from the years 2014–2016 from three different online databases[7] by using relevant search terms (students, higher education, university) in each national context. The data were coded and analysed by using qualitative content analysis (Hsieh & Shannon, 2005). In the first stage of the analysis, all references to students and family were coded under the label 'students as family members'. In the second stage, the material under this label was analysed in a more detailed manner, exploring the ways in which students were represented in relation to family. Google Translate was used, where necessary, in the first stage of the analysis and language assistants in the second stage.

Regarding the data collected from policy actors, we interviewed a civil servant or minister responsible for higher education policy, and representatives of the following organisations: the national body representing higher education leaders; a national organisation of graduate employers (or employers in general); and the national union representing higher education students[8]. The interviews were conducted in English, audio-recorded and fully transcribed before being uploaded to NVivo for analysis. All interviewees were asked a series of open-ended questions about how they understood students, before moving on to ask them about specific constructions, such as whether they saw students as consumers, political actors and/or future workers. While we did not ask specifically about students as family members, this was a theme that was often raised spontaneously, and which came to constitute an important focus of our analysis.

Dominant constructions with media and policy

Students as integral family members: Spain and Ireland

In Spain and Ireland, students were constructed – in both the policy interviews and newspaper articles – as integral members of the family. In the two countries, various types of family involvement in the lives of students were discussed. In Ireland, this included being closely involved in decision-making about which course to apply for and institution to attend, and the provision of financial and practical support (including accommodation) during the student's course of study. The following quotations are illustrative:

> students ... mostly unlike the UK, they stay close to home, so there's ... for a lot of them they are still living at home, and still being expected to be home for you know dinner at 6pm and that sort of stuff.
> (Irish HE leaders' organisation representative)

> I meet a lot of parents at open days here at UCC [University College Cork] and the majority seem to do a very good job in gathering all of the relevant information so they can make an informed decision and give good advice to their kids.
> (Irish Independent, 16.1.2016)

A study by the Irish League of Credit Unions found that nine out of 10 parents support their child through third-level education, contributing on average EUR 421 a month.

(Irish Times, 6.6.2015)

Similar types of involvement were outlined in the Spanish data. Indeed, the interviewee from the Spanish employers' organisation asserted that families were now so involved in higher education decision-making that universities tended to address them, rather than the prospective students, in their marketing activities. Moreover, reflecting on this change, she contended that universities tended to 'treat them [students] more as still little children'.

While similar themes were evident in the data from Ireland and Spain, the positioning of students as family members appeared stronger in the latter, especially in the newspaper articles. Here, and unlike the other countries in our sample, the family was understood as constituting the basic unit of society, and students were viewed as part of this unit, rather than a distinct group in their own right. This message is conveyed in the following extracts, which highlight how expenses and savings in education are relevant to *families* rather than *students*:

The universities, with one and a half million students, are financed mainly with public funds from the autonomous communities, along with the fees paid by families, which have skyrocketed in the last three years in some regions.

(El País, 24.2.2015)

Faced with criticism that warns of a rise in the cost of studies, Gomendio [Secretary of State for Education] asserted that the measure is, in turn, a saving for families.

(ABC 30.1.2015)

Family involvement was not always evaluated in the same way across the two countries, or by the different stakeholders in our sample. In Ireland, for example, parents were sometimes seen by policymakers as having too much influence on their children's choices, and treating them in an over-protective way more generally:

I suspect that ... politicians and large sections of Irish society .... still see them as sort of barely grown-up children. .... And they still need to be herded around and looked after to the n'th degree, which is understandable, and Irish mothers are notorious ... for mothering their children to death, you know, as opposed to saying, right you're off, here's your handkerchief, wipe your own nose

(Irish HE leaders' organisation representative)

They were also contrasted with German students, who were held to be more independent than their Irish counterparts and less reliant on others. Within the Irish media, similar critiques were made about parents' 'over-protective-ness'; this was believed to have a negative impact on students' independence and emotional strength:

> In some cases, parents will contact tutors or lecturers (so much easier now with email) with requests for extensions or pleas of mitigating circumstances. That is beyond embarrassing: if a student cannot manage to navigate such territory themselves, they are failing the basic third-level test of independence…intrusive parents are compounding the problem by not knowing the difference between support and interference.
>
> (Irish Times, 30.1.2016)

Within Spain, there was less convergence between the perspectives of the policy actors and those evident in the media. Several of the policy interviewees, for example, were critical of what they perceived to be the dependence of Spanish students on their families and, reflecting the data from Ireland discussed above, contrasted their dependence with what they saw as the more independent nature of students in other European countries such as Germany:

> … in most cases they are financed by their parents, I mean in some cases, these young people work, but I wouldn't say, my perception is not that this is the majority at all. Unlike I mean other countries are different. …. Because maybe a person that works in another country, in Germany for instance, and is very self-aware of how much it cost to go to university, how much he has to work to afford to study, maybe he's more self-aware of everything, and he's more focused at the end of the day.
>
> (Spanish HE leaders' organisation representative)

Such differences were explained in terms of students' engagement in paid work, and their living arrangements. Spanish students' dependence was thus seen as a consequence of their lower propensity to work alongside their studies, and their assumed preference for living with their parents rather than alone or in dedicated student accommodation.

> here it's not like that at all, first because if you can study in your town or in your city, you do it. And … it's not only the living, you are not supposed to work, if your parents can afford it, you don't work
>
> (Spanish HE leaders' organisation representative)

In these narratives, there is little mention of the impact of national policies or funding arrangements impacting on students' decisions about how to live their lives. In contrast, the Spanish media tended to take a more sympathetic view of familial dependence, typically highlighting the consequences of it for the students and their choices:

> Ainhoa Serrano, a 24-year-old from Madrid, changed from her Tourism degree to vocational social work training when her parents lost their jobs. 'I tried to get to work to pay my tuition and my expenses, but it didn't work out, the studies cost me 700 euros a year, at home we are four and now only my father receives the subsidy.'
>
> (El País, 17.2.2014)

Students as independent actors: Denmark

In contrast to the constructions evident in Spain and Ireland, in Denmark, students were commonly understood as *independent actors*. For example, the policy interviewees pointed to the prevalence of Danish students living alone or with friends, which were linked to ideas about independence and autonomy. Similar assumptions were evident in the media, too. There were relatively few references to students' families within the newspaper articles, and the link between students and parents was typically problematised rather than celebrated, thus emphasising the independent status of students. Moreover, the Danish newspapers differed from those in the other countries by giving more space and weight to the views of individual students, which also underlines their societal positioning as independent actors.

Although independence was generally discussed in a positive manner, this was not true in all cases. Indeed, the interviewee from the Danish employers' organisation claimed that students' learning would be better if they did not have such independent lives, and instead mixed more – socially as well as academically – with other students:

> I think that too much other stuff is taking up their time. I think that ... it's not that they, it's not that I think that they should be home and studying more, I wish they were together with other students more. I wish they were in a learning environment ... much more of their time.

However, and in contrast to some of the assumptions in the quotation above, the media also positioned students as becoming more dependent on their families. Various newspaper articles linked this increased dependency on family to recent reforms. It is claimed that as a result of the 'Study Progress' reforms (which penalise students if they do not complete their studies within a specific period of time), students have less time during their degree to engage in paid work and have thus become more dependent on their parents for financial support. As the following quotations demonstrate, the reforms are seen as problematic not only in terms of students becoming financially dependent on their parents but because of the assumed consequences for social mobility:

When the possibility of having a student job is worsened, it will really matter if you have parents who have the opportunity to help you financially. And it is clear that it will have an effect on your ability to complete a college education if your parents do not have the opportunity to help financially

(BT 14.5.2015)

… the requirement for faster completion [of degree programmes] will be at the expense of social mobility, as it is students from low-education and income families that spend the longest time under the current regulatory framework.

(Politiken 28.3.2015)

Thus, while students were portrayed as significantly more independent than their peers in the other nations, various threats to this independence were also discussed.

Students in position of ambivalence: Germany and England

As we have mentioned above, interviewees in both Ireland and Spain believed that German students were much less reliant on their families than their Irish and Spanish counterparts. However, our analysis revealed a less clear view of student–family relationships in Germany – and also in England – than that suggested in the Irish and Spanish narratives. Indeed, a third, more ambivalent position can be identified in the data from Germany and England. Here, students were typically not discussed as independent (as evident in Denmark), but neither were they seen as an integral part of their families (in the ways outlined in the Irish and Spanish newspaper articles and policy narratives). This ambivalent position is a mixture of both dependence and independence, and articulated rather differently in the two countries, as the following analysis demonstrates.

The newspaper articles in both countries highlighted students' financial dependency on their parents:

87 percent of students are financially supported by their parents, parent support is the largest and most important pillar of student funding, even before the part-time job…

(Süddeutche Zeitung, 30.1.2016)

The bank of mum and dad is feeling the strain as parents try to help their children avoid crippling debts by the age of 21.

(Daily Mail, 12.10.2016)

However, whereas in Germany the financial support from parents is articulated more as a fact, in the English newspapers there is a broader discussion of financial support and its implications. For example, some articles focus on the means-tested nature of student support, and question the expected contribution from parents:

> How much parents earn is taken into account when students apply for maintenance loans and grants – but some say the system is unfair.
>
> (Guardian 30.3.2015)

Others assert that students' financial dependence on their families has extended beyond their parents to the extended family – largely because of high tuition fees – and inter-generational influences are noted:

> Today, many of Britain's 11.8 million grandparents said they have paid, or are planning to pay, £4,000 towards the cost of each of their grandchild's university education.
>
> (Daily Mail 20.8.2014)

Other types of family involvement were also evident in the texts from both countries. For example, parents were portrayed as closely involved in decisions about higher education. In England, choices about both course and institution were commonly constructed, within the newspaper articles, as taken by family units together:

> But we must ensure this exercise [Teaching Excellence Framework] is not an additional burden for those teaching in our universities and that it provides useful information for students, parents, and employers.
>
> (Guardian, 6.11.2015)

> Parents who wish they knew more about university; How can you help your student child make good choices if you didn't go to university yourself?
>
> (Guardian, 29.10.2014)

Similar narratives emerged from the policy actors from England and Germany, who asserted that that there was now increased pressure from parents on children to go on to higher education, as it had become a more normalised transition (as a result of massification), and to work hard while there, because of fears of unemployment. In Die Welt this kind of parental involvement was not necessarily viewed negatively, as parents were seen as having the potential to guide their children towards 'wise' decisions. However, in Süddeutche Zeitung, it was claimed that parents had become more involved in decision-making because of the younger age of students, which had then, in turn, affected the independence of their children:

> From the Turbo-Abitur to the university – many freshers are only 17 or 18 years old … 'Parents@Uni' is the information event at the University

of Düsseldorf, which sounds like youthful Twitter jargon, but is aimed primarily at the parents... Once [university] enrolment was a declaration of independence out of the nursery, into the wild life. Now, the university no longer seems to be the springboard to adulthood, rather the extension of childhood.

(Süddeutche Zeitung, 2.6.2014)

These narratives of increased parental involvement were tempered, however, by assertions about the independence of students. In Germany, the policy actors argued that the 'typical' student profile of being 'young, male, white, living with their parents' is outdated, and there has been an increase in the number of mature students who are less likely to live with their parents – with implications for ideas about independence and autonomy. In England, higher education was seen as offering an important space in which independence could be obtained. The quotation below is from a civil servant working on higher education policy:

I think that the higher education period is one where people, it can be massively transformational for people, and it's a time when they learn different world views, realise that you know the way their parents and their home handled things isn't necessarily the way that everyone does! …. I don't think anyone would go to university simply for the social experience. But I think the, the sort of, the getting away from home and the social experience is actually a really … it comes a big second [after the learning].

Thus, despite the relatively large number of English students living in the parental home during their studies (currently around 25%) (Donnelly & Gamsu, 2018), in this extract we can see the symbolic importance, for some who work in the higher education sector, of students moving into more independent accommodation, and the impact this is thought to have on their status as adults, free from familial influence.

Discussion

In the analysis above, we are clearly focusing on only *constructions* of students – within newspaper articles and the narratives of policy actors. Nevertheless, such conceptualisations are important as they can inform how we understand the world around us and, more specifically, how we think about the relationship between students and their families, and what can reasonably be asked of parents when their children embark upon higher education. They also raise interesting questions about why we see differences between countries – despite policies such as those associated with the European Higher Education Area to increase convergence between national systems of higher education within Europe, and the widely-documented spread of neo-liberal norms across the Global North. In this part of the chapter, we discuss some of the patterns in our data in light of the literature presented above, to explore possible reasons for enduring differences by nation-state and raise a number of questions about various assertions made in the wider body of scholarship.

First, in relation to the *type* of family involvement discussed in the newspaper articles and policy narratives, it is notable that a relatively wide range of involvement is explored. Typically, both sources tend to mention the provision of financial support – and, to a lesser extent, accommodation – by families. However, there are interesting differences in how various types of involvement are perceived. Whereas in Ireland the newspaper articles and policy narratives criticise parents for too intrusive family involvement, reflecting the wider literature discussed above about 'helicopter parenting', in Spain the critical accounts of dependent students by the policy actors are not articulated in relation to parents' intrusive actions but the perceived immaturity of students. In Germany, increased parental involvement is linked to demographics – the younger age of students – yet still loaded with both positive and negative associations. In this regard, the narratives in the English data are different as no criticism is targeted towards students or parents. Instead, questions are asked about how all parents could become more involved in decision-making irrespective of their own educational background. In part, this may be related to the funding arrangements for higher education in England, where the viability of the sector relies on young people continuing to want to progress to higher education, and their families supporting this decision. Furthermore, the narratives across the countries echo the literature on the effects of family involvement, in that it is seen to lead to positive outcomes (e.g. better choices). Nevertheless, our data also reflect what Symeou et al. (2018) see as a shift in parental perspectives – from higher education being viewed as a time for personal growth and self-discovery to increasingly an investment for the future.

Second, our data speak to the various studies that have explored differences in family ties by nation. As we noted above, much of the literature tends to draw a sharp contrast between family practices in northern Europe and those observed in the Mediterranean region. Reher (1998), for example, has suggested that strong family ties tend to characterise relationships in the latter but not in the former. Our data raise some questions about this, with respect to discourses about higher education students, at least. While Reher's thesis would suggest that practices in Ireland and Spain would be likely to differ significantly – because of cultural and social differences associated with their particular geographical location (in northern and southern Europe, respectively) – our data, outlined in the preceding section, have indicated some strong commonalities in relation to how higher education students are viewed by the media and policy actors in these two countries. Indeed, in both nations, students are conceived of as close family members, and the family, rather than the individual, understood as the key unit upon which society is based. Interestingly however, Reher (1998, p. 214) points out that Catholic countries, especially Ireland, in northern Europe diverge from the prevailing 'weak' family patterns characteristic of that region, thus fitting poorly with the north–south comparison. Considering Ireland as an exception in this way would explain the closeness of Ireland and Spain in our data. Thus, while Ireland and Spain differ quite considerably in their geographical positioning within Europe, the similarities evident in our data may be explained, at least to some extent, by their common religious heritage.

The differences between countries, identified in our data, appear also to be associated with the ways in which higher education and higher education students are funded in the various nations (see Table 11.1). Spain, Ireland, Germany and England, where students were constructed, at least to some extent, as family members, differ significantly from Denmark in their fee regime and student support system. While tuition remains free to Danish and German higher education students (studying in their home country) and fees are payable in the other three countries (although in Ireland it is called a student contribution), Denmark is the only country where grants are available to nearly all students, and it is the student's income rather than their parents' that is used to assess eligibility for student support (all students are eligible for a state grant, unless their income exceeds a defined amount). Hence, there are no implicit expectations about familial support. The construction of students as independent actors by the Danish newspapers and policy influencers could then be explained by Chevalier's (2016, 2018) notion of 'individualised social citizenship' in which no expectation of familial support is made for students in higher education.

In Spain and Ireland, fees are means-tested and so not payable by all students. Nevertheless, around 70% of students pay fees in Spain (of, on average, €1081 per year) while in Ireland the comparable figure is 57% (paying the annual student contribution of €3000) (see Table 11.1). The means-tested nature of this fee, and the assumption that, where payable, it will be covered by the family, as well as the family income-dependent grant in both countries, underlines the significance of family as a source of financial support. The commonalities between the constructions of students in Ireland and Spain can perhaps be explained in terms of Chevalier's emphasis on the importance of the 'principle of subsidiarity' in informing social policies (discussed above). The assumptions evident in our Spanish and Irish data, about close parental involvement and students as integral family members, can be seen to be in line with what he argues about countries whose welfare state is influenced by Bismarckian norms – in which families are typically positioned as the primary provider of welfare.

The position of relative ambiguity in Germany and England, outlined in relation to our data above, is also somewhat reflected in their higher education funding policies. To some extent, students are treated as independent individuals: no fees are paid in Germany and, in England, tuition fees are payable by all students, irrespective of parental income, and loans are available to all students to cover these costs (to be paid back when the student's future income exceeds a specified amount). However, the student support system in both countries is means-tested against family income; in Germany, about 22% of the students receive a combined grant/loan (see Table 11.1), and in England, 89% of students take out a maintenance loan, the amount of which is income-dependent (National Statistics, 2018). Although in both countries a relatively high number of students engage in paid work (Eurostudent, 2018; BBC, 2015) to cover the shortfall, it is assumed, at least at policy level, that most parents support their children while studying.

Although, in his analysis of youth citizenship, Chevalier (2016, 2018) draws on both cultural and structural influences, as we have done here, he reaches rather different conclusions – suggesting that, of the countries in our sample, England, Ireland and Denmark can be considered as promoting an individualised form of social citizenship, while in Germany and Spain, a more familialised form is evident. Our analysis points to a more complicated picture and indicates that higher education policies are not always in line with others that affect young people. More specifically, the discussion of English students in national media and by policy actors does not obviously accord with an individualised understanding but instead reflects also elements of familialised social citizenship. Furthermore, while the higher education policies in Germany are in line with a familialised understanding of social rights, our data also indicate that in other ways German students are sometimes positioned as independent actors. The clearest difference between our data and Chevalier's categorisation is, however, most evident with respect to Ireland. Our data indicate that Irish students are not constructed within media texts and policy narratives as independent actors, benefitting from individualised social citizenship, but rather as closely enmeshed within family relationships. Such assumptions also inform higher education policy in Ireland (at least with respect to student funding).

Finally, our data also articulate with debates about the 'Southern Europeanisation' of higher education policy. As we outlined above, Antonucci (2016) has argued that, over recent years, across Europe we have witnessed a growing convergence in the experiences of higher education students and their families, as austerity policies have led to a shift of responsibility for funding higher education away from the state and towards parents. The newspaper articles and policy narratives from our research provide some support for this position, in that in Denmark concern was expressed about students becoming more dependent on their families than had been the case in the past, due to policy reforms. However, we have also shown that, in important respects, students in Denmark are still positioned as independent actors, who are, for example, able to speak for themselves on issues related to higher education. Moreover, we have suggested that the patterns of familial dependency evident in Ireland, Spain and, to a lesser extent, Germany may be less related to the impact of austerity and more to the norms underpinning the provision of welfare. Indeed, the 'principle of subsidiarity' that lies behind Chevalier's (2018) concept of 'familialised social citizenship' can, at least to some extent, explain the construction of students as financially dependent on their families. Even though in all three countries some form of criticism of dependent student–family relationships was articulated, fundamental assumptions about the need of families to support students financially were not questioned. Long-standing traditions and norms may thus be playing more of a role than short-term responses to austerity.

Conclusion

This chapter has explored the ways in which higher education students are constructed, either explicitly or implicitly, as family members within newspaper articles and interviews with policy influencers across five European countries. It has shown that such constructions differ quite considerably by nation-state. Students are, for example, positioned as integral family members in the Spanish and Irish newspapers and interviews, but typically as independent actors in the Danish texts, while family relations are discussed in rather ambivalent ways in England and Germany. On the basis of these data, we have argued that the north–south dichotomy in family relationships, discussed in much of the literature, is played out in more complex ways with respect to higher education. The patterns we observe are seemingly related to structural factors, such as how higher education is funded, but cultural and historical factors as well as religion also have an important role to play in the formation of student–family relationships. Moreover, our data raise some questions about the scale and depth of processes of 'Southern Europeanisation'. While some trends towards this are evident, these tend to be played out in different ways in the various nations and, in some cases, the figure of the independent student remains central to national debate.

Acknowledgements

We are grateful to those policy actors who kindly gave up their time to be interviewed, and to the European Research Council for the award of a Consolidator Grant to Rachel Brooks (award number: EUROSTUDENTS_ 681018).

Notes

1 The principle of subsidiarity originates in Catholic social doctrine which has shaped the approach to social issues more generally in Bismarckian (corporatist) welfares states (van Kersbergen (1995) cited in Palier, 2010).
2 Poland was also included in the larger study but is not discussed in this chapter because of an absence of relevant data.
3 See Esping-Andersen (1990) for a discussion of this typology.
4 Source: European Commission/EACEA/Eurydice (2018)

5 In England graduates start repaying the loan when they earn more than £25,725 per year. In Denmark and Germany repayment is not income contingent, however repayment in Denmark starts one year after graduation and in Germany five years after the end of the maximum period of the BAföG grant (combined grant and loan).

6 The main differences between the two types of newspapers are related to the content. Tabloids devote a lot of attention to the personal and private lives of people and to topics like sports, scandal, and popular entertainment, whereas broadsheets focus more on the public side of life and topics related to politics, economics and society (Sparks, 2000).

7 NexisLexis database was used to retrieve newspaper articles from most of the newspapers. In the case of Denmark, Infomedia database was used, and data from Süddeutche Zeitung was retrieved from Genios-Wiso database.

8 In Spain, it was not possible to interview a member of the national students' union, so we interviewed a member of the national union representing higher education staff instead.

References

Antonucci, L. (2016). *Student lives in crisis. Deepening inequality in times of austerity.* Bristol: Policy Press. doi:10.2307/j.ctt1t89h62

Bathmaker, A-M., Bradley, H., Ingram, N., Hoare, T., Waller, R., & Abrahams, J. (2016). *Higher education, social class and social mobility. The degree generation.* London: Palgrave Macmillan.

BBC. (2015). *Increase in students 'working to fund studies'.* Retrieved from https://www.bbc.co.uk/news/education-33843987

Beck, U. (1992). *Risk society.* London: Sage.

Berg, B.L., & Lune, H. (2012). *Qualitative research methods for social sciences.* 8th edition. New Jersey: Pearson.

Bradley-Geist, C., & Olson-Buchanan, B. J. (2014). Helicopter parents: An examination of the correlates of over-parenting of college students. *Education and Training* 56:4, 314–328. doi:10.1108/ET-10-2012-0096

Chevalier, T. (2016). Varieties of youth welfare citizenship: Towards a two-dimension typology. *Journal of European Social Policy* 26:1, 3–19. doi:10.1177/0958928715621710

Chevalier, T. (2018). Social citizenship of young people in Europe: A comparative institutional analysis. *Journal of Comparative Policy Analysis: Research and Practice* 20:3, 304–323. doi:10.1080/13876988.2017.1320160

Donnelly, M., & Gamsu, S. (2018). *Home or away. Social, ethnic and spatial inequalities in student mobility.* London: The Sutton Trust.

Esping-Andersen, G. (1990). *The three worlds of welfare capitalism.* Cambridge: Polity Press.

European Commission/EACEA/Eurydice. (2018). *National student fee and support systems in European Higher Education – 2018/19.* Luxembourg: Publications Office of the European Union.

Eurostudent. (2018). *Social and economic conditions of student life in Europe.* Retrieved from https://www.eurostudent.eu/download_files/documents/EUROSTUDENT_VI_short_report.pdf

Hsieh, H.-F., & Shannon, S.E. (2005). Three approaches to qualitative content analysis. *Qualitative Health Research* 15:9, 1277–1288. doi:10.1177/1049732305276687

Lamprianou, I., Symeou, L., & Theodorou, E. (2019). 'All we need is love (and money)'! What do higher education students want from their families? *Research Papers in Education* 34:3, 352–372. doi:10.1080/02671522.2018.1452957

Mönkediek, M. & Bras, H. (2014). Strong and weak family ties revisited: reconsidering European family structures from a network perspective. *The History of the Family* 19:2, 235–259. doi:10.1080/1081602X.2014.897246

Moreno, A. (2012). The transition to adulthood in Spain in a comparative perspective: The incidence of structural factors. *Young* 20:1, 19–48. doi:10.1177/110330881102000102

National Statistics (2018). *Student support for higher education in England 2018.* Retrieved from https://webarchive.nationalarchives.gov.uk/20190510151948/https://www.slc.co.uk/media/10180/slcsfr052018.pdf

Palier, B. (2010). *Ordering change: understanding the 'Bismarckian' welfare reform trajectory.* In B. Palier (ed.), *A long goodbye to Bismarck? The politics of welfare reform in Continental Europe* (pp. 19–44). Amsterdam: University Press.

Reher, D. (1998). Family ties in Western Europe: persistent contrasts. *Population and Development Review* 24:2, 203–234. doi:10.2307/2807972

Schiffrin, H. H., Liss, M., Miles-McLean, H., Geary, K.A., Erchull, M.J., & Tashner, T. (2014). Helping or hovering? The effects of helicopter parenting on college students' well-being *Journal of Child and Family Studies* 23, 548–557. doi:10.1007/s10826-013-9716-3

Segrin, A. W., Givertz, M., Bauer, A., & Murphy, M. T. (2012). The association between overparenting, parent-child communication, and entitlement and adaptive traits in adult children. *Family Relations* 61:2, 237–252. doi:10.1111/j.1741-3729.2011.00689.x

Sparks, C. (2000). Introduction: The panic over tabloid news. In C. Sparks & J. Tulloch (Eds), *Tabloid tales: Global debates over media standard* (pp. 1–40). Oxford: Roman & Littlefield Publishers.

Symeou, L., Theodorou, E., Lamprianou I., Rentzou, K., & Andreou, P. (2018). Has family involvement migrated into higher education? An investigation of how administrative staff document the phenomenon in students' university experiences in Cyprus *International Studies in Sociology of Education* 27:1, 78–99. doi:10.1080/09620214.2017.1336934

van Kersbergen, K. (1995). *Social Capitalism: A Study of Christian Democracy and the Welfare State.* London: Routledge.

West, A. & Lewis, J. (2017). *'Helicopter Parenting' and 'Boomerang Children': How parents support and relate to their student and co-resident graduate children.* London/New York: Routledge.

Williams, J. (2011) Constructing consumption: what media representations reveal about today's students. In M. Molesworth, R. Scullion & E. Nixon (Eds), *The marketisation of higher education and the student as consumer* (pp. 170–182). London/New York: Routledge.

Zaloom, C. (2019). *Indebted: How families make college work at any cost.* Princeton: University Press.

Chapter 12

Student millennials/Millennial students

How the lens of generation constructs understandings of the contemporary HE student

Kirsty Finn, Nicola Ingram and Kim Allen

Introduction

The massification of Higher Education (HE) has seen a significant rise in young people attending university over the last quarter century, meaning that young adults born between 1981 and 1996 – so-called 'Millennials' – have generally higher levels of educational qualifications than previous generations. In broader terms, this cohort has, in recent years, taken on significance in wider debates about politics, civic participation, work-life balance and personal relationships. The figure of 'the millennial' is highly contradictory, becoming synonymous with self-interest and a sense of entitlement while at the same time embodying emotional fragility and economic precarity (Allen, Finn & Ingram, 2020). More often, the millennial is imagined through discourses of lack, failure and decline. This emerges in fairly broad terms, however, it manifests with particular veracity in relation to the contemporary HE student, as exemplified by this article in the *Times Higher*:

> Millennials don't read. They don't think as critically as they could. And they're not interested in learning for learning's sake. They want the Dream. They will go into debt to get that degree they believe will help them pursue it, but they have lost respect for knowledge, rigour and hard intellectual work. Working among such entitled puppies makes me feel like an academic platypus out of water.
>
> (Vehko, 2018, para. 30)

Focusing on the UK, this chapter argues that the boom in HE participation since the mid-1990s, and the attendant increasing marketisation of the sector, has important implications for the ways contemporary students are imagined and understood. We demonstrate how the Millennial generation has 'grown up with' the rapid growth in HE participation and, crucially, the creeping normalisation of fees and debts associated with university study. Moreover, their experiences of HE have been set against a backdrop of the Global Financial Crisis (GFC) and austerity, both of which have adversely impacted on the young (Mendick et al., 2018). The impact of this, we argue, is that pervasive public discourses around Millennials, like the one expressed in the excerpt above, have been transposed onto debates about contemporary HE students, regardless of age or social background. 'Millennials' and 'students' are often used interchangeably within popular media discourse, especially those expressing a sense of disdain at declining standards or a sense of entitlement among contemporary students. In this chapter, we show how this engenders narrow and decontextualised imaginings of the contemporary HE student, which obscure important differences within the student body, and individualise the challenges students and graduates face.

Interestingly, the slippage between Millennials (Generation Y) and students neglects that, since 2015, most young students actually constitute Generation Z ('Zoomers' born between 1995 and 2015). We are not suggesting that Zoomers should be conceived as radically different from previous generations, or that generational concepts are unproblematic. Rather, our aim is to highlight how the discursive construction of Millennials has led to partial and problematic imaginings of contemporary HE students. While debts and fees were relatively novel for many Millennials, they are now, to a large extent, 'the new normal' for UK Zoomers. Indeed, the youngest Millennials (born in 1996) entered HE in 2014, just two years after the introduction of higher-level tuition fees in England and Wales. However, for the last 5 years, there have been further changes to fee regimes and the costs associated with HE participation have become accepted, if not necessarily welcome for the current generation. Moreover, as students now graduate with an average £50,000 of personal debt (Belfield, Britton, Deardon, & van der Eyre, 2017), as wage growth remains weak (Costa & Machin, 2019), and as fears about the costs and standards of university accommodation become prominent (Busby, Booth & Blackall, 2019), the material conditions of contemporary students require much closer engagement. We argue here that the generational discourse shrouding debates about students prevents such conversations, ushering in a focus on individual dispositions that deflects attention to the increasingly challenging material context of student transitions in, through and out of HE.

To advance these arguments, the chapter first outlines the rise in generational thinking and dominant definitions of generational cohorts. We reflect on the ways the millennial cohort has 'grown up' with a marketised HE sector in the UK, and how in turn, contemporary understandings of student experiences and values have been subsumed within broader attempts to imagine and define generational change, inequality and crisis. To demonstrate this, we outline two significant representational tropes that characterise constructions of the contemporary HE student. These were identified as part of a wider research project exploring the discursive constructions of millennials (Allen, Finn & Ingram 2019). This involved a search for news articles (using the term 'millennials' in the headline) from UK national newspapers (from September 2017 to September 2019). The search, conducted using the comprehensive online media database LexisNexis, returned 1368 results which were coded by the authors. A significant theme in the news coverage related to university students, and our analysis identified two key representational tropes: (1) *Passive Consumers, Entitled Learners* and (2) *Fragile Snowflakes, PC Warriors*. What we present here is not a definitive or comprehensive analysis of how students are constructed across all media or indeed elsewhere. Rather, our intention is to unpick the ways in which contemporary constructions of students are framed by notions of generation, and we consider the discursive effects of such framings of how students are understood.

Millennials and the HE landscape

While there is no 'official' definition of Millennials, they are usually defined as those born between the early 1980s and late 1990s/early 2000s (Dimock, 2019; Strauss & Howe, 2000; Intergenerational Commission, 2018), with 1981 to 1996 being the accepted range in US research. Millennials are commonly pitted against other generations, most notably Baby Boomers (those born between 1946 and 1964), with whom they are imagined as 'at war'. As noted elsewhere, a focus on intergenerational division can mask the inequalities and diversities *within* generations related to class, gender and ethnicity (Roberts & Allen, 2016; Shabi, 2020). Below we sketch out some of the key changes in UK HE policy which have differently affected students entering the sector since the late 1990s. We draw attention to the *intra*-generational complexities of Millennial experiences of HE in the UK and consider the current context for contemporary Zoomer students.

The millennial cohort and the shifting fees and loans landscape

In the UK, the Millennial generation entered HE at a significant policy juncture, which saw considerable shifts in relation to tuition fees, bursaries, student loans and university participation. As the oldest Millennials (those born in 1981) were coming to the end of compulsory schooling, the Dearing report (1997), commissioned by a British Labour government, paved the way for tuition fees to be introduced across the UK by recommending that working graduates should bear partial responsibility for the costs of their tuition. Acting on the recommendations of the report, tuition fees of £1000 were introduced in 1999 through the Teaching and Higher Education Act 1998. This was the very point at which Millennials were first entering universities, making them the first generation to not have access to free university tuition. The introduction of tuition fees was justified through debates about the growing numbers of young people entering the system, the forecast for participation to continue to increase over 20 years, and an assumption about the continued positive link between HE and graduate earnings (the so-called 'graduate premium'). Within 7 years, this modest contribution to tuition fees was increased under the Higher Education Act 2004. This enabled universities to charge variable tuition fees of up to £3000 per year for students enrolling on courses beginning in the 2006–2007 academic year in England and Northern Ireland, and in Wales for students enrolling in the 2007–2008 academic year. The fees increased significantly to £9000 for those enrolling in the 2012–2013 academic year, following the publication of the Browne Review in 2010. The youngest Millennials (born in 1996) began to enter HE just two years after this increase and are thus among the first swathe of graduates to be leaving university with in-excess of £30,000 debt. The millennial cohort is therefore unique in that they are a generation that have experienced significant changes in tuition fees within a generation, and yet both ends of the generational cohort have very different fee experiences ranging from £1000 to £9000 per annum. The youngest Millennials' experiences of fees and student debt are therefore aligned with that of the subsequent generation (Zoomers), who now face fees of £9250.

Student debt

An obvious outcome of increases in student fees is an increase in student and graduate debt. Crucially, from a generational perspective, Millennials comprise a significant proportion of the first cohort of graduates to exit HE with both fee and maintenance loans. For older Millennials entering the system in 1999, tuition fee loans were not available but income contingent maintenance loans were, and from that year both the average loan amount (of approximately £2000) (see Gayardon, Callender & Green, 2019) and the number of students taking out student loans has steadily increased as new fee regimes were introduced:

> There was a large jump in the average amount owed by those who first became liable to repay from 2010. These cohorts were the first to mainly consist of students who had taken out fee loans for variable fees. The average amount owed by the 2009 cohort (when first liable to repay) was £11,800, £14,700 for the 2010 cohort, £16,200 for the 2011 cohort.
> (Bolton 2019, p. 18)

These figures jump sharply for the first cohort of post-2012 students who meet the threshold for loan repayment. Their average debt, based solely on those who have made the threshold salary for repayment (which was £21000 in 2012 and now sits at £25000 per annum), is reported to be £32000 (Bolton 2019). What the figures do not capture is the average debt of students leaving HE, which under the 2017 system sits at just over £50000. According to the Institute for Fiscal Studies, "[t]he combination of high fees and large maintenance loans contributes to English graduates having the highest student debts in the developed world" (Belfield, Britton, Deardon, & van der Eyre, 2017, p. 2). There have been complex shifts in the way that

HE is funded in the UK since Millennials first entered the HE system and this has seen the move away from a system of maintenance grants available to poorer students to a system of means tested maintenance loans. The result is that 'students from the poorest backgrounds will accrue debts of £57,000 (including interest) from a 3-year degree' (Belfield et al., 2017, p. 2). Their wealthier counterparts, however, still emerge with significant levels of debt, reported to be £43000 for the wealthiest 30 per cent of families, and this is argued to be more than double the amount of debt that students would have incurred if the system had not changed in 2012 (Belfield et al., 2017). Thus, younger Millennials are perhaps much closer in experience and expectation to their Generation Z counterparts than their fellow (older) Millennials. Moreover, while the burden of debt is a normalised feature of labour market transitions for graduates from across the social spectrum, speaking in generational terms obscures entrenched inequalities (e.g. social class, ethnicity) when understanding orientations and outcomes.

Graduate employment and the diminishing returns to education

The fee changes experienced largely by Millennials and Zoomers were initially justified in the Dearing report (1997) by the fact that graduates at the time experienced higher earnings than those without a degree, and therefore a significant return on their investment. There was also an expectation that this positive link between learning and earning would be sustained for future generations. However, this link is less straightforward for both younger Millennials and Zoomers graduating into a congested graduate labour market in conditions of post-crash (and now COVID-related) austerity.

While returns to HE have been diminishing over time (Boero, Cook, Nathwani, Naylor & Smith, 2019), graduates still earn more than those without HE qualifications and this graduate premium becomes particularly acute as their careers become established in their late 20s and early 30s (Belfield et al., 2018). Boero et al. (2019) compared data from different birth cohorts and established that Generation X graduates earned on average 19 per cent more than their non-graduate counterparts by age 26, whereas graduate Millennials at age 25 earned just 11 per cent more than non-graduates from the same cohort.

As the sector has expanded with greater numbers of students from working-class and minority ethnic backgrounds, the idea of the graduate premium has been further questioned. Graduate earnings vary enormously by gender, ethnicity and social class (Britton, Dearden, Shephard & Vignoles, 2016; Ingram & Allen, 2018). Goldthorpe (2016) reveals the link between origins and destination has largely remained the same over successive decades despite a weakening of the link between class of origin and educational attainment. He argues that 'any equalisation in educational attainment that may have been obtained in relation to class origins is being offset by a decline in the "class returns" that education brings' (p. 102). This has implications for considering the differential prospects for Millennial graduates who, as a cohort, are experiencing diminished returns on their investment in HE while also accruing higher debts than previous generations. This bears out in particularly acute ways for working-class and minority ethnic students. These students are not only exiting with higher debts than their White, middle-class counterparts, but their investment in HE is less likely to bear the same fruit in terms of employment status and salary than that enjoyed by graduates of their parents' generation who came from similar origins to themselves.

Imagining the millennial, imagining the student

Having identified how the Millennial generational category has coincided with significant changes to HE and the graduate labour market in the UK, we now discuss two discursive tropes emerging from our media analysis: (1) *Passive Consumers, Entitled Leaners* and (2) *Fragile Snowflakes, PC Warriors*. We demonstrate how these tropes are shaping the ways the contemporary student is imagined within the UK revealing that while the different narratives and articulations of young students do not always sit neatly together, even where there are contradictory interpretations the outcome is often the same. Specifically, these tropes work to shore up particular imaginings of students as departing from an idealised (and imagined) notion of the intellectual, engaged and resilient scholar of the past. Of course, media representations can be interpreted as humorous caricatures. Nonetheless, we contend that they are not purely benign exaggerations and that they work in conversation with policy to bring particular subjects into being (Ball, Maguire, Braun & Hoskins, 2011). We return to this in our conclusion.

Passive consumers, entitled learners

Barely a day goes by without an article in the UK news media about Millennials and, invariably, these include representations of lifestyles and values that have become ubiquitous with notions of narcissism, excess and a sense of entitlement. The millennial label is loaded with mostly negative associations, including a poor work ethic, and millennials have been hailed the 'ME, ME, ME' generation' (Stein, 2013). Millennials are commonly imagined as expecting rewards without investing the requisite effort and for indulging in expensive 'avocado toasts' and lattes rather than saving for a secure future (Levin, 2017). These ideas circulate widely in media and popular culture, having resonance across advanced Western economies where HE participation has increased alongside the millennial generation coming of age. Indeed, the UK press often draw upon on research from the US in order to paint Millennials as 'a generation of "deluded narcissists"' whose 'desire for material gain has been increasing steadily' and whose 'commitment to hard work has been decreasing' (Blair, 2018, para. 3). Elsewhere the connection to students and graduates is more explicit, and news outlets report that Millennials 'are a nightmare to employ' (Hoyle, 2017, para. 10) requiring more guidance than any other age group and presenting both a strong sense of entitlement and poor decision-making skills which impact upon educational spaces.

> Schools and universities are increasingly under pressure to follow some sort of student-led business model. Students not only believe that they're entitled to voice their point of view, but that theirs is the only valid view. This attitude has bled into the workplace.
>
> (Hoyle, 2017, para. 18)

The interlacing of generational discourses with narratives of contemporary students and graduates reinforces the growing perception of (and disdain towards) students as passive consumers and entitled learners. Images of the student as consumer (SAC) are bolstered by political and policy discourse (Brooks, 2018; Sabri, 2012; Naidoo & Williams, 2015) where the SAC subjectivity is encouraged through notions of 'value for money' and a focus on labour market returns. This particular view of SAC, while encouraged within policy, does little to dismantle the dichotomy between students as active, engaged learners on the one hand, and as entitled consumers on the other. Indeed, it appears that if and when students are imagined as consumers, they necessarily cease to be learners (or students or scholars) in any meaningful way. One identity negates the other; it is impossible to be both. As Brooks (2018) notes, a focus on students as *learners* is notably absent in policy. This is revealing of the ways students' own intellectual investments and identities are valued against their financial contributions and roles as paying customers. Thus, when students emerge as consumers, they are imagined as simply going through the motions of university in order to move on to the next phase (Brooks, 2018) and this plays into perceptions of their passivity and entitlement.

This is evidenced in the growing debate about grade inflation, which imagines students as undeserving of their degrees, or at least the particular classification thereof. In August 2019, the *New Statesman* ran a cover story titled *The Great University Con: How the British Degree Lost its Value*. It encapsulates the interconnection between the generational discourse about Millennials as entitled consumers and shores up fears about how this cohort have corrupted (and indeed have been corrupted by) HE and its (increasingly marketised) values. The image presented is of students demanding – and receiving – higher grades than previous generations. This is read as a 'dumbing-down' of degree courses and a decline in intellectual standards. The impact of this 'moral panic' around degree outcomes and supposed 'grade inflation' has evidently been felt by the representative body of UK universities, Universities UK, whose response appears to simultaneously reject and validate claims of 'dumbing down' as 'truth' by demanding transparency from institutions in order to ward off external 'perceptions' rather than address poor practices internally.

A review of academic research reveals that this image of students – as passive and entitled in their new roles as consumers of education – is mostly accepted as truth and thus provides the basis upon which research questions are formulated. At one level, it has been argued that framing HE students as hard-working consumers is reflective of a broader culture of competitive individualism (Brooks, 2018). Going further however, Nixon, Scullion and Hearn (2018) maintain that 'intensifying marketisation heightens the potential for consumer satisfactions and frustrations in HE that are profoundly narcissistic in character' (p. 928). Drawing on interviews with students at an English university, they claim that the SAC model results in students '[s]eeing the only valid purpose of a degree as the personal (largely economic) benefits' (p. 935) it can bring. The image of the SAC is evidently understood as problematic, and the explicit mobilisation of 'narcissism' as a term to characterise student behaviours and values plays into the discourse of the 'ME, ME, ME Generation' outlined earlier. Narcissism is defined as 'self-enjoyment, image-obsession, new forms of media reinforcing self-centeredness and entitlement characteristic of consumer societies' leading to 'a deep sense of emptiness and inferiority which vacillates with a grandiose self-image' (Nixon, Scullion & Hearn, 2018 p. 930-31). It is clear, then, that the new condition or disposition among students is considered to be harmful to those who embody it. It does not seem to vary by gender, ethnicity or social class but represents a more universal characteristic of a cohort growing up with social media and rapid consumerism.

A more critical reading of the passive, entitled consumer trope locates this as a response to students' inability to see or plan for a future which then leads to particular (economic) orientations to the 'here and now'. For example, Harrison et al. (2015) reflect on the binary representations of young students as, on the one hand, leading hedonistic, alcohol-fuelled lifestyles while spending little time studying, and on the other hand as impoverished and struggling. As with broader debates about Millennials, Harrison et al. reveal how these dichotomous images merely distort the debate to the extent that 'the diverse lived experiences of actual students are in danger of getting lost' (Harrison et al., 2015, p. 100). Indeed, within debates about generational thinking, there is already a backlash that illuminates how images of Millennials are figured largely as white, able bodied, urban and privileged (Allen, 2019; Clark, 2019). In UK HE research, there have been attempts to show that while some may have a 'devil may care' attitude towards debt and spiralling costs of study, BAME students, women and those from disadvantaged backgrounds are more likely to simply resign themselves to the structural imposition of indebtedness and adopt 'a "hit and hope" approach to financial planning and decision-making' (Clark, Hordósy & Vickers, 2019, p. 718). Rather than passivity or entitlement then, this research imagines students as participating in HE as a 'perfunctory process' (Esson & Ertl, 2016) as they *insure* themselves against an uncertain future, rather than actively investing in it (N. Harrison, 2019).

While there is considerable academic research which complicates and challenges the image of students as overly-entitled and passive in their consumption of education (Tomlinson, 2017; Abrahams & Brooks 2019; Komljenovic, Ashwin, McArthur & Rosewell, 2018), the questions that the HE community are asking nevertheless proceed from – or are at least haunted by – toxic images and discourses of students as disengaged, utilitarian and outcomes oriented. Although some studies work hard to challenge negative constructions of the SAC model, such orientations apparently run counter to proper, engaged learner identities (Bunce, Baird & Jones, 2017; Nixon, Scullion & Hearn, 2018). Thus, even where there is nuance, and where research has complicated the notion of students as passive consumers and entitled learners (Tomlinson, 2017), the false dichotomy of the consumer vs learner is necessarily bolstered. Thus, active learner engagement is read as an antidote to, or antonym for, consumer orientations. It is unclear to us how, in an era of unprecedented student fees and graduate debt, a consumerist approach can be avoided among the contemporary cohort. As with the discourse around Millennials, it is perhaps more useful to understand how and in what ways consumer-oriented and mediated living are reshaping aspects of social, educational, political and working lives, rather than operating within what we see as an unhelpful and false binary between consuming and learning.

Fragile Snowflake, PC Warriors

The other side of the millennial discourse is their apparent fragility and hyper-sensitivity. In a piece for the *New Republic*, Allen (2019, para. 9) asserts,

> Perhaps no generation has been so gleefully maligned in the press, which has produced a zillion think pieces casting Millennials as entitled, lazy, mayonnaise-hating, over-educated pampered whiners who, in their blinkered narcissism, are selling out the human race. That caricature has slowly given way to a more nuanced picture of a generation profoundly shaped by the events of its time—9/11, the Iraq War, the Great Recession, climate change—and baleful socioeconomic trends: growing income inequality, staggering levels of student debt, stagnant wages.

Evidently, studenthood is a key aspect of the ways Millennial experiences are characterised, and, under the shadow of the Millennial discourse, contemporary students are defined as much by their vulnerability as their rampant narcissism. They are imagined as taking offence (too) easily and as lacking the resilience of earlier generations, as being without humour and demanding apparently absurd levels of political correctness (PC) (Fox, 2016). This construction of students as fragile is most clearly embodied in the term 'snowflake' that has become synonymous with young people and university students in particular (Finn, 2017). This term has become so ubiquitous that it entered the Oxford English Dictionary in 2018. In one newspaper article, 'Snowflake' is defined for the reader, and moves synonymously between conceptions of snowflakes as a generation, and examples of 'snowflakey' behaviour coming mainly from HE students. The piece claims that 'Generation Snowflake is a put-down used to describe the current generation of sensitive *millennials*' and defines snowflakes as those 'aged in their late teens and twenties' who 'embraced their snowflake ways while they were at university' (G. Harrison, 2019, para. 23, our emphasis). The slippage here from the Millennial cohort to teenagers (Zoomers) is revealing of the ways in which supposed Millennial dispositions and values are transposed onto images of the contemporary young student. This view of students as overly-sensitive and too easily 'triggered' has emerged with particular veracity in recent debates around 'free-speech', 'no platforming' and 'safe spaces' within universities. In these imaginings, the contemporary student is constructed as intolerant of alternative views and hostile to free speech:

> Today, many of these unis [sic] are hostile to free speech and determined to shield students from any ideas they don't like. Students unions demand 'safe spaces' - areas where people cannot disagree with or challenge your ideas. Meanwhile, other ways Generation Snowflake is leaving its mark on the world is by introducing 'trigger warnings' and 'no platforming speakers whose opinions they may not agree with.
>
> (G. Harrison, 2019, para. 25)

Constructions of students as overly sensitive and a threat to free speech are promulgated by national newspapers and authorised in the UK by academics such as Professor Frank Furedi (2017) and other prominent figures within HE including university vice chancellors (Crouch, 2017). These ideas also have roots in US academic research, mainly from the field of psychology (e.g. Twenge & Foster, 2010), which has suggested that Millennials lack resilience and 'grit', and face problems in education due to overly protective parenting and a wider culture of infantilisation. The 'therapeutic turn' as it is labelled by UK academics (Ecclestone & Hayes, 2019) has apparently led to a 'sense of emotional fragility' among undergraduates (Furedi, 2017). In instances of students campaigning for no-platforming of controversial speakers, or the removal of statues that represent historical figures with links to the slave trade for example, we see how the HE student is imagined as a politicised subject but in ways that are deemed problematic. Instead of being recognised as legitimate political actors with strong considered views on important historical and contemporary social issues, they figure as censorious and intolerant, whereby their own fragility shuts down debate and threatens democracy. Thus, whereas one might interpret such practices of engaged critique of the university as counterbalancing notions of passivity or entitlement, the discourse around Millennials as PC Warriors undermines students' agency, reducing their calls for different knowledge communities to a type of silliness and hyper sensitivity (Fox, 2016).

Free speech on campus is a fiercely contested issue and continues to garner much energy and attention. However, the notion that it is under threat has been strongly refuted by large swathes of the student population and some sector representatives, and by the government's own inquiries. Indeed, the British parliament's joint committee on human rights found limited evidence of censorship occurring on campuses, nor evidence that students are unwilling to hear or engage in perspectives that are different to their own. The report concluded that 'the narrative that "censorious students" have created a "free speech crisis" in universities has been exaggerated' (2018, p. 20). This view is further compounded by a recent study conducted by the Policy Institute at King's College London, which found that over 80 per cent of students believe that freedom of expression is 'more important than ever' and that universities actually offer a more productive space for this compared to other contexts in the UK (Grant, Hewlett, Nir & Duffy, 2019). As O'Keefe (2016) asserts, freedom of expression and of protest, and also freedom from hate, means that 'students and academic and non-academic staff should collectively decide who to welcome on campus' (p. 89). From this perspective, students are imagined as active participants *and* active consumers, having a hand in shaping campus cultures and transforming the curriculum through practices such as no-platforming and the safe spaces movement. Notwithstanding, Hill (2020) illuminates how for critics of safe spaces and no-platforming, 'debate' is regarded as the *only* legitimate mode of engagement with ideas in the university, and how the suggestion that debate is being curtailed or closed down is automatically attributed to students' own sense of entitlement and deficient scholarly identities. Thus, rather than understanding how contemporary students prefer to engage with and challenge difficult ideas, 'Generation Snowflake' (Fox, 2016) is invoked to demonstrate that students no longer regard universities as space of knowledge but instead, as spaces of comfort (Fox, 2016).

The battle for representation is hard fought and at the same time as populist and academic critiques of the contemporary HE student grab headlines in the UK, more nuanced research about student activism continues apace, albeit quietly. By way of example, research by the 1752 Group, a UK-based research and lobby organisation working to end sexual misconduct in HE, reveals that it is institutions rather than students who prefer to close down debate and create a culture of silence around staff sexual misconduct in universities, mainly through the use of Non-Disclosure Agreements (NDAs) and other forms of institutionalised suppression and silencing. As Page, Bull and Chapman (2019) outline, it is student unions and self-organised feminist groups that have worked to make gender-based and sexual violence in HE visible, via campaigns, discussions and talks. There is, indeed, a contradiction between how students are imagined as vulnerable, censorious subjects, closed off to new knowledge and 'real learning' and the growth of campus activism in various spheres from campaigns against sexual misconduct, the movement to decolonise the curriculum and protests against rising fees and costs of university living. Reflecting on this tension, Danvers (2019) argues that at the same time as critics of contemporary HE and its students decry the creeping anti-intellectual and anti-democratic cultures which supposedly undermine critical thinking 'the academy is simultaneously and inseparably alive with more recognisably "deconstructive" criticality' (p. 3). Citing high-profile student-led movements in the UK, Danvers illuminates the contradiction between everyday critical thinking and political activism, and the kinds of critical learning and knowledge exchange that has come to characterise the values of universities and the value of university graduates. She concludes that critical thinking within HE curricula has been narrowly drawn to refocus criticality as an inward-looking disposition that, in turn, leads to the kinds of 'performative self' that others, like Nixon et al. (2018), understand as narcissistic subjectivities. Critical thinking has become 'an instrumentalised pedagogic performance indicator' and 'something to get "right" within a practice of impermeable boundaries, rather than a practice of questioning or re-writing boundaries' (p. 10). Indeed, when students participate in a more engaged political activism, when they campaign for an alternative vision for HE which has a moral duty to align its interests with those of its members, they are imagined as 'immature, needing authoritative guidance and enforced limitations on their political engagement' (Danvers & Gagnon, 2014, p. 11). The construction of students as snowflakes and PC warriors is not accidental, however. Indeed, it serves the function of delegitimising their political voices through a reductionist discourse that services those in power by deflecting from the need for policy changes that are an inevitable conclusion to the issues that students are raising.

Conclusion

In this chapter we have outlined how the Millennial generation has grown up with the massification and marketisation of HE in the UK, to the extent that representations of the contemporary student are formed in the image of the young millennial; an entitled and passive figure, vulnerable and censorious, privileged yet highly precarious. In many ways, the imagined Millennial student emerges in contrast (and conflict) with their imagined Baby Boomer counterparts; a cohort that experienced HE in the UK at a significantly different social and economic moment. Participation was much lower, of course, but the 'graduate premium' was much more dependable. While the generational label of the Millennial taps into the important material differences facing contemporary students in the UK, it also sends a contradictory message about who students are, how they engage with HE and wider society and what they might expect from their studies and associated 'investments' in learning. This, we argue, has serious implications for the ways contemporary students enter public consciousness and how a diversity of experiences can be known and understood, particularly in terms of social class and ethnicity.

This chapter demonstrates how the dual and overlapping figures of the Millennial and the student lend themselves to derision and critique. Analysis lapses into individualistic discussions of values, dispositions and generational quirks rather than addressing structural transformations that have drastically altered the material realities for current students and graduates in the UK. We conclude, then, by highlighting how such an approach and attendant images of contemporary HE students in the UK further compound debates which position newer cohorts against an idealised and immortalised notion of the student of the past. As others have reflected, this imagined student is, more often than not, male, white, straight, cis-gendered, able-bodied and unencumbered in his learning and engagement (Hill, 2020; Leathwood, 2013). When constructing the contemporary student, writers like Fox (2016) betray their lack of curiosity into how and under what kinds of circumstances the contemporary student body has changed. She writes that,

> the very excitement of undergraduate life was that it represented a completely different experience from school, precisely a break from home comforts. About standing on your own two feet [and represented a time to] get away from small-town preoccupations, the limits of spoon-fed lessons, in loco parentis teachers and being looked after.
>
> (p. 179)

There is no consideration of the fact that many students, such as those who have left the care system (Bland, 2018), those with disabilities or caring commitments (Dent 2020; Loveday, 2015) and those who already hail from challenging and diverse urban contexts might have already had to stand on their own two feet. Neither is there an acceptance that, far from an experiment in self-discovery, HE now carries life-long financial burdens to the extent that it has a responsibility to offer much more than a temporary playground or debating society. It is no coincidence that the contemporary critiques of HE students come at a time when the student body exhibits more diversity than it has in the past and, as Leathwood (2013) argues, the autonomous intellectual scholar, as a student or academic, has long been a subject position that only men could take up. Imagining students as entitled consumers or censorious PC Warriors devalues the emerging practices and priorities of newcomers to the sector and in doing so, allows the ideology of what 'real' students ought to be and do to pass without critique.

To conclude, we see these tropes as integral to the failure to acknowledge the rapid and caustic changes that have taken place in HE since the late 1990s and which shape the material conditions of students and graduates in the UK. Imagining the student as the Millennial, and Millennials as the archetypal student, does little to dismantle the dichotomous 'consumer vs learner' discourse or versions of the consumer that embody active and engaged participation, rather than passivity, entitlement and fragility. In maintaining these tropes, contemporary images of the student as Millennials shores up an idealised student body from an imaginary past, in which all Baby Boomers were benefitted from free education and were white, middle class, able-bodied, cis-gendered and male. Generational labels mask intra-generational diversity and intergenerational reproduction along class and ethnic lines. It is incumbent on HE scholars to recognise that consumerist dispositions to HE are logically engendered through the material structure of the system, and are not in opposition to active learner dispositions. Younger students are navigating this terrain with few points of reference; there is much to learn from their modes of engagement and activism.

References

Abrahams, J., & Brooks, R. (2019). Higher education students as political actors: Evidence from England and Ireland. *Journal of Youth Studies* 22:1, 108-123, doi: 10.1080/13676261.2018.1484431

Allen, K., Finn, K., and Ingram, N. (2019, December 2) *Snowflakes and Smashed Avocados: The discursive construction of millennials in UK news media.* Paper presented at Journal of Youth Studies Conference, University of Newcastle, Australia.

Allen, K., Finn, K., & Ingram, N. (2020, March 31) (Are you) OK Boomer? Discursive constructions of Millennials and generation through COVID-19. *Discover Society.* Retrieved from https://discoversociety.org/2020/03/31/are-you-ok-boomer-discursive-constructions-of-millennials-generation-through-covid-19/

Allen, R. (2019) The Missing Black Millennial. *The New Republic.* February 20 2019. Retrieved from https://newrepublic.com/article/153122/missing-black-millennial

Ball, S. J., Maguire, M., Braun, A., & Hoskins, K. (2011). Policy subjects and policy actors in schools: Some necessary but insufficient analyses. *Discourse: Studies in the Cultural Politics of Education* 32:4, 611–624, doi:10.1080/01596306.2011.601564

Belfield, C., Britton, J., Buscha, F., Dearden, L., Dickson, M., van der Erve, L., Sibieta,L., Vignoles, A., Walker, I., & Zhu, Y. (2018). *The impact of undergraduate degrees on early-career earnings: Institute for Fiscal Studies.* Retrieved from https://assets.publishing.service.gov.uk/government/uploads/system/uploads/attachment_data/file/759278/The_impact_of_undergraduate_degrees_on_early-career_earnings.pdf

Belfield, C., Britton, J., Deardon, L., van der Eyre, L. (2017). *Higher Education funding in England: Past, present and options for the future* (BN211). https://www.ifs.org.uk/uploads/publications/bns/BN211.pdf

Blair, L. (2018, April 12). Do millennials really have a misplaced sense of entitlement? *The Telegraph.* Retrieved from https://www.telegraph.co.uk/health-fitness/mind/do-millennials-really-have-misplaced-sense-entitlement/

Bland, B. (2018). It's all about the money: The influence of family estrangement, accommodation struggles and homelessness on student success in UK higher education. *Widening Participation and Lifelong Learning* 20:3, 68–89. doi:10.5456/WPLL.20.3.68

Boero, G., Cook, D., Nathwani, T., Naylor, R., & Smith, J. (2019). *The return to a degree: New evidence based on the birth cohort studies and the labour force survey*, HESA Report, https://www.hesa.ac.uk/files/Return_to_a_degree_main_report.pdf

Bolton, P. (2019). *Student loan statistics: Briefing paper (1079)*. Retrieved from https://researchbriefings.parliament.uk/ResearchBriefing/Summary/SN01079#fullreport

Britton, J., Dearden, L., Shephard, N., & Vignoles, A. (2016). *How English domiciled graduate earnings vary with gender, institution attended, subject and socioeconomic background: Institute for Fiscal Studies*. (W16/06). Retrieved from https://www.ifs.org.uk/uploads/publications/wps/wp201606.pdf

Brooks, R. (2018). The construction of higher education students in English policy documents. *British Journal of Sociology of Education* 39:6, 745–761, doi:10.1080/01425692.2017.1406339

Browne, J. (2010) *Securing a sustainable future for higher education: An independent review of higher education funding and student finance*. Retrieved from http://www.educationengland.org.uk/documents/pdfs/2010-browne-report.pdf

Bunce, L., Baird, A., & Jones, S. E. (2017). The student-as-consumer approach in higher education and its effects on academic performance. *Studies in Higher Education* 42:11, 1958–1978, doi:10.1080/03075079.2015.1127908

Busby, M. Booth, R., & M. Blackall (2019, November 16). Investigation under way into blaze at Bolton student building. *The Guardian*. Retrieved from https://www.theguardian.com/uk-news/2019/nov/15/fire-crews-battle-blaze-at-bolton-student-housing-building

Clark, T. (2019, January 11). This is what black burnout feels like. *Buzzfeed*. Retrieved from https://www.buzzfeednews.com/article/tianaclarkpoet/millennial-burnout-black-women-self-care-anxiety-depression

Clark, T., Hordósy R., & Vickers, D. (2019). 'We will never escape these debts': Undergraduate experiences of indebtedness, income-contingent loans and the tuition fee rises. *Journal of Further and Higher Education* 43:5, 708–721, doi:10.1080/0309877X.2017.1399202

Costa, L. E., & Machin, S. (2019). *Social Mobility, Centre for Economic Performance*, Paper EA045 http://cep.lse.ac.uk/pubs/download/ea045.pdf

Crouch, G. (2017, September 4). Don't indulge snowflakes: Oxford University Head says Generation Snowflake students need to toughen up and challenge views they disagree with rather than taking offence. *The Sun*. Retrieved from https://www.thesun.co.uk/news/4392155/oxford-professor-toughen-up-snowflake-students/

Danvers, E. C. (2019). Individualised and instrumentalised? Critical thinking, students and the optics of possibility within neoliberal higher education. *Critical Studies in Education* doi:10.1080/17508487.2019.1592003

Danvers, E. C., & and Gagnon, J. (2014). Is 'student engagement' just a mirage? The case for student activism. *Student Engagement and Experience Journal* 3:2. ISSN 2047-9476

Dearing, R. (1997). *The national committee of inquiry into higher education*. London: HMSO.

de Gayardon, A., Callender, C., & Green, F. (2019). The determinants to student loan take up in England. *Higher Education* 78, 965–983. doi:10.1007/s10734-019-00381-9

Dent, S. (2020). *Recognising Students who Care for Children while Studying*. Bradford: Emerald Publishing.

Dimock, M. (2019). Defining generations: Where Millennials end and Generation Z begins. *Fact Tank, Pew Research Centre*. January 17 2019. Retrieved from https://www.pewresearch.org/fact-tank/2019/01/17/where-millennials-end-and-generation-z-begins/

Ecclestone, K., & Hayes, D. (2019). *The dangerous rise of therapeutic education*, 2ndEdition London: Routledge doi:10.4324/9780429401039

Esson, J., & Ertl, H. (2016) No point worrying? Potential undergraduates, study-related debt, and the financial allure of higher education. *Studies in Higher Education* 41:7, 1265–1280, doi:10.1080/03075079.2014.968542

Finn, K. (2017, December 8). Snowflakes and smashed avocados: Exploring the contradictory representations of the higher education generation in times of political crisis and change. Paper presented at SRHE annual conference, Newport, Wales.

Fox, C. (2016). *I find that offensive*. London: Biteback Publishing

Furedi, F. (2017, January 2). Why are millennials so fragile? *Minding the Campus: Reforming Our Universities*. Retrieved from https://www.mindingthecampus.org/2017/01/02/why-millennials-are-so-fragile/

Goldthorpe, J.H. (2016). Social class mobility in modern Britain: Changing structure, constant process. *Journal of the British Academy* 4, 89–111. doi: 10.5871/jba/004.089

Grant, J., Hewlett, K., Nir, T., & Duffy, B. (2019). *Freedom of expression in UK universities*. The Policy Institute at King's College London. Retrieved from https://www.kcl.ac.uk/policy-institute/assets/freedom-of-expression-in-uk-universities.pdf

Harrison, G. (2019, October 24). The kids aren't all right: What does 'Snowflake' mean and who are 'Generation Snowflake'? *The Sun*. Retrieved from https://www.thesun.co.uk/news/5115128/snowflake-generation-meaning-origin-term/

Harrison, N. (2019). Students-as-insurers: Rethinking 'risk' for disadvantaged young people considering higher education in England. *Journal of Youth Studies* 22:6, 752–771, doi:10.1080/13676261.2018.1535174

Harrison, N., Chudry, F., Waller, R., & Hatt, S. (2015). Towards a typology of debt attitudes among contemporary young UK undergraduates. *Journal of Further and Higher Education*, 39:1, 85–107, doi: 10.1080/0309877X.2013.778966

Hill, D. W. (2020). Communication as a moral vocation: Safe space and freedom of speech. *The Sociological Review* 68:1, 3–16 doi:10.1177/0038026119854857

Hordósy, R., & Clark, T. (2018). 'It's scary and it's big, and there's no job security': Undergraduate experiences of career planning and stratification in an English red brick university. *Social Sciences* 7:10, 173

Hoyle, A. (2017, February 17). A generation with a huge sense of entitlement: Bosses complain that millennials are spoilt, full of themselves, averse to hard work and expect 'success on a plate' so what does that mean for society? *The Daily Mail*. Retrieved from https://www.dailymail.co.uk/femail/article-4232696/Millenials-generation-huge-sense-entitlement.html

Ingram, N., & Allen, K. (2018). 'Talent-spotting' or 'social magic'? Inequality, cultural sorting and constructions of the ideal graduate in elite professions. *The Sociological Review* 67:3, 723–740. doi:10.1177/0038026118790949

Intergenerational Commission (2018). A New Generational Contract. The Final Report of the Intergenerational Commission. Retrieved from https://www.resolutionfoundation.org/advanced/a-new-generational-contract/

Komljenovic, J., Ashwin, P., McArthur, J., & Rosewell, K. (2018). To be or not to be consumers: The imperfect alignment of English Higher Education marketization policy and the narratives of first year university students. *CGHE 2018 Annual Conference: The New Geopolitics of Higher Education. Centre for Global Higher Education.* Retrieved from http://www.researchcghe.org/perch/resources/uksa-cg-paper-22.3.18.pdf.

Leathwood, C. (2013). Re/presenting intellectual subjectivity: Gender and visual imagery in the field of higher education. *Gender and Education* 25:2, 133–154, doi:10.1080/09540253.2011.590467

Levin, S. (2017, May 15). Millionaire tells millennials: If you want a house, stop buying avocado toast. *The Guardian.* Retrieved from https://www.theguardian.com/lifeandstyle/2017/may/15/australian-millionaire-millennials-avocado-toast-house

Loveday V. (2015). Working-Class Participation, Middle-Class Aspiration? Value, Upward Mobility and Symbolic Indebtedness in Higher Education. *The Sociological Review* 63:3, 570–588. doi:10.1111/1467-954X.12167

Mendick, H., Ahmad, A., Allen, K., & Harvey, L. (2018). *Celebrity, Aspiration and Contemporary Youth Education and Inequality in an Era of Austerity.* London: Bloomsbury Academic.

Naidoo, R., & Williams, J. (2015). The neoliberal regime in English higher education: Charters, consumers and the erosion of the public good. *Critical Studies in Education* 56:2, 208–223. doi:10.1080/17508487.2014.939098

Nixon, E., Scullion R., & Hearn, R. (2018). Her majesty the student: Marketised higher education and the narcissistic (dis)satisfactions of the student-consumer. *Studies in Higher Education* 43:6, 927–943. doi:10.1080/03075079.2016.1196353

O'Keefe, T. (2016). Making feminist sense of no-platforming. *Feminist Review* 113:1, 85–92. doi:10.1057/fr.2016.7

Page, T., Bull, A., & Chapman, E. (2019). Making power visible: 'Slow activism' to address staff sexual misconduct. *Violence Against Women* doi:10.17863/CAM.38871

Roberts, S., & Allen, K. (2016, April 6) Millennials V baby boomers: A battle we could do without. *The Conversation.* Retrieved from https://theconversation.com/millennials-v-baby-boomers-a-battle-we-could-have-done-without-57305

Sabri, D. (2012). What's Wrong with the 'Student Experience'? *Discourse: Studies in the Cultural Politics of Education* 32:5, 657–676.

Shabi, R. (2020). The war between boomers and millennials befits neither side. *The Guardian.* 14 February 2020. Retrieved from https://www.theguardian.com/commentisfree/2020/feb/14/war-millennials-baby-boomers

Stein, J. (2013, May 20). Millennials: The ME, ME, ME generation. *Time.* Retrieved from https://time.com/247/millennials-the-me-me-me-generation/

Strauss, W., & Howe, N. (2000). *Millennials rising: The next great generation.* New York: Vintage Books

Tomlinson, M. (2017). Student perceptions of themselves as 'consumers' of higher education. *British Journal of Sociology of Education* 38:4, 450–467. doi:10.1080/01425692.2015.1113856

Twenge, J. M., & Foster, J. D. (2010). Birth cohort increases in narcissistic personality traits among American college students, 1982–2009. *Social Psychological and Personality Science* 1:1, 99–106. doi:10.1177/1948550609355719

Vehko, V. (2018, July 19) Millennials: The age of entitlement. *The Times Higher*. Retrieved from https://www.timeshighereducation.com/features/millennials-the-age-of-entitlement

Chapter 13

Exploring spaces in-between

Reimagining the Chinese student in a transnational higher education context in China

Paola R.S. Eiras and Henk Huijser

Introduction

Higher education (HE) is rapidly changing, and perhaps nowhere faster than in China. In addition to outbound Chinese student mobility, there has been an increase in various forms of transnational education (TNE) within the Chinese HE environment over the last 10–15 years (Montgomery, 2016). The contrast between 'traditional' Chinese universities and these transnational universities can be quite pronounced, which in turn creates a learning context that may have an impact on how students construct their identities as HE students and as Chinese youth in a changing political and social landscape. This is especially the case in English as Medium of Instruction (EMI) institutions where students attend an English-speaking university in a Chinese context. This creates a liminal space (Turner, 1967) in which potentially conflicting identities, such as consumers (Brooks, 2018) versus learners, and future workers versus entrepreneurs and innovators, need to be negotiated by (in)dependent adults-in-the-making.

In this chapter, we focus on one group of Chinese undergraduate students in a transnational university in China, to explore how they see themselves as HE students in this context. A specific university, Xi'an Jiaotong-Liverpool University (XJTLU), is used as a case study, and it functions as a specific example of the hybrid spaces of TNE. This chapter is informed by empirical evidence from 31 semi-structured interviews, using an arts-based interview method, with Chinese undergraduate students from XJTLU. This study is grounded in Critical Discourse Analysis (CDA) (Fairclough, 2003, 1995), using a critical realist philosophical framework (Bhaskar, 2008). Discursive constructions of students' identities are analysed and theorised in relation to the articulation between material realities, the students' personal and cultural values and their embodied self and agency. In the process, we identify a range of potential conflicting forces, for example those related to culture, educational backgrounds and nationality, which are part of students' identity constructions.

The research findings show that their negotiated identities are permeated by intersecting and conflicting discourses, practices and positions, while trying to balance a simultaneous sense of being the same as, and different from, others. Overall, we contend that Chinese HE students' discursive identities, in a TNE environment in China, are constructed in spaces in-between, characterised by a sense of continuity and fluid change across time, as well as being maintained and practised over time, thus feeding their inter-subjective sense of who they are. In this chapter, we explore how students at XJTLU negotiate their identities, as HE students and as Chinese people, in the liminal space of transnational higher education in China.

We first discuss the literature with a focus on liminality (in-between spaces) as part of identity constructions and culture negotiation. An overview of the study's methodology is then provided, followed by an explanation of the case study context, and a CDA of the interview data. This analysis centres on processes of identity constructions in the hybrid spaces of transnational HE in China.

Liminality and identity in the hybrid spaces of transnational HE in China

The context of the study that is discussed in this chapter is a transnational higher education institution in China, and the focus is on identity construc-tions within its hybrid spaces. Identity in these spaces can be seen as fluid and in constant flux, which creates a need for students at the institution to nego-tiate their identities among potentially conflicting elements of culture, lan-guage and nationality, which are never quite stable but instead always need to be worked on and renegotiated.

Stuart Hall (1996) has argued that identities are 'positions' and that they '…are never unified and [...] increasingly fragmented and fractured [...] multiply constructed across different, often intersecting and antagonistic dis-courses, practices and positions' (p. 4). For the purpose of this chapter, the term identity is used as a reflexive self-conception or self-image that partici-pants derive from their family, gender, cultural, ethnic and individual sociali-sation processes at both personal and social levels (Stryker & Serpe, 1994; Stryker, 1980; Tajfel & Turner, 1986; Mead, 1934). As such, it is built on personal experience, which in turn draws on a history and a culture, and has linguistic and geographic components (Castells, 2006); it is not fixed but is rather framed by a specific context at a particular point in time, in our case the time when the interviews with participants took place.

Furthermore, individuals may find themselves to be transitionally liminal when they are 'in-between' who they perceive they used to be (a former identity) and who they might become (a desired identity), which was fre-quently found to be the case for the participants in this study. Liminality was first introduced by Van Gennep (1960) in his book *Rites of Passage*, to refer to the main phases to rites of passage, and conceptually developed by Victor Turner (1967) to describe a subjective state of being on the threshold of or betwixt-and-between two different existential positions. It particularly presents a challenge for the enactment of identity. Van Gennep (1960) identified three stages, which are significant for our purposes here: separation (from normal routines and practices); transition/liminal stage (when the subjects of ritual fall into a limbo between past and present modes of daily existence) and (re-)incorporation (in society, with a new status/identity) (cited in Wu et al., 2020). This may be applied to the experience of Chinese students studying at a transnational higher education institution in China, where they move from separation (from their Chinese cultural background and the Chinese education system) to a transitional/liminal stage (where they are confronted by the different realities of a UK-based education system, delivered in English), and finally (re-)incorporation into Chinese society, albeit with a changed identity.

The transitions between these different stages are never completely final and are instead characterised by continuous identity negotiations. As noted above, Turner built on Van Gennep's concept and defined liminality as 'a state or process which is betwixt-and-between the normal, day-to-day cultural and social states and processes' (1979, p. 465). The Chinese students in this study may be seen as occupying a perpetual state of 'betwixt-and-between', or a liminal state, which informs their identity constructions at different stages of their educational journey.

However, this identity construction is not context-free. As Zotzman and O'Regan (2016, p. 140) argue, 'identity is to a large extent a discursive phenomenon, as representations of self and others are co-constructed through language and other semiotic resources.' They go on to note that identity constructions and negotiations involve 'acts of embodiment as individuals perform and display their identities (e.g. through fashion, cosmetics or their latest car or avatar)' (p. 140), and indeed through their language and gestures during the interviews in this study. Moreover, Lemke (2008) questions whether existing power relations are reinscribed and/or challenged in the process of identity constructions and notes that 'discourses of identity often tend to reinscribe more fundamental cultural assumptions which in turn promote a longer-term status quo' (p. 22). Thus, 'as identity constructions are imbued with power relations and ideology' (Zotzman & O'Regan, 2016, p. 140), CDA was considered an appropriate theoretical framework in this study to analyse identity constructions in the liminal spaces of a transnational higher education institution.

Thus, Chinese students' identity constructions in a TNE environment were explored based on their discursive identity constructions during interviews, which focused on how they positioned themselves in discursive interactions both actively and passively, and how they made their choices based on their personal beliefs and values (Bamberg et al., 2012). Differentiation between themselves and other(s), constructed around a sense of uniqueness and a common sense of belonging to groups (e.g. their peers) and/or culture, was an additional part of the analysis of their discursive identities. The tendency to keep a level of identity constancy (and development), while sometimes resisting change across time, is explored through the concept of liminality (Turner, 1967). From a critical realist position (Bhaskar, 2008), symbolic and material realities surrounding the participants' experiences of the transnational university were taken into consideration, as enabling or constraining their discursive identity constructions.

Previous studies on identity development in higher education institutions (e.g. Kaufman & Feldman, 2004; Torres, 2003) have suggested that universities play an important role in creating the context for the development of identities, which include personal traits (e.g. intelligence, race, gender) and identity roles (e.g. HE student, their majors, club member). Thus, a university can be viewed as 'an arena of social interaction in which the individual comes in contact with a multitude of actors in a variety of settings, and through such social interactions and other social influences identities are, in part, constituted' (Kaufman & Feldman, 2004, p. 464). Cross-border HE universities, in the form of transnational partnerships, constitute hybrid spaces where students inhabit in-between (or liminal) spaces, for example when transitioning from secondary school to HE, and from a Chinese educational system to a westernised one. This context and interactions with others within it – including other people, societal norms and/or expectations that evolve from culture – influence how one constructs one's identity (Jones, 1997; Weber, 1998; Torres, 2003). Thus, after the initial separation stage, individuals find themselves in a state of in-between-ness and ambiguity, or the liminal stage (Van Gennep, 1960), which is explored in this study.

Methodology

This chapter is informed by in-depth face-to-face semi-structured individual interviews with a purposive sample (Bryman, 2016) of 31 (9 males and 22 females) students at Xi'an Jiaotong-Liverpool University in China. Interviews were conducted in English because the focus of this study was to understand how these Chinese students constructed their cultural identity in a TNE setting, which uses English as a medium of instruction. Given that students can choose to partake their final two years of study in the UK, Year Two Semester Two Chinese students from all undergraduate courses fitted the recruitment criteria for this study. Participants were recruited through institutional mailing lists, and access to the research setting was facilitated by the good rapport established with XJTLU during the first author's 2-year professional experience at this institution (prior to this study) as an English for Academic Purposes (EAP) tutor.

After full ethical approval by both the University of Surrey and XJTLU, fieldwork was conducted for a period of eight weeks in China in 2018. This qualitative research study was designed to explore identity constructions of Chinese students in a transnational university in China, considering how both material and socially constructed factors (e.g. the Chinese education system, the transnational university, personal and cultural values) could affect the participants' life experiences and self-perceptions. It used an arts-based interview method, for which participants were given A3 white sheets and a pack of colour pencils. Each interview (60–90 minutes) was audio-recorded and transcribed verbatim, as data related to cultural identity were gathered and subsequently analysed using CDA (Fairclough, 2003; 1995).

Although it was not assumed that participants 'needed' different methods to be able to talk about the topic of identity, some aspects of human experience can be challenging for participants to verbalise; in this sense, incorporating visual methods (Boden et al., 2018; Mannay, 2016; Gauntlett, 2007; Gauntlett & Holzwarth, 2006), particularly drawing, was consonant with the adopted analytical lens in helping participants express their subjective experiences around constructions of their identity, and thus open up the possibilities for CDA to be applied. According to Gauntlett (2007), understanding of identity is better derived from creative media explorations, which gains even more validity in a Chinese cultural context. Trust is a crucial element of interpersonal relationships in a Chinese context (Li & Chua, 2016) and takes a while to be established. This is important in the context of this study because it relates directly to how interviewees draw on a range of discourses (or not, if they do not feel comfortable). Providing them with the time to settle into the situation and to 'draw their identity' first likely led to much richer data than may otherwise have been achieved.

The visuals produced by the participants were not seen as data in themselves, but rather used as prompts for discussion, that is, students took their time to draw and started talking about themselves based on their interpretation of their creation. This seemed to facilitate the flow of the interviews through probing without direct abstract questions about identity. As Gauntlett (2007) notes in his study of identity using Lego Play, a combination of three elements when using visual tools – (a) the process and taking time to make an artefact; (b) the artefact itself and (c) the individual's own interpretation of the artefact – can provide participants with the opportunity to consider what is 'particularly important to them before they are asked to generate speech' (p. 183). This approach proved to be helpful as a self-reflection tool, and because it provided participants with time to reflect in preparation for their responses.

Data were then analysed using CDA. According to Waugh et al. (2016), drawing on Wodak (2009), 'most kinds of CDA seek to demystify discourses by deciphering ideologies and to ask questions about the way specific discourse properties are deployed in the reproduction of social dominance' (p. 75). This is of particular interest in this study as such discourses become potentially unstable in the liminal zone of the transnational higher education institution. CDA is therefore used to analyse the data and to explore how identity constructions draw on discourse in the liminal spaces in which participants find themselves.

This chapter focuses on transitional liminality of identities in a transnational university, specifically, as one theme found in the overall data set. This theme emerged as student interviewees often appeared to be uncomfortably wedged between conflicting discourses of 'compliance' (with culturally hegemonic discourses around for example family and filial piety) and 'rebellion' (discourses of individualism). CDA provided a useful framework for analysis in this respect. Before explaining the case study in this chapter, it is important to outline the context of TNE in China, as this constitutes the liminal spaces in which the interview participants constructed their identities.

Transnational higher education in China

TNE in China emerged in the mid-1980s and has grown rapidly since China opened its market to the world after joining the World Trade Organisation (WTO) at the turn of the last century (Harpaz, 2019). The norms, guidelines and regulations of the WTO have influenced not only the way trade and business are managed in China, but also how higher education is run, especially as HE is defined as a service by the WTO's General Agreement on Trade (Mok & Xu, 2008; Huang, 2007; Siqueira, 2005). Since 1978, building up close links between education and the market has been the most prominent direction taken, together with decentralisation of finance and management in the reform of education (Cai, 2011).

In this context, TNE is seen as a means to rapidly boost the capacity of Chinese universities by accessing the world's most advanced education systems, thereby accelerating the process of building human capital and, ultimately, economic development (Li, 2016). Through collaborations and joint ventures, China can capitalise on the demand for foreign qualifications and/ or the shortages available at local universities and, in the long term, build its capacity to deliver its own programmes without foreign partners (Yang, 2008). China's aspiration to become a powerhouse in international education has placed attracting international students firmly on its agenda as part of growing its global influence, economic development and international engagement (Wen et al., 2018).

However, as Oleksiyenko (2018) notes, expanding access to international programmes does not automatically provide students with the skills and cultural knowledge needed to take advantage of available opportunities and to adapt to new locales (Sawir, 2005; Ranta & Meckelborg, 2013; Wang & Chang, 2016, cited in Oleksiyenko, 2018), nor does the presence of foreign students and scholars on a campus guarantee spontaneous cross-cultural interactivity and enrichment (Jaworski, 1993; Burke & Wyat-Smith, 1996; Liu, 2001; Roberts & Tuleja, 2008, cited in Oleksiyenko, 2018). In the context of fast-paced expansion of TNE in China, the impact of such TNE experiences on the way individuals construct their identities is underresearched – this is the focus of the present chapter.

Transnational HE in China takes the form of partnerships between Chinese and foreign universities, and it includes both joint institutes operated in partnership between Chinese and foreign providers, and joint programmes delivered at Chinese universities in partnership with foreign providers (British Council, 2017; Huang, 2007, 2006). Joint programmes are by far the most common type of Sino-foreign cooperation delivering programmes at bachelor's levels and above (MOE, 2014). As of June 2018, there were 2,342 Sino-foreign cooperative schools and projects, of which 1,090 were undergraduate or above (MOE, 2018).

UK providers are the most common partners for undergraduate degree programmes, while US universities lead on postgraduate provision, and Australian ones on vocational education. The fact that China and the UK have worked to create a strong bond through international education and exchange programmes since the early 20th century (British Council, 2017) might be one of the reasons why the UK is predominantly engaged with undergraduate programmes in China when compared to other countries. Most of the educational programmes provided by Chinese and foreign partners are run by institutions concentrated in the eastern coastal areas, the most economically prosperous region in China (Montgomery, 2016).

A current attempt to advocate a 'global template', in the form of curriculum internationalisation, has significant implications for students enrolled in joint programmes in China, who may perceive that the local perspective is overshadowed by a dominant global perspective on education (Yang, 2008). It is interesting in this context that our case study (XJTLU) has an institutional profile of shared control of the curriculum by both Xi'an Jiao Tong University and the University of Liverpool, which is different, for example, from the University of Nottingham-Ningbo (UNNC), where control of the curriculum is guaranteed by the University of Nottingham (Feng, 2013). These specific contexts might impact on students' experiences of TNE in different ways.

Xi'an Jiaotong-Liverpool University: The case study context

Xi'an Jiaotong-Liverpool University is a TNE collaborative institution: a joint-venture between the University of Liverpool (UK) and Xi'an Jiaotong University (China), which uses English as a medium of instruction. Located in Suzhou, in Jiangsu province on the east coast of China, XJTLU was established in 2006 and is accredited by the University of Liverpool.

The institution is classified as a Chinese tier 1 university, which means it is positioned in the top grouping of universities, when student enrolment through the National Entrance Exam, Gaokao, is taken into account. The university employs approximately 500 international academic staff from 50 different countries, with extensive international experience in industry and academia (XJTLU, 2019). XJTLU offers a range of degree programmes including bachelor, masters and PhD degrees. It is a research-led institution and increasing internationalisation remains a cornerstone of the university's mission with a gradual increase of international students. XJTLU students have a choice to do their final two undergraduate years in the UK, and similarly the University of Liverpool encourages its students to spend time studying at XJTLU's campus through their 'Year in China' programme (University of Liverpool, 2016).

In line with most Chinese universities, the Chinese students at XJTLU are required to study and pass a number of compulsory modules in Chinese Culture, Communication Studies and Physical Education in order to be awarded their degree. Except for two modules, Mandarin Chinese and Spanish language courses, all modules of all programmes are delivered in English, which is regarded as the university's *lingua franca* for academic exchange, lecturers, professional services and students across all areas and modules. Students arrive with a range of English proficiency levels and are required to take 2 years of EAP, in order to achieve specific academic language requirements.

The complexities and specificities of transnational partnerships in China call for qualitative studies that can deepen knowledge of cross-border education locally, nationally and globally, and more specifically, of how it impacts on the way students negotiate their identities in these contexts, in our case XJTLU. Thus, this study explores individuals' identity constructions at XJTLU, in the current context of Chinese economic growth and aspiration to become a global power in international education.

Findings and discussion

Identity negotiations in the hybrid space of XJTLU

The interview data showed a strong theme of 'in-betweenness' of participants in this study, or of being in Van Gennep's (1960) transition/liminal stage. As part of their identity constructions and negotiation, they drew on strong and sometimes conflicting discourses of communal culture and individuality, which were expressed in references to family and related obligations (e.g. filial piety) on the one hand, and 'rebellion' against such obligations (expressed in the pursuit of individual choices) on the other. Thus, their transitional liminal position in a transnational environment was a recurrent theme across the participants' responses, where they showed a de-centred attachment to more than one cultural identity. They felt, for example, that they had a Chinese self (e.g., in the figure of conformity) (Hwang, 1999) and an international student self, which would (or would not) overlap through embeddedness across a range of networks in the transnational context in which they found themselves.

Some participants exercised a considerable level of agency in terms of the identity they projected (Goffman, 1959). In expressing their social identities, they drew upon a range of discourses, as well as their own self-perceptions. Their personal identities, as an internalised view of the self as part of which they sought to 'keep a particular narrative' (Giddens, 1991), for

Figure 13.1 Xiao na's representation of her identity

example when attempting to commit to cultural beliefs, were at times in conflict with a desired identity, which became more salient as they found themselves in spaces in-between.

The following quotation from Xiao na[1] is an example of this, as she constructs 'versions of reality' through her discourse of conformity to avoid confrontation and in an effort to be accepted by both her family and her peers. This quotation is based on her drawing (Figure 13.1).

> The grass seems to be the girl, who always listens to her parents and who is always under her parents protection and she knows her parents love her, and it's like this blue glass bottle is not a bad thing, it's a protection to this small grass, but the grass just doesn't want to grow in a limited place, it wants to grow out of something… sometimes she has different ideas from others, and but she doesn't want to tell them, she always agrees with others and, in fact, in her heart, I think she wants to show her opinion, in fact, she is always a good girl but sometimes she wants to break the rules…but maybe I am different now, I think she is much more independent and braver, and before coming to XJTLU, she was a bit shy, she is much more brave and she is becoming more and more independent.
>
> (Xiao na, Female, Applied English undergraduate student)

She draws here on conflicting discourses of filial piety ('who always listens to her parents') and independence and individuality ('she is becoming more and more independent'). However, she sounded uncomfortable and conflicted talking about her own identity, which is reflected in her use of the 'detached' third person, when she mentioned she wished to 'break the rules' and saw herself as a bit 'braver' than she used to be. In this sense, there was an implied discourse of boundaries or resistance (i.e. a desire to cross such boundaries) here.

Xiao na's response showed a desire to put herself in a position of an active 'agentive self-constructor' (Bamberg et al., 2012). To 'break the rules' required Xiao na's higher agency in order to construct an identity of a person who comes across as strong, in control and self-determined, which she portrayed verbally and through her drawing, the latter mirroring her complex linguistic account.

Some participants resisted identity change processes through their TNE experiences and tried to maintain a perception of a consistent self, based on dominant discourses of what it means to be Chinese (Hsiao & Bailey, 2017). For example, when Xiao xu was invited to reflect on how she perceived herself after 2 years in this particular transnational environment, she described how her peers seemed to have changed in the new environment, but she had not; although she sounded like she contradicted herself about her own changes, she did not believe/want her identity to be (re)shaped in fear of not being 'recognised' or accepted by others, and in particular the people she knew and associated with prior to starting at university.

> I would say I'm practically the same compared to others, who changed very quickly. They have changed their way of thinking because they have experienced a lot of different programmes [referring to their studies] … but I haven't had that experience, I wish I did; I don't think they changed because of their experience, I think they have the courage to change... I can take more responsibility by myself now, but what if everybody just hates me? What if my old friends can't recognise me as I was before, I mean, if they think I have changed but I actually haven't changed…
>
> (Xiao xu, Female, Applied Mathematics undergraduate student)

Xiao xu initially attributed her peers' identity (re)constructions around her to being exposed to 'different programmes' at the university and experiences, and then, interestingly, she said it was actually an individual choice, which required courage that she felt she did not have. Thus, she drew on discourses of individuality (with an emphasis on agency and personal responsibility), which are common, in the XJTLU context, among international teachers, staff and her peers. According to theories of student development (e.g. Evans et al., 2010; Chickering & Reisser, 1993), which involves a process of differentiation and integration, 'students struggle to reconcile new ideas, values and beliefs' (p. 35) in the new environment, where there are tensions between social expectations around cultural behaviour and perceived personal identities. Applying Turner's (1967) concept of liminality as in-between positions, the reconstructions of identities (in which the sense of self can be significantly disrupted), manifested as persistently ambiguous, is illustrated here through Xiao xu's resistance to show transformations in the new environment, perceiving her reshaped identity as negative for herself and her peers, in turn creating a fear of not being recognised any longer. Yet at the same time, she notes that 'they have the courage to change', suggesting that she has not.

Another example explicitly shows a student's struggle and negotiation process to incorporate his cultural upbringing, as related to Confucian values, which surfaced through elements such as conformity and obligation to reciprocal favours (Hwang, 1999), and the conflicting ways in which he constructed his relationships and his desired identity. When invited to reflect on the person he thought he was, he drew a cactus (Figure 13.2) and responded:

> mmm… I'm basically likable, but I don't get too close to people…my mum…she taught me that…you can love everything and you hate everything, but there is something outside in the world you have to do… you know…Chinese people pay attention a lot to tradition…For example

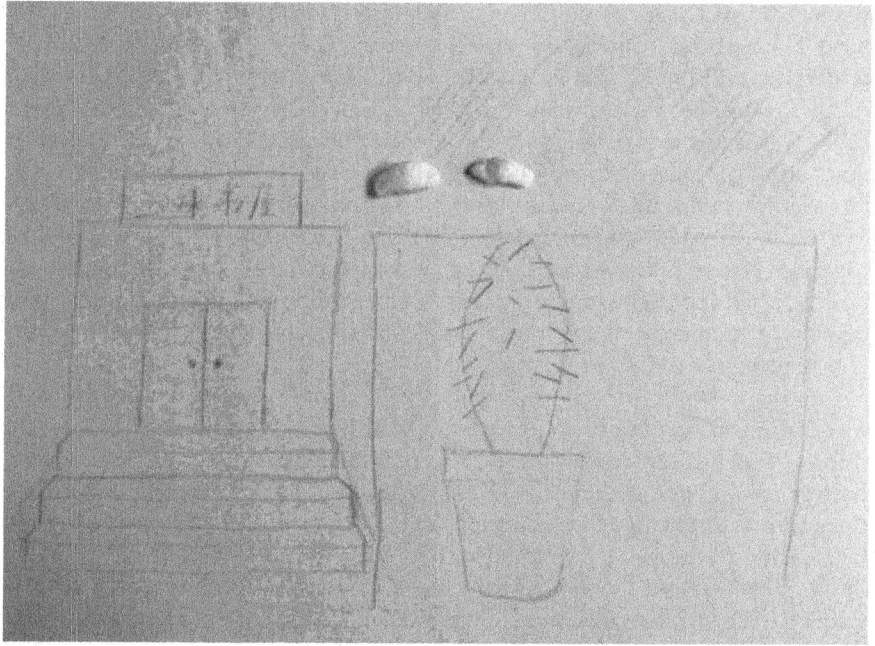

Figure 13.2 Xiao wei's representation of identity

I give you something...it's appropriate for you to give me something back...and also when hanging out with friends[2]... I feel uncomfortable hanging out with 'so called friends'... it's how they act...I know some of them hate each other, but they mask themselves and pretend to like them...and I think it's a Chinese thing...we are taught Confucius values... mmm... 'no individualism'.... but I think everyone should have their own ideas, their own opinion and not be affected by others and...at home, I pay attention to that...because my parents are very traditional...
     (Xiao wei, Male, Financial Mathematics undergraduate student)

Xiao wei's conflict in trying to accommodate his identity (e.g. likable... not getting too close to people) and social identity as a child, student and friend at the university was quite clear in his response, which appeared to impact on his interpersonal relationships. He drew explicitly on discourses of Confucian Chinese culture as a binary opposite to individualism (King, 2018). His relative intolerance of Chinese cultural values of conformity and giving/saving face ('...I know some of them hate each other, but they mask themselves and pretend to like them...and I think it's a Chinese thing...'), for example, showed the spectrum of intersubjective values, implying ethical standards that differentiated him from others ('Chinese people pay attention a lot to tradition and maybe... I think it's a Chinese thing... it's weird for me...I feel uncomfortable'), while conforming to cultural values when he is at home ('at home...I'm very...mm...I pay attention to that...because my parents are very traditional... my family, they are all very traditional'). Some of this may have been about impression management, vis-à-vis both a non-Chinese researcher and his ex-teacher, a context which exemplified the liminal zone of the transnational university. XJTLU, as a TNE institution in China, enables intersubjective identifications with culturally different groups in a fluid and complex manner, but this does not occur without conflict. The cross-border education provision within China brings the local (as in China as a physical space) and the global (as in an international space) very close together. There was a stronger awareness of the participants' 'Chineseness' when embedded in the liminal space of an international bubble in their home country, which created a need for self-reflection and developmental identity constructions.

Identity-related cultural discourses, for example the clear struggle with conforming to his cultural values, to which he referred to as '... a Chinese thing...with which he disagrees', shows how his identity was situated in-between fluid personal identity constructions, and a situationally negotiated one. Interestingly, he also identified with a young generation that seems to be attaching decreasing importance to Chinese cultural traditions: '...nowadays many teenagers don't actually believe that... [referring to Confucian values]'. Yet, at the same time, he needed to negotiate his personal values when he was at home with his family with strong traditional values. His identification with a generation that does not appear to value traditional Chinese culture is part of a process of constant self-recognition (Hall, 1996) that could have been enabled by not only a local transnational context, but also a type of 'everyday transnationalism' (Gu & Schweisfurth, 2015). The latter is aided by ubiquitous modern technology, through which various intersubjectivities, networks and environments can be created and transformed, which was explicitly noted by another participant (Xiao yong):

> Xiao yong: I'm easy going...and I'm inclusive for most things, and I respect people for what they want to be...[...]...I'm bisexual and I like this in western music, Lady Gaga for example contributed so much to the LGBT community...and maybe what shapes me is tolerance for different groups.
> Interviewer: [...] And do you feel comfortable being open about your sexual orientation in China?
> Xiao yong: My parents don't know about it, maybe younger generations started respecting it, not older generations, but it's the same in America [...] and I love China now...for Chinese government they do not show anything against it, they accept this, but they are not against it [...]. I'm proud to be Chinese, and it's because we have a long history, our own cultural values [...] our old traditional values...but at the same time it has evolved.
> (Xiao yong, Male, Information and Computing Science undergraduate student)

Xiao yong's identity transformation was manifested through and from various sources and networks, enabled by globalised communication networks. Similar to other participants in this study, his identity construction was multidimensional, and included shared personal, enacted (i.e. an individual's performed or expressed identity) and relational layers (Hetcht et al., 2003; Jung et al., 2007). Xiao yong was very open and appeared anxious to say as much as he could, while still sounding appreciative of his own culture.

Without having lived abroad, but in the context of increasing interconnectivity, Xiao yong's reflexivity showed wider cultural knowledge and cosmopolitan values, as demonstrated in his openness towards his sexual orientation (which was not openly shared with his family) and an inclusive attitude towards diverse values in his individual experience, which all shaped his identity construction process. He also identified with a younger generation that 'started respecting it, not older generations...', and was aware of a broader LGBTQ+ community discourse worldwide ('...but it's the same in America'), which made him feel that China was no different in this aspect, reinforcing his pride to be Chinese, but positioning his Chineseness as being part of a global community. Yet, there seemed to be an identity threat (Segal, 2010) to being LGBTQ+ in China, exemplified by hiding his sexual orientation from his family, and the apparent prominence of non-Chinese role models that play a part in Xiao yong's identity construction in this respect. Furthermore, the researcher (and first author) being non-Chinese further facilitated his eagerness to talk about his sexuality and other personal values, which may otherwise have remained concealed, and thus allowed him to explore the boundaries of his own identity construction. The latter may also be based on a sense of trust and confidence, developed over time, that it was okay to share such personal values in the liminal space that is the transnational university. As noted, the arts-based element of the interview process further contributed to the building of trust in this respect.

Although Xiao yong was speaking from within a transnational university context, his self-perceived identity was not explicitly linked to his university experience (as per his response), but was partly drawn from global sources and facilitated by technological interconnectivity.

In this sense, and for most participants in this study, not only the transnational university, but a broader context of embeddedness in a range of networks within and outside of China, enabled by technology, contributed to and even exacerbated the liminality of the spaces in which they constructed their situated cultural identities, even if participants showed differing levels of awareness of this process. However, the transnational university definitely legitimised and stimulated this global interconnectivity. This further points to the fact that HE institutions (transnational or not) should not be perceived as completely bounded environments, as students continue to be influenced by a range of significant others outside the university (family and friends, for instance) and virtual networks (e.g. social media and other Internet-related resources), but such institutions do provide a liminal space which forces students to engage with competing discourses in constructing (and re-constructing) their identities.

Conclusion

In this chapter, we have reported on a study that explored the process of identity constructions in the liminal space of a transnational university in China. We have used XJTLU as a case study because it can be seen as a microcosm of the competing forces that impact on identity constructions. It is thus a liminal space in which students negotiate different value systems and in doing so continually construct (and reconstruct) their identities. In other words, in the liminal spaces of the transnational university in China, Chinese students are reimagining themselves and exploring the boundaries of how they can construct their own changing identities. What this study shows is that this is a relational process that is never finalised but instead is in constant flux, impacted upon for example by language, peers (both local and international), teachers, global media and family, among other factors. Within the liminal space of the transnational university, Chinese students are engaged in a process of identity construction that involves reimaging their value system and their cultural position as it relates to potentially conflicting cultural discourses. This process is different for each individual, even if it has similarities based on particular experiences, such as the diverse influences students are exposed to through engagement with teachers from a variety of different countries and cultures. This ongoing process of identity construction is likely to have a profound impact on the ways in which these students see themselves and their place in the world into the future, and by extension on the way China as a nation will reimagine itself in its engagement with the rest of the world.

Notes

1 Participants' names are not their real names in this chapter.
2 Xiao wei was referring to the Chinese cultural value known as *guanxi*: although relationships and personal connection-building are not unique to China, *guanxi* assumes a level of reciprocal favour. Originated from Confucianism, it is a system that emphasises mutual obligation and trust (Tsang and Kwan, 1999).

References

Bamberg, M., De Fina, A., & Schiffrin, D. (2012). Discourse and identity construction. In Schwartz, S. J., Luyckx, K. and Vignoles, V. L. (Eds). *Handbook of identity theory research* (pp. 177–200). New York: Routledge.

Bhaskar, R. (2008; 1975). *A realist theory of science*. Leeds: Leeds Books.

Boden, Z., Larkin, M., & Iyer, M. (2018). Picturing ourselves in the world: Drawings, interpretative phenomenological analysis and the relational mapping interview. *Qualitative Research in Psychology* 16:2, 218–236. DOI: 10.1080/14780887. 2018.1540679.

British Council (2017). Country report: The People's Republic of China. Universities UK International. Retrieved 11 September 2019 at: https://www.qaa.ac.uk/docs/qaa/international/country-report-china-2017.pdf?sfvrsn=12c9f781_10.

Brooks, R. (2018). The construction of higher education students in English policy documents. *British Journal of Sociology of Education* 39:6, 745–761. DOI: 10.1080/01425692.2017.1406339.

Bryman, A. (2016). *Social research methods* (5th ed). Oxford: Oxford University Press.

Cai, Y. (2011). Cross-border higher education in China and its implications for Finland. In Y. Cai and J. Kivistö (Eds.) *Higher education reforms in Finland and China: Experiences and challenges in post-massification era* (pp. 245–260). Tampere: Tampere University Press.

Castells, M., (2006). Globalisation and identity: a comparative perspective. Retrieved August 7 2019 from: file:///C:/Users/pr00256/Desktop/SEPT%202019%20working%20VERSIONS%20after%20HH%20feedback/Castells.pdf.

Chickering, A. W. & Reisser, L. (1993) *Education and identity*. (2nd) ed. San Francisco: Jossey-Bass.

Evans, N. J., Forney, D. S., Guido, F. M., Patton, L. D., & Penn, K. A. (2010) *Student development in college: Theory, research, and practice* (2nd ed.). San Francisco: Jossey-Bass Publishers.

Fairclough, N. (2003) *Analysing discourse: Textual analysis for social research*. London & New York: Routledge.

Fairclough, N. (1995) *Critical discourse analysis.* London: Longman.

Feng, Y. (2013) University of Nottingham Ningbo China and Xi'an Jiaotong-Liverpool University: globalisation of higher education in China. *Higher Education,* 65 (4), 471–485.

Gauntlett, D. (2007) *Creative explorations: New approaches to identities and audiences.* London: Routledge.

Gauntlett, D., & Holzwarth, P. (2006). Creative and visual methods for exploring identities. *Visual Studies* 21:1, 82–91. DOI: 10.1080/14725860600613261.

Giddens, A. (1991) *Modernity and self-identity: Self and society in the late modern age.* Stanford, CA: Stanford University Press.

Goffman, E. (1959) *The presentation of self in everyday life.* Garden City, NJ: Doubleday.

Gu, Q., & Schwesifurth, M. (2015) Transnational connections, competences and identities: Experiences of Chinese international students after their return 'home'. *British Educational Research Journal* 41:6, 947–970. DOI: 10.1002/berj.3175.

Hall, S. (1996). Who needs identity? In S. Hall & P. du Gay (Eds) *Questions of cultural identity.* London: Sage Publications.

Harpaz, M. D. (2019). China and the WTO: On a path to leadership? In K. Zeng (Ed.), *Handbook on the international political economy of China* (pp. 260–280). Cheltenham (UK): Edward Elgar.

Hecht, M. L., Jackson, R. L., & Ribeau, S. A. (2003) *African American communication: Exploring identity and culture.* Mahwah, NJ: Erlbaum.

Hsiao, Y., and Bailey, L. E. (2017). Accommodating and resisting dominant discourses: the reproduction of inequality in a Chinese American community. In R. Elmesky, C. Yeakey, & O. Marcucci (Eds.), *The power of resistance: Culture, ideology and social reproduction in global contexts* (pp. 77–98). UK: Emerald Publishing Limited.

Huang, F. (2007) Internationalisation of higher education in the developing and emerging countries: A focus on transnational higher education in Asia. *Journal of Studies in International Education* 11:3–4, 421–432. DOI:10.1177/1028315307303919.

Huang, F. (2006) Transnational higher education in mainland China: a focus on foreign degree-conferring programs. In F. Huang (Ed.) *Transnational higher education in Asia and Pacific region* (pp. 21–34). Hiroshima: Research Institute for Higher Education, Hiroshima University.

Hwang, K. K. (1999) Filial piety and loyalty: Two types of social identification in confucianism. *Asian Journal of Social Psychology* 2, 163–183.

Jones, S. R. (1997). Voices of identity and difference: A qualitative exploration of the multiple dimensions of identity development in women college students. *Journal of College Student Development* 38, 376–386.

Jung, E., Hecht, M. L., & Wadsworth, B. C. (2007). The role of identity in international students' psychological wellbeing in the United States: A model of depression level, identity gaps, discrimination and acculturation. *Intercultural Journal of Intercultural Relations* 31, 605–624.

Kaufman, P., & Feldman, K.A. (2004) Forming identities in college: A sociological approach. *Research in Higher Education* 45:5, 463–496.

King, A. Y. C. (2018). *China's great transformation: Selected essays on Confucianism, modernization, and democracy.* Hong Kong: Chinese University of Hong Kong Press.

Lemke, J. (2008). Identity, development, and desire: Critical questions. In C. Caldas-Coulthard, & R. Iedema (Eds.), *Identity trouble: Critical discourse and contested identities* (pp. 17–42). Houndmills: Palgrave Macmillan.

Li, F. (2016). The internationalization of higher education in China: The role of government. *Journal of International Education Research* 12:1, 47–52.

Li, Z., & Chua, C. E. H. (2016). A cultural analysis of the difference between interpersonal trust and institutional trust. In *Pacific Asia Conference On Information Systems (PACIS) Proceedings*. Association for Information Systems. http://aisel.aisnet.org/pacis2016/366

Mannay, D. (2016). *Visual, narrative and creative research methods: Application, reflection and ethics.* New York: Routledge.

Mead, G. H. (1934) *Mind, Self and Society from the Standpoint of a Social Behaviorist.* Chicago: University of Chicago Press.

Ministry of Education of the People's Republic of China - MOE. (2014). *List of Chinese colleges and universities in China 2014.* Retrieved August 10 2016, from http://www.moe.edu.cn/publicfiles/business/htmlfiles/moe/moe_2804/201409/175222.html.

Ministry of Education, P. R. China MOE (2018) Notice in Chinese: 教育部办公厅关于批准部分中外合作办学机构和项目终止的通知， 教外厅函〔2018〕39号), Retrieved from https://internationaleducation.gov.au/International-network/china/PolicyUpdates-China/Pages/Article-Chinas-Ministry-of-Education-confirms-formal-termination-of-234-defunct-transnational-education-partnerships.aspx.

Mok, K., & Xu, X. (2008). When China opens to the world: A study of transnational higher education in Zhejiang, China, *Asian Pacific Education Review* 9, 393–408.

Montgomery, C. (2016). Transnational partnerships in higher education in China: the diversity and complexity of elite strategic alliances. *London Review of Education.* 14:1. DOI: 10.18546/LRE.14.1.08.

Oleksiyenko, A. (2018). *Global mobility and higher learning.* London & New York: Routledge.

Segal, L. (2010). Genders: Deconstructed, reconstructed, still on the move. In M. Wetherell & C. T. Mohanty (Eds), *The Sage handbook of identities* (pp. 321–338). London: Sage.

Siqueira, A.C. (2005). The regulation of education through the WTO/GATS. *Journal for Critical Education Policy Studies.* Retrieved September 12 2019 from: http://www.jceps.com/?pageID=article&articleID41.

Stryker, S. (1980). *Symbolic interactionism: A social structural version.* Menlo Park, CA: Benjamin Cummings.

Stryker, S., & Serpe, R. T. (1994). Identity salience and psychological centrality: equivalent, overlapping, or complementary concepts? *Social Psychology Quarterly.* 57, 16–35.

Tajfel, H., & Turner, J. C. (1986). The social identity theory of intergroup behaviour. In S. Worchel & W. G. Austin (Eds). *The psychology of intergroup behaviour* (pp. 7–24). Chicago: Nelson Hall.

Torres, V. (2003). Influences on ethnic identity development of Latino college students in the first two years of college. *Journal of College Student Development* 44, 532–547.

Tsang, E., & Kwan, K. (1999). Replication and theory development in organizational science: A critical realist perspective. *Academy of Management Review* 24:4, 759–780.

Turner, V. (1967). *The forest of symbols: Aspects of Ndembu ritual.* Ithaca (NY): Cornell University Press.

Turner, V. (1979) Frame, Flow and Reflection: Ritual and Drama as Public Liminality. *Japanese Journal of Religious Studies* 6:4, 463–572. doi: 10.18874/jjrs.6.4.1979.465-499.

University of Liverpool (2016). *Year in China programme.* Retrieved September 14 2019 from: https://www.liverpool.ac.uk/study-abroad/outbound/what-is-study-abroad/year-in-china/.

van Gennep, A. (1960) *The rites of passage.* Chicago: University of Chicago Press.

Waugh, L., Catalano, T., Al Masaeed, K., Do, T. H., & Renigar, P. (2016). Critical discourse analysis: Definition, approaches, relation to pragmatics, critique, and trends. In A. Capone & J. Mey (Eds.), *Interdisciplinary studies in pragmatics, culture and society* (pp. 71–135). Cham: Springer.

Weber, L. (1998). A conceptual framework for understanding race, class, gender, and sexuality. *Psychology of Women Quarterly.* 22, 13–22.

Wen, W., Chen, Q., & Wu, S. N. (2018). The "one belt one road" initiatives and international education in China. In *China blue book of education* (pp. 171–187). Beijing: Social Sciences Academic Press.

Wodak, R. (2009) *The discourse of politics in action. Politics as usual.* London: Palgrave.

Wu, S., Li, Y., Wood, E., Senaux, B., & Dai, G. (2020). Liminality and festivals – insights from the East. *Annals of Tourism Research,* 80. doi: 10.1016/j.annals.2019.102810

XJTLU (2019). *XJTLU Fees.* Retrieved September 11 2019 from: https://www.xjtlu.edu.cn/en/study-with-us/admissions/fees.

Yang, R. (2008). Transnational higher education in China: Contexts, characteristics and concerns. *Australian Journal of Education* 52, 272–286.

Zotzmann, K., & O'Regan, J. P. (2016). Critical discourse analysis and identity. In S. Preece (Ed.), *The Routledge handbook of language and identity* (pp. 139–154). London: Routledge.

Chapter 14

Between international student and immigrant

A critical perspective on Angolan and Cape Verdean students in Portugal

Elisa Alves and Russell King

Introduction

International student migration/mobility (ISM) has been studied from diverse perspectives. Key topics for attention have included students' motivations to study abroad, their experiences and integration in the host society, the efforts of universities and other higher education institutes (HEIs) to attract them, and government policies on ISM (Riaño & Piguet, 2016). However, the actual meaning of the term 'international student' remains somewhat elusive. According to King, Findlay and Ahrens (2010), it has been studied through two main lenses: a statistical-geographical one, focused on defining, quantifying and mapping the flows across international borders; and a more sociological perspective, focusing on students' motivations, perceptions, experiences and identities, often linking and contrasting the societies of origin and destination.

From the perspective of host countries in Europe, North America and Australia, the sociological literature points to a certain way of life among international students: they are seen as young, mobile cosmopolitans (Bilecen, 2016; King & Raghuram, 2013), possessed of the economic, social and cultural capital to be considered an elite population (Brooks & Waters, 2011; Murphy-Lejeune, 2002). In fact, many authors go further and suggest that international students are 'an elite within an elite', in the way they are positively selected within the pool of higher education students, and that their international exposure gives them further advantages which can be 'capitalised', leading to increasing inequality within the overall population of students and graduates (Bilecen & Van Mol, 2017). Put another way, going abroad to study, especially at a 'world-class' institution, bestows social distinction and upward socio-economic mobility among international students and their families (Findlay, King, Smith, Geddes & Skeldon, 2012; Waters, 2012).

While we accept this general theoretical argument about ISM and the social reproduction of elites, we are wary about considering international students as a homogeneous class. Our analysis in this chapter will nuance the meaning, experiences and embodiment of international students, based on primary research on Angolan and Cape Verdean students in Portugal. These two groups of international students have long been the most numerous in Portugal, dating back to colonial times (Costa & Faria, 2012; França, Alves & Padilla, 2018). Angolan and Cape Verdean labour migrants have also been two of the largest immigrant communities in the country (Malheiros, 1998). This latter situation creates a social perception of the international students from these countries as underprivileged immigrants rather than an elite or a cosmopolitan category.

The chapter unfolds as follows. Next, we discuss different meanings of the term 'international student'. This is succeeded by a brief section on methods. The main body of the chapter presents research findings, based on semi-structured interviews with 49 research participants – final-year students and graduates – most of whom were interviewed twice. We find that many students feel themselves, and are made to feel by the racialised reaction of the host society, as somewhere 'in between' international students and immigrants.

International students: Multiple understandings

According to most definitions, an international student crosses an international border to study in another country; but this is not necessarily the same as being a 'foreign student'. In its *Education at a Glance*, the OECD (2018, p. 225) clarifies the distinction:

> **Foreign students** are those who are not citizens of the country in which they are enrolled and where the data are collected. Although they are counted as internationally mobile, they may be long-term residents or even be born in the 'host' country. While pragmatic and operational, this classification may be inappropriate for capturing student mobility because of differing national policies regarding the naturalisation of immigrants. ... **International students** are those who left their country of origin and moved to another country for the purpose of study. The country of origin of a tertiary student is defined according to the ... 'country of prior education' or 'country of usual residence'.

The above distinction is crucial, especially when making international comparisons of statistics on ISM, but there are other complexities to bear in mind. The differentiation between 'national' and 'international' students can be sociologically problematic (Jones, 2017). On the one hand, international students might know the language of the foreign country, might have studied there before and be familiar with its academic system. On the other hand, a 'national' student might not know the language well, perhaps because he or she is a naturalised migrant or refugee, or belongs to a minority ethnic and linguistic group. What is more, students of migrant heritage who are 'visibly different' might be perceived as 'foreign' students, whereas in fact they are resident nationals.

Further complexity arises when we consider motivations. For many migrants and mobile people, including students, the decision-making process involves multiple motives. The aim of studying abroad might, or might not, be the principal reason for the move; either way, it could be mixed with other purposes. Obtaining a student visa might be a pragmatic route to enter a country when the main reason is something else – to work, to get refugee status or to raise a family. This leads to an interesting semantic about whether students who are spending a study period abroad, and are perhaps simultaneously engaged in other things, such as part-time work for an income, should be regarded as migrants or as mobile people. As indicated at the very beginning of this chapter, 'ISM' stands for both international student migration and international student mobility. In the broader literature on migration, and reflecting the so-called 'mobilities turn' in studies of Western societies (Cresswell, 2006; Urry, 2007), the main distinction between migration and mobility focuses on length of stay and degree of embedding in the host society. In one of the first detailed studies of students moving within Europe, Murphy-Lejeune (2002, p. 5) summed up this distinction as follows:

Migration [is] a decisive final movement leading to a long-term social integration and assimilation, implying a slow but intense transformation of the individuals concerned. Mobility [implies] a shorter kind of integration, where personal transformations may be more peripheral.

Subsequently the migration–mobility dialectic was applied to two binary situations within ISM. Students who moved for entire degree programmes, commonly 3 years or more, were migrant students, whereas those who moved within a degree programme, for a semester or year abroad, were mobile students (King & Raghuram, 2013). The second mode of distinction is based more on geography: students moving within Europe are engaged in mobility, whereas those coming from outside Europe or Western countries are student migrants (King, Lulle, Morosanu & Williams, 2016). In this latter scenario, historical and colonial relations may also play a part, since the students are moving along the same channels as the larger volumes of economic migrants looking for work in the former colonial metropole. Examples are Indians in the UK, students from the Maghreb countries in France, from Latin America in Spain, or from Portugal's former African colonies (including Angola and Cape Verde) in Portugal. According to Rozenweig's (2006) 'migration model' of international student movement, 'student immigration' occurs when the protagonists come from countries with low returns to education and poor opportunities for remunerative employment for returning graduates, so that a period of study abroad is followed by applications for better-paid jobs in the host country.

From the etic categories imposed by researchers, statisticians or host-country governments, we move to the emic perspective of the international students who, on the whole, do not see themselves as migrants.

Ask them if they are migrants, and they will reply no, they are international students...Purposely or unwittingly, they distance themselves
from migrants, who are constructed in their minds as people who move
for work and who are more likely to be poor people or refugees.

(King et al., 2016, p. 15)

The quotation above refers to intra-European student movers, where the
dominant construction among EU institutions, which applies also to temporary labour migration, is to label this as 'mobility' (thereby stressing its tem-
porariness) rather than as 'migration' (which implies a 'threat' of permanent
settlement). However, even within Europe, this distinction is problematic,
reflecting geopolitical discrimination. On the one hand, 'Western' European
students are viewed as unproblematic *mobile students* who will probably move
on and, even if they do elect to stay, are welcome to do so; on the other hand,
migrant students from the 'Eastern', post-2004 accession countries are viewed
with a marker of territorial stigmatisation (Wilken & Dahlberg, 2017). The
experience of students from countries like Poland and Romania is reinforced
by their need to work part-time to support their studies. Because of their
stigmatised nationality, they are then viewed by employers as akin to less-
educated labour migrants and offered only menial, poorly paid jobs. Outside
Europe, the exploitation of international, especially non-white, students is
also confirmed, for instance in Australia (Nyland et al., 2009; Tran, 2017).
These studies have the effect of further distancing international students from
the ideal of the cosmopolitan international individual who is viewed as a mix
of some kind of cultural tourist and proto-expat (Bilecen, 2016).

The cases we explore in this chapter concern two international student
communities in Portugal, from Angola and from Cape Verde. Our data
report only individuals who left Angola and Cape Verde and went to Portugal
with the main purpose of completing a course, which means a focus on international students (as opposed to foreign students) and on degree mobility.
For an unbiased reading and discussion of the results, we adopt a neutral
position regarding the use of the terms *mobile students* vs *migrant students*.
As the outcomes of our study will show, Angolan and Cape Verdean students
in Portugal do not always see themselves as 'typical' international students;
nor does the host society view them in that way. Some of them feel more like
immigrants, living in precarious conditions and struggling to survive. Both
within the university and in the wider society, they are made to feel rather
like 'second-class' international students. Detailed evidence for this will now
be presented, following a brief outline of our research methods.

Methods and participants

The core research instrument for this research was the in-depth semi-structured
interview carried out with 49 Angolan (26) and Cape Verdean (23) students
and former students, most of whom were interviewed twice, making 85

interviews overall. The interviews were designed to ascertain participants' educational and socio-economic background, their motivations and expectations regarding the choice of Portugal, their social and academic integration in the host society (the main theme of this chapter) and their mobility projects after graduation. Most were interviewed in the final year of their degree and then later as part of a follow-up strategy. This strategy aimed to evaluate whether students were able or not to accomplish their mobility projects, and why. The first-round interviews took place when students were enrolled in a Portuguese HEI; the re-interviews were one or more years later, when they were either further on in their studies or already graduated. Most were conducted during the period 2017–2019, except a few pilot interviews in 2013. Both face-to-face and online interviews were carried out, mostly in Lisbon but a few also in other university cities. The interviewees comprised a mix of student levels – bachelor, master and doctoral students, as well as (in the second-round interviews only) recent graduates. All were engaged in degree mobility; none were credit-mobile students. Equal numbers of men and women were in the sample.

Participants were initially accessed from the authors' personal networks and an online survey,[1] followed by the snowball technique. The objectives of the research were explained to all the participants and written consent forms were signed. Fictitious names were given to all participants to ensure their anonymity. The quotations selected in the next sections of the paper give 'typical' indications of their experiences, thoughts and feelings, highlighting the way they position themselves in Portugal, including their reactions to the views of Portuguese society towards them.

The main reasons behind interviewees' move to Portugal were better education, access to specialised fields of study, acquisition of a scholarship, the shared Portuguese language and the presence of support networks in the host country. They were enrolled in both public and private HEIs in Portugal, with a predominant focus on social science programmes of study, plus small numbers enrolled in courses on engineering, health studies and architecture.

Most of the participants saw themselves as belonging to the middle class in their home countries. Despite this, some differences between the two national groups were noted, which are in line with official statistics (DGEEC, 2016) and other studies (Pedreira, 2015). The Angolans tend to come from more privileged and well-off family backgrounds. Parents are mainly civil servants, business owners and professionals, many of whom had themselves studied abroad. Without specific questioning or prompting, several described their lifestyle back in Angola as having 'perks' such as housemaids and their own cars. Moreover, they were more likely to be enrolled in private HEIs in Portugal and on postgraduate programmes. By contrast, the Cape Verdeans were more likely to be undergraduate students in public HEIs and to be the beneficiaries of grants and scholarships to study in Portugal. Most parents of Cape Verdean students have only basic education and work in construction, factories and other less-skilled jobs; those with higher education – mainly fathers – were civil servants.

Student, foreigner or immigrant? Hierarchies in the classroom and in employment

From the interviews, it is possible to see that Angolan (A) and Cape Verdean (CV) students see themselves with reference to a range of identifications – as an international student, foreigner or immigrant – according to their individual perception and also depending on the situational context. The idea of being a foreigner was related to being in a different place to one's home country and experiencing a feeling of 'otherness'. Answering a question about what things he would like to change in the university, Afonso (CV), a graduate student, said HEIs should give city maps and things like that to students from abroad, because, in his words, 'It's a little bit like, not the same, but like being a tourist abroad'. Afonso's hesitancy about identifying as a tourist is an interesting self-reflection and certainly does not accord with the perception of the 'white' Portuguese population of the 'black' Africans in their midst. For Afonso, the idea of being like a 'foreign tourist' related to how he felt in his daily encounters in and outside the university, where he saw himself as a 'visitor' who clearly did not 'belong' and was perhaps 'passing through' – and far from the image of a wealthy foreign tourist or expatriate.

The self-perception as a foreign tourist was not a widespread view. Much more common were hybrid articulations of 'student', 'immigrant' and 'African', most of which translate into feelings of 'difference' and 'distance' between themselves and the majority host society, including the majority student population.

One area where feelings of everyday difference and rejection were frequently experienced was the university classroom. Several participants reported 'splits' in student groupings along nationality lines. These divisions are not created by the interviewees, nor by their tutors and professors, but by the other students, who appear to see 'immigrant' students, especially Africans, as a threat to their academic success.

> Especially with us, Africans and immigrants, the problem of student working groups is that nobody wants to form a group with us. There is the stigma among the other students that Africans are dumb. So nobody includes you in their group. And if they do, they never accept your opinion, because the opinion of an African doesn't count.
>
> (Ana, CV, Bachelor's degree student)

This quotation, and several others, suggest that differences among students are split along the lines of nationality and geographic origin, and by implication 'race'. This result is in line not only with studies on 'East-West' student and academic mobility in Europe (Amelina, 2013; Wilken & Dahlberg, 2017) but also with research in other regions: for instance, in the United States, where Dominican students (Urban, Orbe, Tavares & Alvarez, 2010) and Asian students (Quinton, 2020) face similar discrimination, or in South Korea and with 'other' Asian students (Byun & Jung, 2019; Suh, Flores & Wang, 2019). Ranked in terms of relative desirability as a friend or project collaborator, in Portugal it seems that the African is at the bottom. Note, too, how Ana uses the labels 'Africans' and 'immigrants' and not 'international students'.

Our participants were also alive to more subtle status divisions, including within the majority Portuguese students between those from the city and those who hail from rural and provincial districts of Portugal. This was picked up by Mario (A), a graduate student who has returned to Angola:

> Even today, Portuguese society has a very strict stratification. Not only for foreigners, but even for the Portuguese, for example those come from the countryside... Portugal is a country of families, of surnames, so if it is difficult for a Portuguese [from a rural area], how much worse is it for us, who come from another country.

In Portuguese higher education, social and ethnic differentiation is expressed in a multi-level hierarchy. At the top level of 'academic citizenship' are the Portuguese students, with some social-class and cosmopolitan-orientation divisions between those from Lisbon and from well-known families, and those from peripheral regions of the country. At the next level come 'European' foreign students and, finally, the Africans. The latter group are classified by their geographic origin and skin colour and are further defined by Portuguese colonial history as culturally inferior (Vala, Lopes & Lima, 2008). This feature of colonial legacies is also felt by African international students in other postcolonial contexts (see, for instance, Daniels, 2014). As a result, the interviewees often felt that they had to work extra hard to 'prove themselves' – the same syndrome noted by Amelina (2013) for Ukrainian students and young researchers in Germany, who struggled to overcome their ascribed status as second-class academic citizens.

Parallel to the academic sphere, access to employment followed the same logic of exclusion and categorisation. Participants found that the only jobs open to them were unskilled ones which did not respect their status as international students but, rather, their assumed status as immigrants.

> Here, we don't find good work opportunities in our area of study, because what we can get here is, like, work at McDonalds, or in supermarkets, or in cleaning, and so we find things are very tough.
>
> (Isabel, A, Bachelor's degree student)

The harsh reality of finding work in Portugal to financially support their studies – which for many participants was a necessity – is all the more shocking for those who had already started a professional career in their home country, for instance as a teacher or an accountant. Hence the 'social price' they had to pay for the privilege and prestige of studying in Portugal (which would ultimately 'pay off' when they returned home) was to be deskilled and confined to typical 'immigrant work' sectors of the Portuguese labour market. As Luís (A), a graduate, said, reflecting back on his perceptions on arrival in Portugal and subsequent disillusionment:

> No one tells you about the nature of your work, how it will impact on your education. You think, 'OK, I'll get a job to support my studies'. And [in Angola] I used to work as a teacher... so I was not thinking about immigrant work, on construction sites, or in shopping centres... that did not cross my mind. I was looking at myself as a more or less qualified person. I thought I was going to get a job that matched my skills and my student status.

The finding is clear: the realities of life in Portugal, where the job market is hardly buoyant even for Portuguese qualified young people, pulls Angolan and Cape Verdean students away from thinking of themselves in terms of a 'superior' conceptualisation of being an international student, and pulls them towards an ascribed, and sometimes also internalised, identity as African immigrants in Portugal.

Mobile class positions

The evidence presented above clearly indicates the ways in which Angolan and Cape Verdean students are made to feel like 'immigrants' during their time in Portugal. The denigration that they experience at the hands of Portuguese students is made worse by the structural discrimination they face in the employment market. Between these two domains – the student sphere and the paid-work sphere – there is a kind of toxic relationship. Most African students need to do part-time work to help them survive financially. Yet they can only get 'immigrant' work, not typical 'student' jobs. This not only downgrades their social status and morale but also negatively impacts their studies. The need to work, and their general lack of economic resources, prevents them from participating fully in 'student life', so they may have to miss some classes, project meetings or outings with their student colleagues. In these ways, African students feel detached from the academic environment which should be the main anchor of their lives in Portugal.

Their residential distribution also reinforces the students' separation from the 'mainstream' of Portuguese student life. Most of the participants found themselves living in 'immigrant areas' of the city, where accommodation is cheapest, or staying with relatives who had previously migrated to Portugal (Arenas, 2015). Hence they inhabit a different urban social geography to Portuguese students, who live either with their parents in better-class neighbourhoods or, if from outside the city, in student halls of residence or shared student flats.

The loss of social and economic status and the imposed switch from 'international student' to 'foreigner' and 'immigrant' are, arguably, all the more difficult to bear given that most of the participants, especially those from Angola, belong to the upper or middle class in their home countries. This class identification derived initially from their parental family background, and for others also from the fact that they had a professional work experience before moving to Portugal for further study. The following quotations, from two graduated students, are typical illustrations of this deeply-felt downward class mobility:

> When I was in Angola I lived with my parents. I was upper-middle class... It was like having your life really organised, no hassle, nothing to worry about... I had no worries about paying water, electricity, gas, shopping... Here, not anymore. Here I feel like I'm working just to pay bills. Here, I won't say I'm low class, but certainly lower [than at home].
>
> (Leonor, A)

> [In Cape Verde] I think I'm middle class. In Portugal [I feel] low class, because it's different. I'm in a foreign country so, of course, I don't have those privileges I had at home... Imagine, in Cape Verde, I have a large house, there is a person who cleans, a maid. Here there is no maid; it's me who has to clean, cook, iron and wash.
>
> (Ricardo, CV)

Our findings indicate that Angolans experience this downward social mobility more acutely than Cape Verdeans, mainly because Angolan students come from a more wealthy family background, due largely to the country's oil and mineral resources, whereas in the fragmented archipelagic Cape Verde the middle class is smaller and poverty is more widespread.

As well as 'objective' markers of social-class depreciation, such as disposable income, employment and residential conditions, the Angolan and Cape Verdean participants also felt treated badly in their everyday contacts with the host population. Alice (A), a graduate, gave a revealing example of this discriminatory treatment in a public hospital:

> They give us a treatment that is not quite the same... I had such an experience in the hospital... It was something like this... I had to ask if there was anything to pay. And OK, the lady could have simply said to me 'No, nothing to pay, it is exempt'. But she looked at me and said 'This is not like Angola [implying a corrupt country]; here it is all for free'.

Quite apart from this kind of treatment being an indication of the residual racism that still pervades Portuguese society (as in all European societies, to a greater or lesser extent), many participants tried to draw lessons from their experiences. This was manifest in two main arguments. The first chides Portugal for not paying proper attention to what international students can offer to the country, with the result that, when they graduate, the foreign students simply return home or, quite often, move on to other countries where their qualifications are more appreciated.

> I think Portugal is missing the opportunity to benefit from the immigrant youth who are studying here... What I notice is that there seem to exist specific jobs for immigrants... And many of these young immigrants, after graduating here, do not return to their countries. They come to Portugal, Portugal provides higher education, gives them everything, but then they go to England, Spain, Germany, Luxembourg.
>
> (José, A, Master's student)

The second kind of statement that recurs in several interviews is the way that participants say that they 'learn', from their experience in Portugal, of how immigrants should be properly treated.

> Cape Verde... has been receiving many immigrants, mainly from Africa and the Chinese, in recent decades. I have always respected people as human beings, but I never paid much attention to the possible problems or needs [that those immigrants] might have. Now I pay special attention, and have solidarity for any immigrant. Now I'm more sensitive to the problems of immigrants.
>
> (Eunice, CV, Master's student)

The final stage in the social mobility trajectory is what happens after graduation in Portugal. Geographically, three pathways are possible: return to the home country; staying on in the host country; or moving on to another country. We have analysed these alternative spatial trajectories in more detail in another publication (Alves, King & Malheiros, 2021); our focus in the present chapter is more on the class mobility implications. Most participants agreed that the pay-off for all the sacrifices – personal (separation from family), financial (struggling to survive through poorly-paid 'immigrant' jobs) and psychological (social-class demotion) – is the expectation of an improved socio-economic status back home. This status improvement is interpreted in two ways – reversing the downward social mobility endured in Portugal and enhancing one's status (especially regarding income and career) over what it would have been had the individual remained in the home country and not studied abroad. Hence, in economic terms, the period spent studying abroad represents an investment in human capital which is then capitalised when the return takes place through the ability to use the Portuguese qualification to get a well-paid job (Rozenweig, 2006).

In practice, this meant staying on in Portugal until the degree qualification is obtained, even if this resulted in living in worsening material and psychological conditions; better to grit one's teeth and endure, rather than returning home without the completed qualification. For some participants, this meant deferring the return so that additional human capital could be accumulated, either by progressing to a higher degree or by getting some professional experience in the Portuguese job market as a graduate from a Portuguese university. The next quotation illustrates this theme of how to maximise a 'successful' return.

> I never thought of staying [in Portugal]. But I stayed on to do the Master's in order to increase my knowledge, to improve my CV... In Angola, there are already lots of graduates, and with only the first degree I would not be able to achieve anything... With the Master, I will be earning well and have a better life.
>
> (Paula, A)

Interestingly, Paula rejected the idea of staying longer-term in Portugal because of the rather closed nature of the Portuguese graduate labour market and the scant chance she would have of parlaying her qualifications into a professional career there:

> With the education I have, I will not be valued as much here... in terms of salary and career, as I would in my home country. Here there aren't many good opportunities... You can only get them through acquaintances and connections... and here I don't know anyone. The only work I could get would be in catering or cleaning. And I don't see myself, with my higher education, a first degree and a Master's, doing that kind of work!

As well as the ability to capitalise on Portuguese degree qualifications, which are much more highly valued than degrees from Angolan or Cape Verdean HEIs, the general benefit of having had an 'international experience', especially in the former colonial metropole, also brings a reputational benefit, as pointed out in the next short interview extract:

> There is a feeling in Cape Verde that those who study abroad, especially in Portugal, have a broader vision, and are better able to be successful in the competition for jobs.
>
> (Sónia, CV, Master's student)

Based on the experience and perceptions of our participants, their social-class journey comes full circle once they have graduated and are in the throes of moving back to their country of origin. For most, it looks like the long and hard pathway through the Portuguese higher education system will be compensated with their arrival back home, where they can best reap the rewards of a 'prestigious' foreign education, international exposure, and a corresponding social and cultural enrichment. Their experience illustrates the shifting status of African student-migrants, contrasting their positionality in Portugal, where they are seen, and hence made to feel, like immigrants rather than international students, and then, following return to Angola and Cape Verde, where they are seen as professionally qualified cosmopolitans. For Angola, Augusto and King (2020) document how Angolan graduates with degrees from Portugal and elsewhere are valued much more highly than those with degrees from local universities. This relationship, between Angola and Cape Verde on the one hand, and Portugal on the other, is strongly underlain by the historical experience of Portuguese colonialism. The colonial legacy of Portugal reinforces the idea of Portugal as the metropolis, the centre of knowledge production and of the valued Portuguese language and culture, and also a step into Europe (França, et al., 2018), while Angola and Cape Verde remain the former colonies, with limited human and academic capital.

Student, no matter what

There is a sizeable minority of the participants who have been able to resist the 'immigrant' stereotype and instead stress their identity as international students. This minority exists in both national groups, but in a different form in each. However, they are united in insisting that their primary purpose in moving to Portugal was always to study, and that everything else is secondary to that. The Angolans in this subgroup have a higher socio-economic profile, are often engaged in postgraduate study, following a first degree either in Portugal or in Angola, and are likely to have attended and/or be attending private HEIs. Given their wealthier family background, they have not needed to work to support their studies. They live in their own rented – or even owned – apartments, generally in 'good' areas of the city, and are often sharing with other family members, like the case of João (A), a student who came initially for a Bachelor's degree and was now doing a Master's:

> We found accommodation in S. Sebastião, near *Corte Inglès* [an up-market shopping centre]. We rented there until we bought our own residence. Now we live in Alto dos Minhos, where it is not possible for a low-income person to afford to live.

On the other hand, the Cape Verdeans who see themselves primarily as international students are mostly undergraduates who came to Portugal on study grants and who live in university halls of residence.[2] They mix with other students, including other international students, and hence partake in a multicultural academic environment. At least in the residential setting of university-owned accommodation and shared student flats, these students reported harmonious relations with their room-mates and friends:

Last year I lived with two Portuguese girls, and this year with a Portuguese and a Bulgarian… I never had a problem sharing a room. I was always lucky. The first year I was with a Portuguese, and then in the second semester with a Brazilian… we never had any problems, we were always getting on well.

(Filipa, CV, initially a Bachelor's degree student,
now doing a Master's)

Hence, regarding oneself as an international student, rather than an immigrant or a foreigner, results from different factors: socio-economic background, degree of academic engagement (e.g. 'full immersion' as a student as opposed to part-time worker) and personal self-determinism.

Conclusion

Defining international students is a far-from-straightforward task and different approaches can subtly change the meaning and quantification of the phenomenon (King & Raghuram, 2013; Raghuram, 2013). Although ISM can be considered a form of migration and therefore subject to some of the common rules governing migration theory, notably investment in human capital, many of the drivers of ISM are different from those shaping other forms of migration, such as labour migration (Findlay, Stam, King & Ruiz-Gelices, 2005). In the case of internationally mobile Angolan and Cape Verdean students considered here, the nature of their mobility seems to be constantly under interrogation, both by themselves and by outside observers. Are they really international students, or are they also immigrants looking for work? To what extent is an international life, or permanent residence abroad, the primary aim of their move to Portugal? How do they differ from the large numbers of their fellow-nationals who have preceded them as immigrants in Portugal?

Some of the answers to the above questions are clear; others less so. Undoubtedly, the way Angolan and Cape Verdean students see themselves in Portugal, and the way they are seen by mainstream Portuguese society, are fundamentally shaped by the students' geographical and social origins in the ex-colonial African periphery of the former Portuguese empire. Both before and after the independence of the African colonies in the mid-1970s, large migratory flows were directed towards Portugal, with the result that stable immigrant populations from Angola and Cape Verde (as well as from Mozambique and Guinea-Bissau) were established in Lisbon and other major Portuguese cities. These communities' workers entered the lower echelons of the Portuguese labour market, doing jobs in industry, construction, services and care-work (Malheiros, 1998). The African origin and black skin of these established immigrant-worker groups created an assumption that all black Africans, including students, would be poorly educated, low-status labour migrants. This helps to explain some of the difficulties faced by the participants, both in the academic setting and when it came to seeking work alongside their studies.

Answers to the other questions are more ambivalent. While a minority of the participants – mainly well-off Angolan postgraduates and Cape Verdean undergraduates on scholarships – were keen to maintain an 'international student' identity, most of the interviewees seemed to reluctantly accept their designation as 'immigrants', using this word to denote themselves in their narratives. We suggest two reasons for this. The first is that they have internalised the Portuguese 'colonialist' view of them as part of a broader immigrant population emanating from the former colonies. The second possibility is that they see their stay in Portugal as not solely about acquiring an academic qualification and then immediately returning home with the degree certificate in their hands, but as part of a broader and longer-term project of accumulating a range of academic, professional and 'life' skills. While most of the participants did indeed express a commitment to going back to their home countries at some point in the future, many related how their plans had changed and become more open-ended since their arrival in Portugal. Some mentioned a revised aim of staying on and perhaps acquiring Portuguese nationality, which would then give them freedom of movement elsewhere in Europe (Alves et al., 2021).

Where our study and its key results find common ground with other research on ISM is in studies of East-West student movements within Europe. Wilken and Dahlberg (2017) show that students from the 'accession' countries in Denmark can only find the precarious jobs associated with Eastern European immigrants and cannot benefit from the kinds of professional work experience available to Danish students. In a somewhat different vein, Amelina (2013) has uncovered the professional academic exploitation of Ukrainian postgraduates and researchers in Germany; her informants seemed to be reluctantly willing to accept heavier workloads and even to take pride in this.

In these two cases, clever students are solicited as desirable migrants because of their potential, once they have graduated and gained experience, to contribute to the development of the countries they move to. This does not seem to be the case with Angolan and Cape Verdean students in Portugal, where there are few explicit policies to encourage students to stay on to contribute to the Portuguese skilled labour market, which in any case is still recovering from the devastating effects of the post-2008 economic crisis. Hence, the question remains open as to whether Angolan and Cape Verdean students in Portugal are engaged in student mobility or student (im)migration.

This chapter has highlighted some conflictual aspects regarding the concept of international students. It was our aim to show that, far from being a homogeneous category, the construction of international students is dependent on students' geographic and social origins, on the culture of the host country and on the nature of the host country's relationships with the international students' origin countries. Not to be overlooked, additionally, are students' personalities, self-perceptions and ambitions. In the particular case of Portugal, Angola and Cape Verde, the colonial past is a cornerstone, still promoting an order based on race and skin colour. This means that there is further scope for studies of ISM to confront issues of racism and discrimination within a postcolonial theoretical and geographical setting.

Acknowledgements

This research was supported by an individual research grant from the Portuguese Foundation for Science and Technology, held by Elisa Alves (PD/BD/114272/2016). The interviews were conducted by the first author, with inputs into the design of the interview schedule, sampling strategies and interpretation of results from the second author. We also thank Jorge Malheiros and Sonia Pereira for their advice at the research design stage.

Notes

1 This survey is not discussed here; further details on request from the first author.
2 In Portugal, access to public university residences is usually based on household incomes and it is cheaper than other forms of student accommodation such as private room rental.

References

Alves, E., King, R., and Malheiros, J. (2021). Are you just going to study or do you plan to stay on? Trajectories of Angolan and Cape Verdean students in Portugal. In D. Dedgjioni and C. Bauschke-Urban (eds) *Student Mobilities from the Global South*. London: Routledge, in press.

Amelina, A. (2013). Hierarchies and categorical power in cross-border science: Analysing scientists' transnational mobility between Ukraine and Germany. *Southeast European and Black Sea Studies* 13:2, 141–155. doi:10.1080/1468385 7.2013.789670

Arenas, F. (2015). Migrations and the rise of African Lisbon: Time-space of Portuguese (post)coloniality. *Postcolonial Studies* 18:4, 353–366. doi:10.1080/13 688790.2015.1191982

Augusto, A., and King, R. (2020). 'Skilled white bodies': Portuguese workers in Angola as a case of North-South migration. *Geographical Journal* 186:1, 116–127. doi:10.111/geoj.12334

Bilecen, B. (2016). International students and cosmopolitanisms: Educational mobility in a global age. In A. Amelina and K. Horvath (eds) *An Anthology of Migration and Social Transformation: European Perspectives*. Cham: Springer, pp. 231–244.

Bilecen, B., and Van Mol, C. (2017). Introduction: International academic mobility and inequalities. *Journal of Ethnic and Migration Studies* 43:8, 1241–1255. doi:1 0.1080/1369183X.2017.1300225

Brooks, R., and Waters, J. (2011). *Student Mobilities: Migration and the Internationalization of Higher Education*. London: Palgrave Macmillan.

Byun, B. K., and Jung, H. (2019). From policy rhetoric to reality: The experiences of Southeast Asian science and engineering graduate students in Korea. *Asia Pacific Education Review* 20:4, 607–623. doi:10.1007/s12564-019-09588-y

Costa, A. B., and Faria, M. (2012). *Formação superior e desenvolvimento. Estudantes universitários africanos em Portugal.* Coimbra: Almedina.

Cresswell, T. (2006). *On the Move: Mobility in the Modern Western World.* London: Routledge.

Daniels, T. P. (2014). African international students in Klang Valley: Colonial legacies, postcolonial racialization, and sub-citizenship. *Citizenship Studies* 18:8, 855–870. doi:10.1080/13621025.2014.964548

DGEEC (2016) *Estudantes Iscritos no Ensino Superior Portugues, 2011/12 a 2015/16.* Lisbon: DGEEC, MEC.

Findlay, A. M., Stam, A., King, R. and Ruìz-Gelices, E. (2005). International opportunities: Searching for the meaning of student migration. *Geographica Helvetica* 60:3, 192–200. doi:10.5194/gh-60-192-2005

Findlay, A. M., King, R., Smith, F., Geddes, A. and Skeldon, R. (2012). World class? An investigation of globalisation, difference and international student mobility. *Transactions of the Institute of British Geographers* 37:1, 118–131. doi:10.1111/j.1475-5661.2011.00454.x

França, T., Alves, E. and Padilla, B. (2018). Portuguese policies fostering international student mobility: A colonial legacy or a new strategy? *Globalisation, Societies and Education* 16:3, 325–338. doi:10.1080/14767724.2018.1457431

Jones, E. (2017) Problematising and reimagining the notion of 'international student experience'. *Studies in Higher Education* 42:5, 933–943. doi:10.1080/03075079.2017.1293880

King, R. and Raghuram, P. (2013). International student migration: Mapping the field and new research agendas. *Population, Space and Place* 19:2, 127–137. doi:10.1002/psp.1746

King, R., Findlay, A. M., and Ahrens, J. (2010). *International Student Mobility Literature Review.* London: HEFCE.

King, R., Lulle, A., Morosanu, L., and Williams, A. (2016). *International Youth Mobility and Life Transitions in Europe: Questions, Definitions, Typologies and Theoretical Approaches.* Brighton: University of Sussex, Sussex Centre for Migration Research, Working Paper No. 86.

Malheiros, J. M. (1998). Immigration, clandestine work and labour market strategies: The construction sector in the Metropolitan Region of Lisbon. *South European Society and Politics* 3:3, 169–185. doi:10.1080/13608740308539552

Murphy-Lejeune, E. (2002). *Student Mobility and Narrative in Europe: The New Strangers.* London: Routledge.

Nyland, C., Forbes-Mewett, H., Marginson, S., Ramia, G., Sawir, E., and Smith, S. (2009) International student-workers in Australia: A new vulnerable workforce. *Journal of Education and Work* 22:1, 1–14. doi:10.1080/13639080802709653

OECD (2018). *Education at a Glance 2018.* Paris: OECD Publishing

Pedreira, I. (2015). *Os Estudantes da Comunidade dos Países de Língua Portuguesa (CPLP) no Ensino Suprior Português.* Lisbon: DGEEC, MEC.

Quinton, W. J. (2020). So close and yet so far? Predictors of international students' socialization with host nationals. *International Journal of Intercultural Relations* 74, 7–16. doi:10.1016/j.ijintrel.2019.10.003

Raghuram, P. (2013). Theorising the spaces of student migration. *Population, Space and Place* 19:2, 138–154. doi:10.1002/psp.1747

Riaño, Y., and Piguet, E. (2016). *International Student Migration*. New York: Oxford University Press. doi:10.1093/OBO/9780199874002-0141

Rozenweig, M. R. (2006). Global wage differences and international student flows. In S.M. Collins and C. Graham (eds) *Brookings Trade Forum 2006: Global Labor Flows*. Washington DC: Brookings International Press, pp. 57–96.

Suh, H. N., Flores, L. Y., and Wang, K. T. (2019). Perceived discrimination, ethnic identity, and mental distress among Asian international students in Korea. *Journal of Cross-Cultural Psychology* 50:8, 991–1007. doi:10.1177/0022022119874433

Tran, L. T. (2017). 'I am really expecting people to judge me by my skills': Ethnicity and identity of international students. *Journal of Vocational Education and Training* 69:3, 390–404. doi:10.1080/13636820.2016.1275033

Urban, E. L., Orbe, M. P., Tavares, N. A., and Alvarez, W. (2010). Exploration of Dominican international students' experiences. *Journal of Student Affairs Research and Practice* 47:2, 233–250. doi:10.2202/1949-6605.6081

Urry, J. (2007) *Mobilities*. Cambridge: Polity Press

Vala, J., Lopes, D., and Lima, M. (2008) Black immigrants in Portugal: Lusotropicalism and prejudice. *Journal of Social Issues* 64:2, 287–302. doi:10.1111/j.1540-4560.2008.00562.x

Waters, J. (2012) Geographies of international education: Mobilities and the reproduction of social (dis)advantage. *Geography Compass* 6:3, 123–136. doi:10.1111/j.1749-8198.2011.00473.x

Wilken, L., and Dahlberg, M. G. (2017). Between international student mobility and work migration: Experiences of students from the EU's newer member states in Denmark. *Journal of Ethnic and Migration Studies* 43:8, 1347–1361. doi:10.1080/1369183X.2017.1300330

Chapter 15

Conclusion

Sarah O'Shea and Rachel Brooks

Introduction

This book has brought together a diversity of perspectives that seek to deconstruct the ways in which students, as individual actors and cohort types, have been defined and negotiated. The intent is not to 'smooth out' or untangle these representations but rather to reveal their complexity and how such constructions reveal deeper, often hidden, political and institutional agendas. By focusing on a seemingly accepted or taken for granted social role, in this case that of the university student, this book grapples with the myriad of possible understandings attached to this position and in so doing highlights the deeper political connotations that are inherent in student positionality.

This is an important topic as without a deeper understanding of our university student populations, the enduring issues of participation and retention can only be partially addressed. Globally, we know that these populations are increasing in number and also diversity; Marginson (2016) reports that, between 2007 and 2013, the worldwide number of tertiary students multiplied over six times. This drive to access university is generally defined in terms of opportunity including better employment and financial futures (O'Shea & Delahunty, 2018; O'Shea, Stone, Delahunty & May, 2018; Marginson, 2016). However, in this move from an elite system to one characterised by mass participation, we have a fragmented understanding of how different student cohorts both imagine and experience this higher education space or how these populations are imagined and constructed.

The complexity of the university setting has been somewhat underestimated with a general assumption that we 'know' who our university students are. However, what the chapters in this book attest to is an enduring 'mis-recognition' (McNay, 2008) of various student cohorts, a mis-recognition that invariably reflects dominant values and judgements, often positioning some student types as the 'other' to an assumed norm. Such a situation essentialises students and works 'to subtly reproduce inequalities through shame and shaming' (Burke, 2018, p. 15). Exposing the constructs and subtle propagation of this reproductive naming is ultimately key to understanding how we can ensure equal participation across higher education systems.

In recognising this as an international phenomenon, contributors to this publication discuss understandings of higher education students in various nations across the globe, including Australia, China, Denmark, England, Germany, Ireland, Poland, Portugal, Spain, Thailand and the UK. This international insight is complemented by cross-disciplinary focus and the integration of broad theoretical applications. Of particular interest was how these conceptualisations sometimes 'jostle uncomfortably' in relation to each other, with different stakeholders portraying students in somewhat contradictory or divergent terms.

This publication deliberately draws attention to how the 21st century student is buffeted by a range of conflicting and powerful forces; in exploring these forces, the intent has been to better consider the ways in which understandings of 'the student' are shared across and within nation-states. Scholars have contributed their unique analysis on how such understandings expand beyond the position of learner and include the role of consumers, political actors, future workers and dependent adults-in-the-making. Interestingly within this diversity lives commonality: this is not to say that each chapter is similar but rather that regardless of location or student types, correlations are apparent. This final chapter provides an overview of these commonalities as well as highlighting the theoretical and empirical innovations that have emerged from across these contributions.

Conflicts in the 'making' of university students

The combination of increased participation in higher education alongside the drive to improve the economic viability of countries and states has not only led to more students attending university but also a greater range and type of individual choosing this educational pathway. This growth in student diversity has arguably thrown into sharp relief conflicts within the sector, and the ways in which these contradictions are understood and played out by individual actors features strongly in a number of these chapters. For example, in Chapter 6, Sykes interrogates the ways in which student populations are still unhelpfully defined as either 'traditional' or 'non-traditional'. The former implicitly referring to the idyll of the university student as school leaver, a 'coming of age' mythic that resonates with access to the requisite material and emotional wealth needed for success. The non-traditional student is then positioned as the 'other', a displaced figure that exists in the shadows of the mainstream.

Divides like this one are simplistic and also an unnecessary obfuscation of the complexity of student populations. For Sykes, naming students in this limiting (and 'senseless') fashion only serves to 'demonise' cohorts, attributing certain behaviours or attitudes to groups which have little foundation or relevance to actual reality. These constructions, according to Sykes, are not simply perpetuated by institutions but equally may be enacted by the students involved, even when, as Sykes explains, 'their own experiences do not necessarily correspond with its main precepts.'

Chapter 9 similarly considers understandings of the 'traditional' learner but in this case explores how this assumption can be disrupted by a partnership model of learning. This model is characterised by collaboration in learning where the educative responsibility is shared across the teaching and learning realms. In this chapter, Eloise Symonds draws out the conflicts that exist between depicting students as 'traditional learners' but then expecting them to perform as partners in learning – the contradictory nature of both positions is unpacked in the context of two universities. Symonds argues that the case studies point to how the development of a collaborative and partnership model of learning is unsettled by continued institutional alignment with more transmission-based models of learning. This transmission model forces the student into the role of passive recipient with the lecturer assumed to be the all-knower or expert. Such roles are historically placed and reflect a hierarchy of power that is not only contested but equally limits the nature of the university experience; as Symonds points out, such differences ultimately promote 'discord' for students who are forced to do additional work reconciling a matrix of 'different approaches' and 'different outcomes'.

The broad theme of 'conflict' features strongly in a number of the book chapters particularly in terms of the various identity positions or labels available to contemporary students. In Chapter 12, Allen, Finn and Ingram unpack the term 'millennial' exploring how this nomenclature has 'narrowed' thinking about students and the recognition (or misrecognition) of this cohort. These authors consider how the millennial generation (born between 1981 and 1996) has 'grown up' with a higher education system characterised by fees, debt and also, austerity. The resulting marketisation has imbued a radically different understanding about university attendance demonstrated by media representations which variously construct these learners as either 'passive consumers/entitled learners' or as 'fragile snowflakes, PC Warriors'. Drawing on UK newspaper articles, Allen et al. detail how such constructions effectively 'frame' the ways in which students are understood, essentially silencing or obscuring the diversity that we know exists within contemporary student populations.

Continuing the theme of hidden conflict, Lumb and Bunn interrogate the ways in which social imaginaries construct and constrain university learners. In this chapter (Chapter 8) epistemological notions of studenthood are related to a critique of employability in order to disrupt preconceived notions of how to 'be' a student. Lumb and Bunn foreground the contested nature of understandings about 'employability' revealing how the construction of this term increasingly 'patterns the purpose of study'. As this chapter and others attest, such constructions of students not only limit perspectives or definitions but also, have wider political and ideological connotations. For example, Lumb and Bunn point out how implicit understandings of 'employability' work to benefit industry rather than individual learners, this discourse of employability ultimately contributing to the sustenance of the 'precarious' labour underpinning the flourishing and growth of contemporary economies.

Perhaps unsurprisingly, the contested undertones of such constructions reveal wider contradictions spanning social and cultural spheres. This is clearly highlighted by Calver and Michael-Fox in Chapter 10, in which documentary representations of UK students are critically analysed. Following a recent upsurge in 'student life' documentaries, the authors draw upon media theory to explore how these representations reflect broader 'socio-cultural' concerns about university learners. These representations are also framed around 'risk' with either the individual learner presented as being 'at-risk' and in need of protection or else as posing 'a risk' to themselves and others. What such depictions offer is more than just a series of stereotypes or 'tropes' but rather insights into broader social and cultural norms at play in British society. Echoing Sykes' analysis of the traditional and non-traditional student, Calver and Michael-Fox's chapter highlights an enduring duality with early documentaries depicting the traditional student as being 'risky' with behaviour such as binge drinking and promiscuity featuring but contrasting this with more recent documentaries showing students as being 'at-risk' from predatory colleges or financial debt.

The chapters in this book reveal different facets of understanding about university students in terms of the imagery drawn upon, the language applied and the activities attributed to these populations. However, what each chapter also reveals is the ways in which such facets are constructed and embedded within dominant political and policy discourse; such constructions arguably say more about the society that perpetuates them than the individuals they refer to. For Danvers and Hinton-Smith (Chapter 5), it is the lack of any embodied or emotional understanding of our student populations that ultimately limits perceptions. Drawing upon their work with young people involved in Widening Participation activities, Danvers and Hinton-Smith point to the disempowerment and disassociation caused by categorising individuals in terms of 'blunt' postcode identifiers. Such categorisation has powerful implications for those being named and also ignores the complex political and social structures that people exist within.

The next section further situates these complexities within a broader geographical context revealing how students are positioned as actors in an increasingly international global education economy.

Players in a global setting: Students within the international realm

Chapters 13 and 14 both interrogate constructions of international students; Eiras and Huijser (Chapter 13) explore the identity-making of Chinese students within 'transnational university' settings which offer a hybrid education across nation states. Drawing on the concept of 'liminal space', the authors argue that these particular transnational systems offer individuals the possibility of negotiating various and sometimes conflicting identities as both university students and also, in their participants' case, Chinese culture. The students in this study were perceived as occupying an 'in-between' space negotiating both an existing or former identity and also considering a future or desired one. The chapter reveals the intricate negotiations required as Chinese students move from a traditional Confucius-style education environment into a HE system based upon a UK model, while simultaneously ensuring a future reincorporation into Chinese society. The Angolan and Cape Verdean students in Alves and King's study (Chapter 14) who are enrolled in a Portuguese university context, experience a different type of conflict but are similarly located in an 'in-between' space. As these authors explain, the colonial history of this state leads to a tension between these students being categorised as 'international student' or as 'immigrant'. In this way, the construction of these students is situated within a national agenda that appears to discriminate on the basis of both geography and social origin.

This international scrutiny of students is also the focus of Chapter 4, where Uerpairojkit and Burford turn their attention to Thai students and the ways in which this cohort is constructed according to four key imaginings: 'future worker, preserver of culture, customer and the "new gen" student'. Drawing upon online materials, these authors indicate how the dominant imaginaries of Thai university participants reveal a level of antagonism and even fear; much like the UK students in Calver and Michael-Fox's TV documentaries (Chapter 10), these students are 'othered' in this imagery, often sexualised and presented in antithesis to dominant socially acceptable roles. These online representations deviate sharply from the policy documents analysed, which highlight both enduring and traditional notions of student as 'future worker' or 'consumer'. These traditional perspectives jostle uncomfortably with the more recent depictions of learners or the 'new-gen' students characterised in terms of being an entrepreneur or degree seeker.

In Chapter 3, Sarah McDonald attends to the relational nature of student identity formation focusing on Australian female first-in-family students and their relationships with their mothers, exploring how familial relationships impact on the transition into university. McDonald shows how the 'unrealised aspirations' of mothers can impact on their daughters, increasing the pressure to succeed. Equally, McDonald points out that these female actors (both mothers and daughters) are generally 'playing the game of HE' at a disadvantage due to classed or gendered behaviours. Similarly addressing the themes of family and also media representations of students, is Chapter 11, in which Lainio and Brooks highlight how students across five European nations are constructed as family members. Drawing upon content analysis of newspaper articles and interviews with policymakers, these authors highlight a clear typology of how students are constructed in relation to their family identifying 'integrated', 'independent' or 'ambivalent' positionality. Understanding this relationship is particularly key in a higher education context where financial responsibility for university study is increasingly the burden of the entire family rather than the individual learner.

Returning to the Australian context, O'Connor (Chapter 7) focuses on the online student and explores the tensions between 'instructivist' and 'constructivist' understandings of this learner cohort, particularly the ways in which students are constructed as either 'engaged and empowered' learners, or as 'vulnerable' and in need of support. Finally, Patfield, Gore and Fray (Chapter 2) attend to the imaginings of prospective university students to explore how they construct their future university self. These authors argue that rather than prospective students 'buying into' the student as 'consumer' dominant imagery, the participants in their study, all of whom were still at school, articulated a number of alternative types that informed their perception of future university selves. Such perspectives are somewhat silenced in the dominant imagery of the higher education student and serve as a timely reminder that key to understanding how university is perceived requires a need to return to the players themselves – the students.

Delineating the field: What can this book offer?

As the previous sections have indicated, this book is a rich resource and provides both methodological and theoretical insights. This section draws together some of the key themes as well as an overview of additional contributions to the field. This is not an exhaustive list but rather a summative overview of some key 'take-home' messages.

Tensions in depictions of studenthood

A number of these chapters highlight the demise of the 'ideal' or taken-for-granted student type instead variously pointing out that this is constructed, unrealistic and contrary to the realities both experienced by individual learners and also presented within the media or political agendas. For example, the students in the TV documentaries featured in Calver and Michael-Fox's chapter (Chapter 10) seem to conform to a 'risky' student imagery – those who drink excessively or avoid study. Equally, Finn et al. (Chapter 12) focus on the newspaper reporting of students born between 1981 and 1996, revealing how the representations utilised serve to 'shore up particular imaginings of students' that are very removed from an idealised or imagined version of the student type that is a 'resilient scholar of the past'. These chapters and others reveal how the positioning of 'students as learners' is absent from policy and instead the roles of 'consumer', 'risk taker' and 'hedonist' are often foregrounded. Such understandings do not account for the more relational or embodied nature of university attendance and instead emphasise an individualised relationship that can be negatively interpreted as both 'passive' and 'entitled'. This is just one example of many in this book where there is a tension between versions of studenthood exemplified across the sector.

Diverse methodologies and foci

The chapters in this book not only present diversity in terms of findings but equally the methodologies used and the data generated are rich in complexity and insights. This deliberate and careful methodological work is demonstrated across studies. For example, Danvers and Hinton-Smith (Chapter 5) describe evocatively how they adopted Kvale's (1996) traveller motif as they journeyed alongside their young school student participants. Outlining their role in focus groups, these authors explained how they intentionally strived 'to gently guide' the participants ultimately 'wandering together with' them to frame and support emerging insights about Widening Participation. These authors explore the difficulties of conducting research in this space and the need to avoid adopting the role of, what they term as, a 'transient stranger' in order to enable a much deeper exploration of the affective impact of transitioning into university spaces and places.

A number of the studies refer to a range of mediums and modalities in order to unpack the domain of studenthood. Drawing upon Fairclough's Critical Discourse Approach, Chapters 9 and 13 both explore spoken discourse in combination with images to develop a holistic understanding of how subject positionings were conceived and understood by participants. In Chapter 13, Eiras and Huijser further complement this approach with an arts-based interview method that encouraged participants to 'sketch' their experiences of identity construction during the interview, an important first step in establishing trust and also, opening up dialogues.

Calver and Michael-Fox (Chapter 10) provide a detailed textual analysis of UK documentaries over 10 years to expose contradictory thinking about student behaviours and characteristics. Drawing upon analysis of both dialogue and narration, the many contradictions and complexities of student representations are drawn out and interrogated. Interestingly, in these media, there is no reference to older, part-time or distance students, instead these documentaries focus exclusively on 18- to 21-year-olds, a narrow construction of what the 'student experience' is, which precludes the diversity of students that actually attend higher education. Finn et al. (Chapter 12) also draw attention to the limiting nature of language and terminology, highlighting how the term 'snowflake' defines students in largely deficit ways as needing 'safe spaces' and being anti-activist. Closer analysis of policy documents, however, reveals how it was higher education institutions rather than students who demanded less debate, exposing how institutions can be censuring bodies that 'delegitimise' political voices and 'deflect' any need for change.

Finally, McDonald's chapter (Chapter 3) draws upon narrative case studies to reveal the complex situations of two first-in-family students. These case studies provide the reader with insight into the diverse lived experiences of two young women as they make the transition to university. This piece also offers a departure from common themes explored in relation to first-in-family students and their family's attitude to university attendance. Too often this work focuses on the conflicts that arise between family members. McDonald's work instead sheds light onto how relationships, particularly those with parents, can positively reinforce and support movements into HE; a much-needed alternative perspective for the field.

Diversity of conclusions drawn: Final thoughts

We largely consider the role of university students as being a 'taken-for-granted' one, an accepted and somewhat unchallenged type. However, this book has revealed the highly contested and variable nature of this role and how the positioning of contemporary students exposes deeper political agendas and understandings. The 'risky' nature of university attendance features strongly in these chapters and yet what is generally publicly articulated is the value of higher education enrolment, the seemingly endless opportunity this participation brings, with little recognition of the contradictions that can result at an individual learner level. Danvers and Hinton-Smith (Chapter 5) refer to this as a 'hyper positive' portrayal and argue that recognising the illegitimate nature of this presentation requires ongoing scrutiny and critical analysis of our university systems and their associated constructions.

Lumb and Bunn (Chapter 8) draw upon an 'Ames Room' motif to encourage the reader to step back from a particular viewpoint in order to deliberately seek out the 'concealed dimensions' within a scenario. These authors equally warn that unless alertness is retained by the 'viewer', it is easy to 'step back' into accepted perspectives and accept the 'illusion' once again. This scrutiny might be uncomfortable, particularly for those who work within this system but it is clearly vital for the ongoing development of higher education. Continually questioning the student identity and recognising its constructed nature contributes to deeper understanding of the hidden tensions within the sector. Such understandings, presented in this book, will contribute to wider debates across the disciplines of education, sociology, gender and social policy ultimately continuing the conversations about the ways in which our understanding about students is both highly contested and deeply constructed.

References

Burke, P.-J. (2018). Re/imagining widening participation: A praxis-based framework. *International Studies in Widening Participation* 5:1, 10–20.

Kvale, S. (1996) *An Introduction to Qualitative Research Interviewing.* London: Sage.

Marginson, S. (2016). The worldwide trend to high participation in higher education: dynamics of social stratification in inclusive systems. *Higher Education* 72, 413-434. doi:10.1007/s10734-016-0016-x

McNay, L. (2008). *Against Recognition.* Polity: Cambridge, UK.

O'Shea, S., & Delahunty, J. (2018). Getting through the day and still having a smile on my face! How do students define success in the university learning environment? *Higher Education Research and Development* 37:5, 1062–1075. doi:10.108 0/07294360.2018.1463973

O'Shea, S., Stone, C., Delahunty, J. & May, J. (2018). Discourses of betterment and opportunity: Exploring the privileging of university attendance for first-in-family learners. *Studies in Higher Education* 43:6, 1020–1033. doi:10.1080/03075079. 2016.1212325

Index